Praise for *The O Neuro-Linguistic Pr*

Finally! Forty-two years later the true origins of NLP are revealed which up to now have only been the subject of mystery and legend. This is a must-read book for any student of NLP. In it we learn what actually happened during the first nine years of NLP and which set the stage for everything that has followed.

Today everyone claims to be one of the developers of NLP. Now we learn who the real developers actually were. Further, we are reminded that the Meta Model is the genuine heart of NLP and that it can only be mastered through ongoing practice. We learn that there were three and not two creators of NLP and are introduced to Frank Pucelik, who tragically many people in NLP have never heard of. Frank lives in Odessa in the Ukraine and continues to pioneer developments in NLP for business and works with at-risk young people.

John Grinder makes several points that the NLP world today desperately needs to hear and apply. He warns of the danger of content, categories, and pre-mature labeling and redirects us to focus on process. He also emphasizes the power of patterning, modeling, and testing in the creation of new applications.

In short, devour this book, imitate the same rigorous methods that were used by the developers, and bring this rigor to develop the next generation of NLP.

Wyatt L. Woodsmall, PhD,
NLP Master Trainer and Master Modeler

Different voices, different histories ... this multiplicity of sometimes conflicting perspectives is a salutary reminder that, as NLP has been at pains to point out, we each have our own map. Or as Robin Williams once said, "Reality – what a concept!"

Ian McDermott, founder of International Teaching Seminars

This is a big important book for the distinct and radical field of NLP, its trainers, practitioners, and critics. With contributions from a core of the original developers from the 1970s, here is an inspiring, sometimes contradictory, multilayered account of the cultural and intellectual background, the key colorful characters, the playful collaborations, the role of artistry and the creative unconscious, the adventures in modeling, research, and rigorous testing as well as some fine examples of early successful NLP applications.

This book sets the scene for the real questions being posed: What really is NLP? Where is it going? Is it now merely a set of techniques you can learn by rote in a few days? Or does NLP still offer a subtle, skills-based, and fundamental opportunity to further expand and deepen our knowledge and practice of the arts of human communication, learning, and change?

The Origins of Neuro-Linguistic Programming is an exceptional and essential read for everyone involved in NLP and interested in contributing to its future.

Judith Lowe, MD and Principal Trainer of
NLP Training Institute/PPD Learning Ltd

Thank you John Grinder and Frank Pucelik for your work in providing us with an account of how neuro-linguistic programming began as a seed and grew rapidly during the 1970s. NLP is now in its fifth decade and for the first time we have a reliable book that offers a history of NLP.

The Origins of Neuro-Linguistic Programming is both a story and collection of stories. The theme of the main narrative is the creation of NLP; the collection of stories is a rich anthology from the people who were there at the beginning and others who came along after the foundation was in place. The accounts in this book capture the commitment of Grinder, Bandler, and Pucelik as well as the spirited people they attracted to radically experiment with patterns of human excellence.

What makes this book exciting are the multiple voices narrating their personal experience of NLP during the heady days of 1970s. However, there is much more than history in these pages. If you focus at a deeper level you will find something very rich which is often missing in modern NLP – the fearlessness, the radicalism, the desire to experiment, the commitment to model, and the willingness to undertake thousands of hours of practice. Without these elements we would not have NLP today.

As you read and enjoy the voices from these pages, you may want to consider how NLP would be more colorful in the current age if we embraced the attitude of the individuals who gave us so much in inspiring and creating the field of neuro-linguistic programming.

Michael Carroll, founder of the NLP Academy and co-founder of the International Trainers Academy of NLP

An enjoyable, exciting, and informative adventure through the brilliant and quirky origins of NLP. This book is a hymn to the spirit of curiosity, creativity, collaboration, and adventure.

Julian Russell, Executive Coach and Director of The Life Talent Programme

We have been waiting almost 40 years for this book – a first-hand account by some of the people who were there at the beginning at one of the most creative times in history. *The Origins of Neuro-Linguistic Programming* can be enjoyed as several interwoven narratives, and you can model the modelers for their process of discovery, testing, trial, and feedback. Whichever filter you choose, this engaging book will provide more about the original spirit of NLP.

James Lawley and Penny Tompkins, authors of
Metaphors in Mind: Transformation through Symbolic Modelling

The Origins of Neuro-Linguistic Programming

TO NICOLE
GOD SPEED & A
GOOD WIND.

The Origins of Neuro-Linguistic Programming

edited by
John Grinder and R. Frank Pucelik

Prologue and Epilogue by
Carmen Bostic-St. Clair

Crown House Publishing Limited
www.crownhouse.co.uk
www.crownhousepublishing.com

First published by

Crown House Publishing Ltd
Crown Buildings, Bancyfelin, Carmarthen, Wales, SA33 5ND, UK
www.crownhouse.co.uk

and

Crown House Publishing Company LLC
6 Trowbridge Drive, Suite 5, Bethel, CT 06801-2858, USA
www.crownhousepublishing.com

British Library Cataloguing-in-Publication Data
A catalogue entry for this book is available from the British Library.

ISBN
978-184590858-4 (print)
978-184590863-5 (mobi)
978-184590864-3 (epub)

LCCN 2012951284

Printed and bound in the UK by
Gomer Press, Llandysul, Ceredigion

To Richard Bandler

Your voice is not here, only echoes of it. Your intelligence, your fear-lessness, and your presence are apparent in many of the narratives. We formed a team, the three of us, then the two of us, and against all odds, we succeeded in creating something distinct and radical and set it free in the world.

It was a great adventure!

John Grinder
Frank Pucelik

Contents

A Suggestion to the Reader

Carmen Bostic-St. Clair

Welcome to the *process* of discovery. This book is a step back in time, composed of a series of articles written today, some 40 years later, by individuals who came together in Santa Cruz, California during the years 1971–1979.

A time when the Dow Jones Industrial Average was still under 1000 points, a new car cost less than $4,000, and the kidnappers of Patricia Hearst were demanding $70 of food be given to every needy Californian. The time is 1970s, an era of change and protest. Bob Marley's song, "I Shot the Sheriff," along with songs by Paul McCartney and the Rolling Stones, could be heard blasting from the radios of brightly decorated VW vans; *Jesus Christ Superstar* was playing at the single screen cinema crowded with long-haired men and women wearing fringes, bell bottoms, and fatigue boots – smells of clove, tobacco, and other substances filled the turbulent air.

We ask you to enjoy the process of experiencing the discoveries as they unfold in the vivid and animated descriptions by some of the individuals who have written articles for this book; as you enjoy, we ask you to engage in a process that is congruent and consistent with the experiential teaching practices which were utilized by Richard Bandler, Frank Pucelik, and John Grinder during trainings on or near the University of California at Santa Cruz.

Words on paper do not really capture the full impact of a brief moment in time, so we are suggesting as you read that you utilize some of the well-known original processes of the field. We ask you to set the stage – to set your computer, television, or whatever device on which you listen to music and tune it to the sounds of the 70s. While enveloped by these sounds, we invite you to transport yourself to the campus as described through the eyes of the writers; to gaze through the redwood forests and capture glints of the shimmering Pacific Ocean melding with the horizon; while you are observing the gentle movement of the deer, listen for the call of the red tail hawk as you briskly rub your arms to ease the chill and become aware that the cool breeze carries the fresh scent and taste of salt. You have arrived at the campus – step lightly into the shoes of these young, eager individuals as the adventure unfolds.

The stories that you will read here are descriptions of experiences as remembered by the students and participants at training events that occurred during the creation by three men of the field known today as neuro-linguistic programming (NLP). The *field was created*, the original patterns known as Classic Code NLP were largely *not created;* rather the preponderance of these patterns were *uncovered, assimilated,* and *explicated* through the process of NLP modeling. These are patterns which you and I perform unconsciously hundreds of times during a day. To provide you with a way of thinking about these unconsciously performed processes, we ask you now, in this moment, to think about instances during your day when you replay the sound of someone's voice and immediately recall their image. How frequently do you realize that you have unconsciously noted the posture, gestures, and general physiology of an acquaintance and find yourself surprised that you are able to anticipate what they are about to say and/or do? How many times a day do you spontaneously ask for specificity of a noun or verb? How often in a business context, or when speaking to a detail-oriented person, do you find yourself asking to see or hear an example of the bigger picture?

The genius of creating a structure from these random natural intuitive processes and presenting them as explicit patterns, was first published in the *Structure of Magic, Volume I* by Bandler and Grinder. The impact of this work is captured by Virginia Satir, as she writes in the Foreword to that book:

> Knowing what these elements are makes it possible to use them consciously and, thus, to have useful methods for inducing change.

One way to look at these explicit patterns is to view them as a coded keypad that can be used to open an on-demand system to use when and where we chose.

If, at any point, while reading these articles you become puzzled by conflicting dates, processes, naming, or connections, relax, enjoy your read. In the Epilogue I pull together such loose strands and braid them into a continuity to provide an integrated description and possibly will solve some of those puzzles.

We *could* assume that you have had some introduction, experience, or background in Neuro-Linguistic Programming, and therefore, have an interest in the creation of the field; this is one possible assumption, among many available. We have not made that assumption; experience in NLP is not a prerequisite. This book is a drama about human beings who came together to make something new in the world.

As I remind participants in my seminars, "a pattern discovered is a pattern owned by the discoverer." Notice within these articles which writers seem to own their discovery. They were treated to excellent teachers who utilized the inductive method of teaching; each of whom, I hope, embodied that process and transferred it, in turn to you – their own students.

Carmen Bostic-St. Clair
San Francisco, California
October 2012

INTRODUCTION

Reflections on *The Origins of Neuro-Linguistic Programming*

John Grinder

This book has as its purpose a description of the origins of Neuro-Linguistic Programming (NLP). Note, please the use of the indefinite article *a* in the phrase, *a description* of *Neuro-Linguistic Programming.* The co-editors of this book, Frank Pucelik and John Grinder, were two of the three prime movers in the creation of NLP and one or both of them were present at the majority of the events described herein that define the origins of NLP. A third voice, that of Richard Bandler, is not present in this book as he elected not to participate.

The presentation of the origins of a field presents an interesting challenge for a number of reasons – among them, the fact that memory is reconstructive.

Here is easily the most responsible act I, as an author and a co-editor, can offer you as the reader of this book. It takes the form of a warning. In approaching what you are about to read, keep in mind the following three points in what you encounter in this volume:

1. *A significant portion of what is described never happened!*

According the latest models of memory processes, memories are *not* stored as intact units to be retrieved and displayed. They are stored in distinct physical locations (the primary cortical areas for each of the corresponding input channels) of the central nervous system; more specifically in separate representational systems. The connections among them are mediated by synesthesia circuitry.

To *remember*, then, is to reassemble portions of experience stored in separate locations into what appears (in the present) to be a coherent representation of some experience in the past, one that satisfies the present intentions and requirements of the person doing the remembering. Such present intentions and requirements of the person remembering operate as filters on the search mechanisms that reconstitute the *memory*.

Thus, all such representations are ultimately, and profoundly, works of fiction. By the way, the fact that they are fiction is NOT a disqualification, simply an epistemological warning about the veracity of what you are reading.

So, what do you suppose is the probability of getting these pieces reassembled so as to match the archival representation of some omniscient, ever present (and non-existent) audio visual 360 degree recording apparatus in the sky?

2. *Memory is selective and essentially incomplete!*

Thus, *memories* can be expected to vary as a function not only of the state, intentions, and filtering that existed at the time of the actual event but also as a function of state, present intentions, and filtering of the person reconstructing the *memory* in the present. Distinct portions of the reconstruction being reported will be identified and presented and others will not. As the state, intentions, and requirements of the person remembering shift, so will the representations of what occurred. Some of these differences will depend on the granularity of the representation (its specificity) and whether it is confined to a specific logical type of representation – description, interpretation, and evaluation (assuming that the person making the reconstruction, or indeed the reader, can make the distinction among these varying modes of representation). This is unlikely as the vast majority of the members of the fourth estate have yet to notice or are unable or unwilling to respect.

Test it for yourself – remember the last dinner you ate in a restaurant. OK, ready – make a representation of what occurred ... Got it!

Cool, but what about the color of the border of the menu? Did the servers actually present the fresh dishes from one side of the diner and remove the used dishes from the other side? How were the portions of the dinner arranged on the serving platters? Were the chargers color coordinated with the flowers on the sideboard (what sideboard!)? Who spoke first after the ordering was complete? Did the following speakers at the table replicate the rhythm of the first speaker's voice or was there a significant contrast? Did the volume of sound in the restaurant rise and fall with a certain temporal frequency? Did the texture of the side dishes complement the texture of the main dish? How clearly could you hear the sounds of the kitchen where your food was being prepared? How frequently did the people sitting beside each other mirror the others' physical movements as compared with people facing one another either at the same table or the one to your left as you sat at the table? Did the chairs you all sat in make a loud sound when moved during the seating ritual? Was the waiter/waitress right or left handed? Was the tablecloth arranged as a square or a diamond with respect to the table it covered ... a flurry of questions, most of little or no interest for most people.

The point here is that in reconstructing a *memory*, you are confronted with the task of selecting from among a very large (although finite) set of possible things to represent. Those things that actually end up in your reconstruction are there as an indicator of your intentions and interests, now, as you reconstruct the *memory*. In the provocations above about your dinner at the restaurant, I confined myself largely to physical aspects of the event. What if we were to venture into the relationships implicit at that table and the complex operations implied by these relationships? Now the situation gets even more complex. If you were able to compare what you reconstructed with respect to the dinner in the restaurant with this archive, do you suppose that your reconstruction would contain more or less than the archival file referred to above. Surprisingly, the answer is both – you would find a vast array of things that were not reconstructed in your representation and some things in your representation would NOT be present in the archive captured by that ubiquitous recording system in the sky.

There are higher level differences that emerge in addition to the essentially incomplete and selective nature of your reconstruction of the dinner. Was your representation biased, focusing largely on the visual aspects of that dinner/restaurant event? Was any attention given to the sounds of the environment (the restaurant)? What about the tastes and combinations and sequences of tastes, the developing of various topics in the conversation, and how the feelings of the people at the table shifted with the development of the conversations about these various topics?

3. *Does it really matter what happened historically?*

What *is* the point of examining the historical development of something as complex as the birth of a new field? Are you hoping to catch a glimpse of the processes of discovery, possibly even with the intention of using such processes in making comparable discoveries yourself? Are you so naive as to think that two human beings confronted with the "same" set of stimuli (experiences) will respond in the "same" way? The *same*'s are in quotes to remind you that the same set of stimuli are NOT the same when processed through distinct neurologies. Is it really relevant to you as a researcher to know how someone else with a completely distinct background responded to the stimuli that were available at the origin of NLP? Do you really think that playing the music of and dancing to Congolese traditional rhythms, and training and riding Arabian trail horses ... will assist you in becoming a better modeler? Does having developed a set of effective patterns help guide young people out of the thick jungle of drugs towards a lighted path from which some of them can then reach back and guide their former mates? Is it really an advantage to speak some eight languages; or have a deep appreciation of battlefield injuries and the corresponding life-saving interventions required; or know how to derail a train with a minimum of plastic explosives; or hit a golf ball 300 yards down the middle of the fairway; or to have a deep computational competency in automata theory; or how to rig a automatic watering system for horse trough; or ...

Personally, I don't think so. But then, it is very dangerous to generalize from a sample of one.

Yet, as I move around the globe offering training, conferences, and demonstrations, one of the most frequent questions is the history question: *What happened at the origin of the field now known as NLP?* and *How did it happen?* What ensues, if the person asked is willing to accept the question, is a series of bedtime stories, meeting the requirements of the speaker's present intentions in presenting themselves to strengthen the image of whoever the speaker is and what s/he wishes the audience to carry away with them.

So, step back a moment here before plunging into this maelstrom and ask yourself the obvious question:

What is the relationship, if any, between the *technology* of modeling and the *history of discovery, assimilation, and coding of patterning in the field now known as NLP?*

Isn't the point of this simple but difficult adventure called the modeling of genius to detect, assimilate unconsciously, code, and disseminate the patterning of geniuses? If this cycle of deep learning has any point, it is to make available the patterning of geniuses in a learnable form that integrates these patterns of genius into the performance of people wishing to achieve higher quality and more effective results in their worlds of application. This results in the raising of the bar in that profession. For example, the modeling of Dr. Milton Erickson required some 10 months or so between first contact and the coding of the patterning (see *Patterns of the Hypnotic Techniques of Milton H. Erickson,*

M.D. Volumes I and *II*).[1] How many people have the time (10 months) as well as the tolerance for the inherent ambiguity of the task of modeling and the competency to code the assimilated patterns into a description that would allow others to gain access to these patterns without this enormous investment of time and talent?

In medieval Europe, the accumulated tacit knowledge of various professions, say, for example, of masonry, was passed from master to apprentice through direct modeling – there were no shortcuts. The apprentice mason prepared the site, carried the materials, did the clean up, and whilst doing all this, if this apprentice were to succeed in becoming a mason, he would notice and mark how, specifically, the master mason approached the various aspects of actually building that structure, setting up that foundation, and executing the plans of the architect.

I recognize that the depth of integration of the patterning is quite distinct (at least initially) as a function of the method of assimilation. If learning the patterning is accomplished inductively and through unconscious assimilation, the patterns belong in a deep sense to the learner. Such a learner then has the leisure to revisit such patterns and may then ferret out the essential elements of the patterns and their sequencing – the formal pattern itself or some functional equivalent.

Those learners following a conscious approach will certainly upgrade their game; whether they ever achieve the depth of integration of patterning arrived at inductively is an open question. In our present context, few people, if anyone, are prepared to enter the strange and disorienting world of deep inductive learning, thus, the niche of modeler emerges.

So, what will you do with these reconstructed tales flowing down through the decades since their actual occurrence, and channeled through the intentions, interests, and self-images of the people offering these representations?

Good question!

The Fundamental Strategy

Frank and I have considered how to manage these issues. We have settled on a specific strategy. We have determined to pursue the minimization of these particular classes of distortion by calling upon a large number of people who were physically present and participated in or observed some of the events that are herein described. A few are names that are widely recognized in the present day field of NLP; most are people who are unknown and largely inactive with respect to the patterning of the NLP of today – people who have no particular clear known agenda. Mark carefully what they report.

You will find in this book the voices of people who moved resolutely, wandered, and/or often stumbled (most of all the co-authors of this book) through these events, each of whom carried with them specific personal agendas and perceptual filters which ensured that their perceptions and thus subsequently their reconstructed *memories* of these events would be quite distinct, especially with the passage of time (now some 40 years). Many of these differences arise through the ubiquitous and selective perceptual filtering that necessarily results from the strong limitations of the bandwidth of consciousness (7 + or – chunks of information).

I would venture that few of the distortions that occur in such reconstructions are deliberate. This lack of explicit awareness of the filtering and its consequences, and the unconsciously motivated personal agendas of the people responsible for these deviations from what actually happened (now largely unknowable), makes such distortions all the more problematic, both with respect to the task of discovering what the distortion is/was and what it is/was a distortion of – that is, deviations from what actually happened.

But surely one of the most obvious and powerful conclusions from the development and deployment of patterning over the last four decades in NLP, and easily verified in the reader's own experience, is the astonishing diversity in the descriptions that emerge from any single event when described from the distinct perceptual positions of the people who directly participated in or witnessed the event in question.

Indeed, I would caution the reader to consider the following: the more prominent the name/reputation of the writer of the description, the more likely the distortions (operationally defined as deviations from a correspondence with the record captured by great 360 degree audio/video recorder in the sky – which fortunately or unfortunately does not exist). This is the sense of *unknowable* as in the paragraph two above this one. Note please that this applies with full force to the words that you are presently reading.

This is as accurate a statement for a relatively common event, such as whose idea was it, really, to organize that birthday party for a mutual friend, as it is for that rare event – the creation of a new field of patterning such as NLP. None of it is to be taken at face value.

There are two distinct issues here. First, anyone with an appropriate background and some thought can comment on what they perceive as the predecessors of NLP or any other set of developed patterns. Certainly, practitioners of the Philosophy of Science have done this service for many branches of science (see especially the fine work of Thomas Kuhn in *The Structure of Scientific Revolutions* on the development of portions of modern physics[2]). Through their research into the birth and development of what later became incorporated into standard models or sets of patterning, these practitioners have succeeded in connecting discrete and heretofore unconnected work, sometimes in a single field, sometimes across fields, that had previously been considered distinct. Such studies can be highly useful and instructive.

This is a distinct issue from what the creator or co-creators of a discipline had access to, what they were aware of at the time and in the context of the creation of that discipline. It is interesting to consider the differences between these two issues as captured by the following two questions.

The first question is:

> *Where did the ideas that turn up in some new model or set of patterns come from historically?*

This is surely an issue worthy of the attention of researchers with a synthetic bent – a history of the development of the ideas involved. As examples of the high value of such work, I cite two cases from Kuhn. The first is from *The Structure of Scientific Revolutions*:

> With scientific observation ... the scientist can have no recourse above or beyond what he sees with his eyes and instruments. If there were some higher authority by recourse to which his vision might be shown to have shifted, then that authority would itself become the source of his data, and the behavior of his visions would become a source of problems. The period during which light was "sometimes a wave and sometimes a particle" – was a period of crisis, a period where something was wrong – and it ended only with the development of wave mechanics and the realization that light was a self-consistent entity different from both waves and particles. In the sciences, therefore, if perceptual switches accompany paradigm changes, we may not expect scientists to attest to these changes directly. Looking at the moon, the convert to Copernicanism does not say, "I used to see a planet, but now I see a satellite." That locution would imply a sense in which the Ptolemaic system had once been correct. Instead, a convert to the new astronomy says, "I once took the moon to be (or saw the moon as) a planet, but I was mistaken." That sort of statement does occur in the aftermath of scientific revolution. If it ordinarily disguises a shift of scientific visions or some other mental transformation with the same effect, we may not expect direct testimony about that shift. Rather we must look for indirect and behavioral evidence that the scientist with a new paradigm sees differently from the way he had seen before.

> Let us then return to the data and ask what sorts of transformations in the scientists' world the historian who believes in such changes can discover. Sir William Herschel's discovery of Uranus provides a first example. On at least seventeen different occasions between 1690 and 1781, a number of astronomers, including several of Europe's most eminent observers, had seen a star in positions that we now suppose must have been occupied at the time by Uranus. One of the best observers in this group had actually seen the star on four successive nights in 1769 without noting the motion that could have suggested

13

another identification. Herschel, when he first observed the same object twelve years later, did so with a much improved telescope of his own manufacture. As a result, he was able to notice an apparent disk-size that was at least unusual for stars. Something was awry, and he therefore postponed identification pending further scrutiny. That scrutiny disclosed Uranus' motion among the stars, and Herschel therefore announced that he had seen a new comet. Only several months later, after fruitless attempts to fit the observed motion to a cometary orbit, did Lexell suggest that the orbit was probably planetary. When that suggestion was accepted, there were several fewer stars and one more planet in the world of the professional astronomer. A celestial body that had been observed off and on for almost a century was seen differently after 1781. It could no longer be fitted to the perceptual categories (star or comet) provided by the paradigm that had previously prevailed.

The shift of vision that enabled astronomers to see Uranus, the planet, does not, however, seem to have affected only the perception of that previously observed object. Its consequence were more far-reaching, probably, though the evidence is equivocal, the minor paradigm shift force by Herschel helped to prepare astronomers for the rapid discovery, after 1801, of the numerous minor planets or asteroids. Because of their small size, these did not display the anomalous magnification that had alerted Herschel. Nevertheless, astronomers prepared to find additional planets were able, with standard instruments, to identify twenty of them in the first fifty years of the nineteenth century. The Chinese, whose cosmological beliefs did not preclude celestial change, had recorded the appearance of many new stars in the heavens at a much earlier date. Also, even without the aid of a telescope, the Chinese had systematically recorded the appearance of sunspots centuries before these were seen by Galileo and his contemporaries. The very ease and rapidity with which astronomers saw new things when looking at old objects with old instruments may make us wish to say that, after Copernicus, astronomers lived in a different universe. In any case, their research responded as though that were the case.[3]

The second case is also from Kuhn, this time from his book, *The Essential Tension*. The topic this time is the phenomenon of simultaneous discovery:

> Between 1842 and 1847, the hypothesis of energy conservation was publicly announced by four widely scattered European scientists – Mayer, Joule, Colding and Helmholtz – all but one working in complete ignorance of the others. The coincidence is conspicuous, yet these four announcements are unique only in combining generality of formulation with concrete quantitative applications. Sadi Carnot, before 1832, Marc Sequin, in 1839, Karl Helmholtz, in 1845, and G. S. Hirn in 1854, all recorded their independent convictions that heat and work are quantitatively interchangeable, and all computed a value for the conversion coefficient or an equivalent. The convertibility of heat and work is, of course, only a special case of energy conservation, but the generality lacking in this second group of announcements occurs elsewhere in the literature of the period. Between 1837 and 1844, C. F. Mohr, William Grove, Faraday and Liebig all described the world of phenomena as manifesting but a single "force," one which could appear in electrical, thermal, dynamical, and many other forms, but which could never, in all its transformations, be created or destroyed. That so-called force is the one known to later scientists as energy. The history of science offers no more striking instance of the phenomenon known as simultaneous discovery.

> Already we have named twelve men who, within a short period of time, grasped for themselves essential parts of the concept of energy and its conservation … The present multiplicity sufficiently suggests that in the two decades before 1850, the climate of European scientific thought included elements able to guide receptive scientists to a significant new view of nature. Isolating these elements within the works of the men affected by them may tell us something of the nature of simultaneous discovery.

> Before proceeding toward that objective, however, we must briefly pause over the phrase "simultaneous discovery" itself. In the ideal case of simultaneous discovery two or more men would announce the same thing at the same time and in complete ignorance of each other's work, but nothing remotely like

that happened during the development of energy conserva-tion. The violations of simultaneity and mutual influence are secondary. But no two of our men even said the same thing. Until close to the end of the period of discovery, few of their papers have more than fragmentary resemblances retrievable in isolated sentences and paragraphs. Skilful excerpting is, for example, required to make Mohr's defense of the dynamical theory of heat resemble Liebig's discussion of the intrinsic lim-its of the electric motor. A diagram of the overlapping passages in the papers by the pioneers of energy conservation would resemble an unfinished crossword puzzle. Nor is the problem of divergent discoveries restricted to those scientists whose formulations were obviously incomplete. Mayer, Colding, Joule, and Helmholtz were not saying the same things at the dates usually given for their discoveries of energy conserva-tion. In these years their papers have important areas of overlap, but not until Mayer's book of 1845 and Joule's publi-cations of 1844 and 1847 do these theories become substan-tially coextensive.[4]

These examples offer ample indications of the treasures buried and ready to be unearthed by the astute historian with a background in the disciplines implicated in the research – in this endeavor to connect various lines of research and thought historically in the development of discoveries and advances, in this case, in astronomy and physics. I also regard Kuhn's work as setting a high standard for solving precisely such puzzles.

Then there is a second and quite distinct question:

How did the creator or set of co-creators discover and develop the ideas, the practices, and the concrete actions in their research that ultimately carried them to a successful creation of the model involved?

Obviously, from the above discussion, the answers to these two ques-tions can be expected to diverge. In particular, note that the answers to this second question are available only in the memory traces in the neurologies of the direct participants in and observers to that creation. Independent of what the larger intellectual milieu was at the time of the creation of the model, this second question is fascinating in the sense that it asks about the creator's or co-creators' states of knowledge at the time of the creation of the model. All this touches strongly on issues of innovation, and the distinction between these two questions offers fertile ground for information leading to useful discussion about how to create contexts that promote innovation and the creation of new models: a subject worthy of its own and separate consideration.

Clearly, then, this book provides material uniquely relevant to the second of these two questions. The beginnings of the discussion concerning the first question have been initiated and partially addressed in other work (see, for example, chapters 3 and 4 of *Whispering in the Wind* by Carmen Bostic-St. Clair and John Grinder).[5]

The reader will have to actively pursue these issues to appreciate what occurred and what the participants actually knew, taking into account the distinct perceptual positions from which these reports are offered and teasing out what specific filters might account for the differences in the various descriptions and interpretations offered here. We trust that the reader will approach these questions in the spirit of discovery, much as a detective would , ferreting out what is common among these contributions and what is distinctive in order to decide for themselves what actually occurred.

John Grinder
Bonny Doon, California
September 2012

PART 1

CHAPTER 1

Lots of "Times," Some Easy, Some Fun, Some Hard

R. Frank Pucelik

I graduated from high school in San Diego, California in 1963. Went to Community College and after three semesters quit. Not a good idea to quit college in 1965. Received my letter from Uncle Sam a few months later and joined the Navy before my 90 days were up. Did too well on the intelligence tests in boot camp and found myself assigned to Hospital Corpsman School directly from boot camp. Spent a wonderful year working in a military hospital and playing golf in Japan, my first duty station, after my abbreviated military medical school.

The Marine Corps needed medical corpsmen and I was transferred to the Marines in 1966. Went to infantry training back in San Diego where I also went to boot camp and Corps School, then off to the 2nd Battalion 9th Marine Regiment smack in the middle of the jungle in Southeast Asia. Not a fun year: spent 10 months in the jungle (I Corp) with a Marine Platoon and three months at a field medical hospital (A-Med) in Phu Bai, South Vietnam. When I left Vietnam I was stationed at the Naval Hospital in San Diego, California, which was also my home town, for the last seven months of my four-year military obligation. This seven months was a great gift to me. I was at home but not actually out of the military yet. Really needed this "halfway" time to try to get back to being a human. It helped a lot and served as a partial re-entry to human-hood.

So I spent four years doing my duty and then back to the college in San Diego I had quit before joining the military. This time around my attitude and desire were of a different caliber than the first time and I excelled at everything: perfect grades, took part in every activity, and a lot more golf. Married the sweetheart I had met in the military after the war, we gave birth to our son, and I went to work trying to get the war and my childhood out of me. I majored in psychology and political science. Not much progress on the self-healing during the two years I spent in college but learned a lot about several different psychological systems and had a lot of fun. In 1970 I transferred to the University of California at Santa Cruz (UCSC) to finish my bachelor's degrees in both psychology and politics.

So, here I was in hippy city, being fresh out of the military, and fresh out of a college dominated by military veteran students. Wow, what a shock. In those days UCSC was really academically difficult to get into and they were not accepting many kids. Only the best could get in. However, the UC system at that time was allowing a number of veterans "special admission" opportunities and so, there I was surrounded by the smartest kids I had ever seen. Most of them were four to six years younger than myself but incredibly well educated. Luckily I was a good talker and a reasonably self-assured character by this time, so I was able to cope and over time "kind of" fit in. Loved the university and was able to immerse myself more deeply in the process of finding out what was wrong with me and working hard to become someone even I could like and respect.

In mid or late 1971, I was doing peer counseling and teaching some younger students how to do Gestalt, which I had studied extensively at college in San Diego. I was also doing a lot of training for other peer counselors to do "talk downs" for students who had taken LSD and were having a "bad trip." For me this was pretty easy stuff. Screaming and relatively violent clients were not much to deal with after being in Southeast Asia. My reputation was "the guy who could handle any counseling drug crisis," and I liked the respect and reputation that went with it.

About this time I met a guy named Richard Bandler who was a lot like me. He didn't seem to care about much and not much could bother him, especially crying, screaming college students. We fit together pretty well and we began doing Gestalt training groups together. We were doing two or three group training sessions a week and making some good pocket change in the process. After a few months of doing these groups together, Richard invited a new "hotshot" linguistics professor to come visit our groups to see if there were linguistic or other patterns he could observe from our behaviors and/or ideas that could help us be better than we already were. After three or four sessions with John Grinder (the new hotshot linguistics professor) observing our training groups and asking us questions about our language patterns and other patterns he had noticed, we knew we were on to something really special. In my opinion it was during these two or three Gestalt training group sessions that NLP/Meta was born. The excitement I felt during these early times with John and Richard became a driving force that never left me during the following six or so years that we spent together (actually it still hasn't left me and I assume it never will).

For the first several months of our interactions it was just John, Richard, and myself, but we rapidly started adding group members. During John's university classes and during Richard and my Gestalt training classes, we would find people we liked and/or people would come to us and ask to join the "study group" we had formed. So, we were off and running. In my opinion, this group of people were the "first generation" NLP folks. They included Joyce Michaelson, Trevelyan Houck, Marilyn Moskowitz, Jeff Paris, Lisa Chiara, Ilene McCloud, Ken Block, Terry Rooney, Jody Bruce, Bill Polansky, Devra Canter, and one more person who is choosing to stay anonymous. Also, there were a few people during these early years who were on the edge of what we were doing: Terry McClendon (who became much more connected and active later with Robert Dilts), Paul Carter (a close friend of Steven Gilligan and partner for several years), David Wick (head of Youth Services and good friend as well as excellent leader and student of NLP), Gary Merrill (a close friend of Judy DeLozier and was in many groups with the Meta kids), Michael Patton (without whose help and friendship I might not have ever graduated from UCSC – a good counselor and colleague at Youth Services), Peter Gaarn (also a powerful counselor at Youth Services), and Pat LeClair (Head Counselor at Youth Services who constantly supported our "innovative" work with the clients). During the first two years, the group of people named above were the ones primarily involved in the experimenting.

It was during these two years of experimenting that the Meta Model and other foundation models were formalized. We spent a lot of time copying the "great" therapists (sometimes in person, sometimes on video, and sometimes via manuscripts) to learn their language patterns and then formalize their "tricks" so we could use them equally well. We spent an incredible amount of time and energy, during all six years and all three generations, doing Gestalt sessions with each other on every conceivable problem we might have: family reconstructions with each other until everyone's families had been analyzed and reconstructed many times for each of us; psychodrama from every possible perspective; parts parties by the hundreds (each practitioner with each member of the team); and dream therapy with every dream that could possibly have any significance for each of us, by each of us. Then, evaluating the patterns (verbal and non-verbal), refining the patterns as much as possible, then testing for quicker, better results. We kept practicing until we were pretty convinced that this particular technique or process could not be done better or faster.

We observed that the "masters" were often sloppy and inconsistent in their use of change behaviors and, by understanding the patterns they used and using them systematically, we believed we were faster and better than they were. We spent much of our time accumulating their "licks" and testing our competence on each other, with our friends, and with the clients several of us had while working with the Santa Cruz Counseling Center (Youth Services). It seemed obvious that in most cases the "masters" had learned their change patterns over many years of trial and error and actually didn't know what pattern they were observing or what systematic behavior or language they were using to affect the change in the clients. We confirmed this many times when questioning the "masters" themselves. It also seemed that they relied on very few patterns and were not flexible. We now understood very clearly what was happening when a therapist was very effective with one client and completely ineffective with the next. The problems that clients had also had patterns and the "helpers" needed to be effective with the pattern the clients used to create their problem. It seemed to us that the "helpers" could not help the client if the client's problem was not "rooted" in the pattern the "helper" could recognize and work with effectively. Today that sounds ridiculously simple but in 1973 this was quite a revelation for us.

This meant that potentially we could find the patterns of many different great communicators and put them together into a package of skills that one practitioner could learn and use. During these early years we played with the patterns of Carlos Castaneda, Carl Rogers, Virginia Satir, Fritz Perls, Gregory Bateson, John Lilly, and others. This, of course, allowed us to understand the most common misjudgment made in psychotherapy. We understood that any model provided by a school or style of psychotherapy was destined to fail more often than not. We also understood that it is the client's model, or group of patterns, that is far more important for the therapist to respond to than the "helping" or "healthy" model the therapist brings to the session. Of course, it is therefore necessary for the therapist to adjust the therapy system to fit the client, not the client to fit the therapy. We spent some time taking the "healthy" models from the different systems of psychotherapy and carrying them out to their logical conclusion, as if they were a real or complete personality structure. What great fun it was to be a complete "Gestalt" person, or a total "Transactional Analysis" person, or a "Freudian" person (be careful with this one). This process helped us understand quickly the limits, incompleteness, and contradictions of the "systems" that were often the guiding principles of psychotherapy.

During this time the nature of my relationship with Richard slowly changed. Originally Richard and I were the dynamic duo. By the middle of 1973 (very possibly earlier in Richard's mind), Richard and John had become the dynamic duo and I was (functionally) the "leader of the pack" of students. Some of the later students never quite accepted this role on my part but that was the way it was until the middle of 1976. I now think some of the later troops – like Robert Dilts, Stephen Gilligan, Jim Eicher, possibly Leslie Cameron, Judy DeLozier, David Gordon, and the rest – never knew how the "Meta people" got started. I never thought about it in those days. I never cared. We were having too much fun, learning a lot, and I was starting to feel like a "real" human being.

On one occasion when we were playing with dream therapy models, mixing Gestalt dream work with psychodrama and Virginia's "parts parties," John led me through the painful process of "living out" my recurring Vietnam nightmare. A long and frightening three or so hours, but John and the guys involved stayed with me and it changed me forever. I was finally able to finish some of the worst memories, guilt, and closed-off feelings that were bubbling out of me at the worst moments and in the worst way. Until that session, with John's guidance, I believed that the craziness put in me by the jungle was there to stay. The transformations from that session with John have continued, in a good way, all my life.

The Meta people met John, Richard, and myself one or two times a week for three to five hours and worked without John and Richard two to four more times a week, often for four to six hours at a time (I was part of all of these groups). Several of us also worked together at Youth Services, and had classes and organizational groups together in the university.

It was during '73 and '74 that my emphasis was divided between learning patterns, working with the patterns we were learning at Youth Services in Santa Cruz, organizing experimentation meetings, working with the Meta people honing our skills, trying to finish with the war and the craziness that was the legacy of my childhood, and finishing my degree work at the university. John and Richard, of course, were key to my personal and professional development; John in a more direct manner and Richard as an attentive antagonist.

During late '73 and early '74 several key people joined the process. This was the time when Robert Dilts, Steve Gilligan, Jim Eicher, Leslie Cameron, David Gordon, and Judy DeLozier became involved. During '74 and '75 an incredible amount of our focus was given to the unconscious models, including Milton Erickson and others. We learned and experienced every trance phenomenon we could find or read about. We spend hundreds of hours working with each other and anyone else we could get to let us put them into "trance," most of the time with their permission. We learned the process of "deep trance identification" where you become another person at the most basic level possible.

The idea was to learn from them as fast and as completely as possible. We "became" every person we could think of who had something "magic" to teach us. We had a hard time getting Steven to be Steven during this time and I spent a few strange days the first time Leslie was Virginia. Leslie and I were very close at the time, life partners, working partners, both on the NLP team and at Youth Services. When she became Virginia she was very polite and obviously did not know me. That is a very uncomfortable feeling when someone you know very well does not know who you are. I was very relieved a day later when Leslie was back in Leslie's body.

Our merry band continued experimenting during '75 through '76, copying, experiencing personally, evaluating, testing, practicing, and refining everything we could find that we thought was worth learning. The models and techniques we were developing were becoming publicly known and people from the other side of the hill (San Jose, San Francisco, Palo Alto, Berkeley, and all points east from Santa Cruz) wanted to study our "discoveries." Most of the Meta people were doing training programs of one kind or another. We had moved into informal teams. Leslie and I worked a lot together and focused on education and family systems. I spent some of my happiest years living with and working with Leslie. She was a great friend, an incredible life partner, a wonderful and fearless learner, and the best trainer I have ever observed (besides myself, of course).

By this time Byron Lewis had moved to Santa Cruz and joined the group. He was and is one of the people in the world that I have the most admiration for. Byron is one of those rare people who does what he says he will do, and always to the best of his ability. Worth his weight in gold. We were friends from the day we met and still are today.

Leslie Cameron, Ken Block, Michael Patton, Peter Gaarn, David Wick, Pat LeClair, and myself all gave a great deal of time and focus to the education system of Santa Cruz County and the problems being experienced by the young people of the greater Santa Cruz region, including the surrounding cities. We worked as a team providing training for the area teachers, working directly with the schools and the agencies responsible for dealing with "troubled youths." We each had clients appointed to us through Youth Services (a department of the Santa Cruz Community Counseling Center). This was the legal entity responsible for providing psychological services to the people in the Santa Cruz region. Pat LeClair was the Supervising Psychologist and David Wick was the Program Director. Both were committed and dedicated to the challenge that confronted the team. The rest of us were the counselors and trainers sent into the field to accomplish the impossible. David Wick has added his unique perspective to this book. You will read what it was like to be involved with us Meta people, and what the reactions were from the schools and the community at large from the work done by the team at Youth Services (see Chapter 4).

We were excited to be using our skills in the "real" world and with clients that other psychologists had so much trouble working with successfully. This was truly a test of our ideas and skills. We learned, succeeded in our goals, and loved working with "our" kids and "our" schools.

By the middle of '75, many of the original Meta people had graduated from UCSC and moved on to the rest of their lives. We were all doing a lot of training and work in our areas of interest. Steven Gilligan and Paul Carter were entrenched in Ericksonian activities, Leslie and I in family systems and education, and the rest of the troops doing their best to continue their focus areas. Training groups were continuing on a regular basis. The people from "over the hill" were coming to Santa Cruz to learn from us. John and Richard would orchestrate challenging and interesting training groups. They would meet with the Meta kids before the training group started and give us directions on what they wanted us to teach the regular group. When the regular training session started they would give each of the Meta people a few of the group participants (6 to 15) and we would lead them through learning experiences. The fun part of the game, for us Meta kids, was when John or Richard would come to us, during our training process, and observe our work, evaluate our abilities, and change our goals – possibly several times during the evening – and still lead a coherent and valuable training program for the participants from over the hill.

Sometimes they would take us from our group of participants and place us with a different group and tell us to continue with the program that the other trainer was doing before we arrived. Of course, we often didn't know what the other trainer was doing and John or Richard would not tell us. We had to figure out what the other trainer was doing by testing and observing, mostly using non-verbal feedback. Wow, was this challenging sometimes. We understood that two different training programs were taking place at the same time. The program for the Meta kids was at a different level than the program for the participants from over the hill. Of course, they would observe long enough and control enough to make sure that the program for the participants from over the hill would be a high quality and valuable experience.

When the program for the regular participants was finished and they had all left, then the program for the Meta kids would continue in earnest. We would tell what we learned, what had given us the best clues about what the other trainers had done with their groups before we took over, what difficulties we had encountered and how we tried to get past those difficulties, whether successful or not, get feedback from each other and summaries of the event, and then there would be feedback to each of us from John and Richard. Of course, we had great learning experiences, not always easy and sometimes not fun until later. I am sure you can understand what I mean.

It was about late '76 or perhaps early '77 that my life changed abruptly and completely. Leslie was invited by Richard to join himself, John, Judy, and Eric (my son) to visit Milton Erickson. Of course, she jumped at the chance and I was really happy for her. When she returned from the trip to Arizona my life was suddenly different. When she returned she was indifferent to me and would barely talk or interact with me at all. It was obvious that something had changed and I fought against the obvious conclusion I did not want to believe.

Within a couple weeks, Richard came to me to inform me that I was no longer welcome to be involved with the team or any of the team members in any way, for any reason. I chose to honor his "request" for reasons of my own. That was the day it became obvious that I no longer had my living partner, my working partner, my learning team, my source of income, or my friends (they were all members of the Meta kids). After some time to get used to this situation (actually a few months), during which Paul Carter and Stephen Gilligan gave me a place to live and showed incredible patience and respect, I loaded up all my personal belongings, and of course my dogs, and headed for Nebraska. I spent about eight months being a counselor for farmers and "town folk" (they didn't like psychological people so I had to work through the preachers and the local priests who were glad to have the professional help) in a farming community where I had originally started my life. It was really interesting living in a community of 600 people after spending the last 28 or so years in San Diego and Santa Cruz.

I spent my free time working as a volunteer with the local animal doctor. Did a lot of surgery on different animals, enjoyed seeing all the farms, meeting all those incredible people, and learning as much as I could about animal medicine. The vet and I became fast friends. I learned a lot from him. I loved the place and loved the experience but soon I'd had all I could take (life in that community was a bit slow and a bit too predictable for me), packed up my truck and my dogs, and headed for San Diego. I was back home and starting over again.

While visiting the Institute of Transactional Analysis (TA) in La Jolla, the Gestalt Institute in Pacific Beach, and the Center for the Studies of the Person, also in La Jolla (this was the institute started and run by Carl Rogers), I discovered a great desire from the people in San Diego to learn about NLP, so after a few months I opened the San Diego Meta Institute (SDMI). I found and invited some of the Meta kids who were no longer involved with John and Richard in Santa Cruz to join me in San Diego. To my great surprise and pleasure, several of the early troops joined me and we spent a fun and exciting four or so years living, learning, and teaching NLP to the San Diego psychological and business communities. Marilyn Moskowitz, Jeff Paris, Byron Lewis, and Lisa Chiara from the Santa Cruz Meta kids, and two great students of psychology and NLP, Tim Criswell and Steven Lorei, from the San Diego area joined us to complete the training/learning staff at SDMI.

During this time, Byron and I both earned our PhDs from United States International University's program conducted through the TA

Institute in La Jolla. I was a lecturer in the PhD program (teaching NLP to the TA and PhD students at the Institute) and Byron was also working with PhD candidates in the same program. The SDMI was active and provided constant training programs in the many fields we had patterned during the six or so years we had spent in Santa Cruz. We all continued to add applications to our bag of tricks and enjoyed each other's feedback and company.

In 1983 I was invited to move to Oklahoma and become a negotiator for a man who owned and operated oil wells in the central US. His promises made it hard to turn down plus I was offered all necessary financial support for opening a branch of Meta Institute there. I accepted the offer, loaded my truck and dogs again, and headed for Norman, Oklahoma. I gave my "blessing" to the San Diego troops and the leadership of SDMI to Marilyn. They continued the SDMI program for a few years after I left and then closed it down and went on with their own lives. In 1983 in Oklahoma the oil business went belly up (my timing for joining this business was not exactly the best) and by the middle of 1984 my NLP training company (Oklahoma Meta Institute) was supporting the oil and gas people I had joined the year before. They left the oil business, so did I, and Oklahoma Meta Institute continued to do very well. I did a lot of training throughout the Midwest and really got used to the central US culture and liked it.

Good people, very conservative, and very religious, took some getting used to, for sure. I had to learn how to teach NLP with the proper connections to the Bible. Not too difficult for a good Catholic schoolboy like myself (I had gone to a Catholic school in San Diego for the first eight years of my schooling – great education in those days). My short time living and working in Nebraska also helped me get ready for Oklahoma. Met and married a wonderful Oklahoma girl in Norman (yes, got married again). We shared life for several years. She is one of the best people I have been lucky to share time with. We still talk and care for each other today. Worked with a lot of companies and spent a lot of time on the road. I also spent a lot of time with my son, Eric, traveling the professional Motocross circuit. He was, by this time, an accomplished professional racer and I had the desire to spend as much time with him as I could. John Grinder, Judy DeLozier, and I would meet as often as possible at his races and at each other's homes when we could. John was my son's stepdad by this time and Eric often had to put up with having four parents with him. I think he enjoyed us all. I hope so. I considered myself an incredibly lucky man. If I had the opportunity to choose a stepfather for my son, of all the men in the world, I would have chosen John.

During this time I was often asked to teach staff counselors at young people's residential treatment programs for drug addicts and alcoholics. Whenever I was at these programs I always had the feeling that the programs were not effective – and this is stating it very mildly. It always seemed to me that the clients in the programs were simply learning how to successfully lie to the staff. Whenever I got close enough to the kids to get the truth from them, they confirmed my worst fears. These programs were shams at best and mostly more damaging than helpful. I thought a lot about the program structures, the staff, and what the goals of the programs actually were. These programs were designed either to make money (the rich kids' programs) or to create a place to put the kids so they were not on the streets for a while (poor kids' programs) or as a place to hold them until they were old enough to put in prison. That is where most of them were going and it seemed that everybody (i.e., the professionals in the field) knew it but just would not say it out loud.

I could not work with these people *and* keep my mouth shut. I went to the head of the worst of the poor kids' programs I had seen and gave him a challenge. I told him, "Your program sucks. I can build a real program, if you are interested, but I want complete control for three years." He told me he would think about it. He called me a week later and asked when I was ready to begin. Now I had to put my money where my mouth was. I spent the next three or so years, while running Meta Institute Oklahoma, spending time with my son traveling to his races and creating and running two treatment programs (one for young people and, later, one for adults) in the Oklahoma City area.

I recruited great staff and we created a model using the practices and principles from NLP, conjoint family systems, Gestalt, quality business practices, and the best of the "therapeutic community" systems I had been studying. During the third year of our operation, we (the House of Life) were selected by a research team from the US government (a national program called Youth at Risk) as the best young people's treatment program in America. The success rate of the best programs I had seen before the House was less than 1%, if the people were counting honestly. Most did not count at all and I knew why. We wanted to get to 75% (no one had ever credibly gone above 10%) but in the four years I led the program we never got there. At the end of the fourth year we were just over 60% (using the strictest criteria I had seen in treatment programs). I left the program in Oklahoma in 1988. That program lasted for several years but slowly returned to the state it was in when I found it (270 clients in the previous three years with no evidence of any positive results of any kind for any of the participants) and does not exist today. I still interact with many of the graduates from that program on Facebook. My kids forever.

In 1987, while living in Oklahoma, I was contacted by a friend of mine in California. She told me she had some Russian psychologists visiting her and three of them wanted to meet me because of what I was working on and what I knew about Gestalt, NLP, and drug treatment. She said I was the only person who knew all three of these things at a high level and could she send me the Russians.

I said sure and the next day I met my first Russians at the Oklahoma City airport. They were planning to stay for three days but they stayed for three weeks. We had great fun. I showed them as much as I could and we became friends quickly. They invited me to visit Russia and a few weeks later I found myself getting off a plane in Moscow. What a shock. I found myself walking into a time warp: I was instantly back in 1935. I loved it. I found a lot of very educated professional psychologists who could not do anything. We fit together perfectly. I didn't know much, compared to them, but had a lot of skills and could do almost everything they wanted to know how to do. It was a trainer's heaven. I found large numbers of highly educated professionals, eager to learn, and ready to try anything. No more intellectual bullshit arguments so common to training programs in the United States. They simply wanted me to show them how to accomplish goals and supervise their attempts to copy what I had demonstrated. Wonderful energy, hungry students, and 11 time zones of need. I traveled back and forth a few times and moved to Moscow completely in late 1989.

I have experienced so many incredible events here. I have been the first American ever to visit many cities all across the Russian world, experienced great chaos, witnessed incredible tragedy, felt grave danger, done lots of "miracles," created hundreds of powerful friendships, helped and trained many thousands of people, helped hundreds of businesses, and been given the gift of an incredible life by the people who live in these 11 time zones. I ran the wild side of the crazy times (the wild 90s) here in Russia, the Ukraine, and the Baltics. I chased the big money deals that were getting people rich quick, like lots of other foreigners. Of course they all failed for some reason or another, but I always kept my hand in the training business as well. Slowly moved away from the NLP world here in the CIS (Commonwealth of Independent States – called the Soviet Union before the "fall"). I moved steadily towards business consulting, which had been my primary business in Oklahoma before I came to the CIS.

In 2000 I decided to stop doing what I didn't know how to do and concentrate on what I did know how to do. During my travels I had discovered a city that really seemed to fit my heart and my style. Odessa, Ukraine, stole my heart the first day I came to visit and do some training programs. I was living in Moscow at the time and it only took me a couple of months to pick up my stuff, my Russian family (oh ya, got married again to a powerful young Russian woman named Tatiana and received a 6-year-old daughter in the process) and moved to Odessa. Been living here ever since. Took a year out of Russia once to move to Santa Cruz and help my friend John Grinder build his home, and earlier spent a year in San Diego working with my lifelong friend John Remley (seems I like my Johns too). Except for these two years I have been living and working in Russia and the Ukraine (and a few other countries) for the last 23 years.

I am now head of Pucelik Consulting Group (PCG), headquartered in Odessa, Ukraine. We have "branch" offices in Saint Petersburg and Vladivostok. My company is made up of 15 young Ukrainian professionals. They are proud, smart, dedicated to the mission of PCG, and a joy for me to work with these days. They are healing the chaos that is their world today. I am sure this team of young professionals will carry on the mission and objectives we presently work towards when I "hang up my spurs." We provide training and consulting on business issues and NLP all over Russia, Kazakhstan, Turkey, Egypt, Poland, Lithuania, Latvia, England, and more. I welcome you to visit our web page at www. frankpucelik.com if you are interested in what we are doing these days. Click on the (en) on the opening page if your Russian is not up to speed. We also sponsor and supervise treatment programs for young drug and alcohol addicts. There are now five programs similar to the program I built in Oklahoma, but better, now operating in Russia and the Ukraine. We don't have the restrictions or the documentation requirements that strangle most programs in the United States. We have three programs near Moscow and two near Odessa. We are in the process of opening three more programs and look forward to the day when there are hundreds of these programs all across the CIS and Europe. I don't hold out much hope for the United States to get a clue.

So, what do I say about the road I traveled to get to where I am now? It was long and often hard. I fought for many years to find a person in my skin who I could respect. I came close, very close, to giving up many times. I somehow found the will to stick with the fight (thank you Eric). I tried everything and studied everything I could find to help me; all the systems I tried were interesting and yet didn't do what needed to be done for me. I always wondered how each claimed to be the "real" one that was sure to help, and never did. I always thought it was my failure, not the system and certainly not the failure of the "peoplehelper" sitting on the other side of the table or pillow or whatever was between us that day. Then came Santa Cruz and the Meta kids. John, Richard, Terry, Marilyn, Joyce, Gary, Ken, Jeff, Lisa, Judy, Paul, Steve, Leslie, Byron, Patrick, Ilene, Michael, Peter, David, Pat, Tim, and Hedges helped me learn a way to build the person I had always wanted to find inside. The war blew out the garbage that had been deeply entrenched from my younger years but left its own unique mark.

Richard has his own type of special genius, of course. I know how much I owe to this special man. I hope I was somehow a catalyst and a resource for him. However, John has given us all ideas, tools, models, and the integrity to move forward into the "study of excellence." Without John Grinder many thousands, perhaps millions of us (me for sure), would not have accomplished most or perhaps any of the incredible contributions we have all made to the quality of the lives of the millions we have touched.

The "Originals" that Chose Not to Contribute to This Compilation of Chapters

This book would not be complete without mentioning a number of people who contributed substantially to the birth of NLP but who, for one reason or another, could not or chose not to contribute to this collection. I recognize them here.

Trevelyan Houck

Smart, energetic young woman always ready to find needed information and ready to work as "client," "helper," "experimentor." Always helpful and good at bringing people together for fun or work. A great and valuable member of the team. One of the first generation troops.

Terry Rooney

Calm, smart, steady young woman. Great trance subject. We often used her skill to test very deep trance phenomenon. Super counselor, great experimentor, and an important integrator on the team. She was also one of the very early generation of Meta people. Good friend to all.

Ken Block

Ken was very well educated and had lots of ideas about what should or could be done. A natural leader/organizer. When the group got a bit fractured it was usually Ken that would call us together and get things coherent again. Good at being a "devil's advocate" when one was needed, but equally good at being "one of the troops." Ken was incredibly valuable on the team and often a catalyst for important pattern discoveries. He had the ability to be "bull headed" when that was needed, and I assure you it was needed from time to time. Very strong and lovingly patient when needed. Rare qualities in one person. He had them both.

Jeff Paris

Jeff was our resident "devil's advocate". Fought against everything and believed nothing until we could prove its value to him. Great value to the team. Jeff could not hide the fact that behind the mustache was a guy who was really a good guy. He tried to hide but we all knew who was inside the wall. Diligent, excellent communicator, pedantic to the extreme. He was exactly what the team needed. His role and contributions to the overall results of the first four or so years can't be overlooked. We all owe Jeff for the important role he filled.

Lisa Chiara

Lisa was a steady, intelligent influence on the team. She was ready to play and have fun when it was time but would powerfully switch to great experimentor and researcher, when needed. Helped Marilyn keep the "loose cannons" grounded. Lisa was careful and diligent when we were experimenting with a new pattern or technique. She would carefully watch out for the process and the people involved. We relied on her to keep us grounded, focused, and "safe" from our own excesses.

Marilyn Moskowitz

Marilyn was the "rock" (rock in a very good sense) of the team. She was solid, loving, always grounded, and helpful to the troops thousands of times. We all respected her and paid attention to her ideas and instructions. She supported the team members extremely well, picked up the pieces when necessary, and always followed up on processes to make sure we were alright and supported, if not by her personally, then by someone else, at her suggestion. Careful, strong, solid, and a trance subject to rival even Terry.

Gary Merrill

Gary was a loving, diligent young man. Careful to the extreme, however, ready anytime to practice or try new patterns when we discovered them. Helped Marilyn secure the wild kids like myself, Steven Gilligan, Paul Carter, Terry Rooney (from time to time), Bill Polansky, Joyce Michaelson, and Trevelyan Houck. Later (1974 until 1977) Judy DeLozier, Robert Dilts, and Leslie Cameron helped Gary and Marilyn. This was not easy sometimes but Gary was always up to the task. Gary was dependable, open to learning, gentle when needed, and strong when the time was right. He was a super friend to both myself and Judy and he is still the same wonderful character today. I have been lucky to meet with him a few times lately and found the same guy with a "few" years under his belt and a lot of wisdom to go along with the energy and style that was so important to all of us in the early days of NLP.

Devra Canter

Devra was a talented, honest, hardworking young woman. She was willing to dig deep when necessary and a great counselor. Amazing empathy skills, very easy to care for, and very easy to trust. Great contributions to the team.

Jody Bruce

Jody was a gentle, intelligent, reserved young woman. Quiet in a room full of people who were always ready to talk. We learned that when Jody made the effort to say something to the group or contribute to the discussion, it was a good idea to give her the room and listen carefully. Jody was a sensitive, insightful woman who gave us many clues to subtle observations most or all of us had missed. Another one of our champion trance subjects. John, Richard, Leslie, or I would always look for Jody, Terry, or Marilyn when we wanted to examine a newly discovered trance technique or altered state phenomenon.

Leslie Cameron

Leslie was a major factor on the NLP team even though she joined us after the first three or so years were already done. She was brave, fearless, and a diligent experimenter. She is one of the best psychotherapists I have ever seen work and the best trainer I have ever seen (outside of myself, of course). She had great natural talents in the area of communication and worked in the communication field for several years before joining us in Santa Cruz. When she added the skills of NLP and used her courage to stretch herself way beyond her prior perceived limits, she emerged as a true leader in the field of NLP and proved it for many years.

I was lucky to be her working partner for several years. The projects we worked on, with people like Ken Block, Michael Patton, and David

Wick, were extremely successful (as documented by David in his chapter in this book). We achieved goals no one had seen accomplished in Santa Cruz County before.

I believe when we encounter NLP people with an incredibly high level of personal integrity, we should look to Leslie and John and say thanks.

Bill Polansky

Bill was an incredibly smart young man. Always gave the team plenty of interesting material to work with. When we needed a client to work with to examine a particular new skill or pattern, Bill was always ready to step up. He could always be counted on to make things interesting. Bill was with us for a couple of years during the very beginning times. When he moved on, he was missed.

Ilene McCloud

Ilene was one of the very early NLP troops. She was extremely articulate, well educated, and a ferocious debater when appropriate. Often we would attack models, trying to find the weak spots or flaws in them and when Ilene came after your work (we each had the responsibility to research and present popular or important models to the team) you had better be ready and well prepared. This skill of hers helped create and insure the quality and depth of the material now known as NLP. We relied on her often to lead the processes of discovery and evaluation. She was a great communicator, a great friend, strongly loyal, afraid of nothing, willing to "step up" at the tough times, and invaluable to the early work done by the Meta people. When she left she was also missed.

David Gordon

David was always helpful and respectful of all of us. He was willing to try new patterns or examine the models that were being presented. Good man, good heart. David made many valuable comments and important contributions to the process of discovery that we were all involved in on a day-to-day basis. Gentle but strong. Well educated but never pretentious. Amazing young man we all liked and admired.

Paul Carter

Paul was Steve's partner and was always on the edge of the Meta people. He specialized in Erickson's stuff and he and Steven Gilligan worked together for several years. He participated with the Meta team often but not constantly and could always be counted on to find new ways to get something accomplished. Paul was always positive and helpful. He simply believed that what we wanted to do could be done if we just found the right way to get it done. This was so valuable as a general attitude and Paul had it, always.

CHAPTER 2

My Road to NLP

Terry McClendon

I was born in Albany, California in 1947 and grew up in the town of Richmond in the San Francisco East Bay area. Our house was located on top of the hill with a view to the San Francisco Golden Gate Bridge. It bordered on bush land and provided wonderful opportunities to explore the valleys, trees, and streams with my two siblings.

At the end of my senior high school year neither college nor work held much appeal to me. What I wanted were some new experiences. I opted for the United States Marine Corps as my way out of Richmond. I had no greater ambition than to travel and experience what the Marine Corps had to offer. The Vietnam War was raging and I volunteered to go overseas for a tour. Looking back, my experience in Vietnam was the turning point of my life: it germinated my adult character. I was shot twice, had malaria, was mortared, tramped the jungles and mountains, and had a near-death experience. I discovered a wealth of personal resources that I could later draw upon.

My last posting in the Marine Corps was as a military policeman (MP) guarding a naval base at Brunswick, Maine. My experience as an MP sparked my interest in becoming a police investigator. I left the Marine Corps after four years and enrolled at Diablo Valley College, located approximately 20 miles east of San Francisco. On the first day of registration the police science course was already filled, so I stepped into the next line which happened to be for an introductory psychology course.

Serendipitously, one of my psychology teachers was John Stevens (later Steve Andreas). He and his wife Connirae edited some early NLP books including *Frogs into Princes*, *Reframing*, and *Transformations*.[1]

Steve was very into Gestalt therapy at the time. It was said that if you cried in Steve's class you would get an A.

The psychology courses excited me so I transferred to the University of California at Santa Cruz (UCSC) to further my studies. UCSC was a logical choice; apart from the reputation of its large psychology department, it also offered a flexible learning environment and, of particular appeal to me, was its setting among the redwoods.

My whole experience at UCSC was fantastic and it was exciting to be on the cutting edge of a new communication technology (neuro-linguistic programming – NLP). I would leave an NLP group session late at night, go home and type up my notes of those early sessions. I still have my original notes from 1972 to 1975. I was able to draw on what I was learning in these groups when studying for my master's degree, particularly in being able to bridge old and new approaches to psychology and personal development.

A few years after leaving UCSC, I was in contact with Steve and Connirae Andreas once again as they gave Robert Dilts (my then business partner) and me our first "jet-set consulting job" when he flew us to Boulder, Colorado to conduct an introductory NLP training. Steve also introduced us to his mother, Barry Stevens, author of the Gestalt book *Don't Push the River*[2] and friend of Fritz Perls. Barry came to Robert and me for help after having a mild stroke. A little hypnosis greatly aided her in the use of her affected arm.

The events and experiences that have had the most significant impacts on me, both professionally and personally, include: (1) Gestalt with Richard, (2) parts parties, (3) the Meta Model, and (4) hypnosis in the Santa Cruz Mountains.

Gestalt with Richard

During my fourth year at UCSC, in the winter of 1972, Richard Bandler was a fellow student in one of my psychology courses. At the time I did not know him personally, but became aware of him as he talked about the lack of practicality in the information we were then learning.

In contrast, he saw Gestalt therapy as being a practical approach as it focused on using present experiences to achieve greater clarity and awareness.

In 1972, Richard taught a Gestalt therapy "student-directed seminar" under the supervision of a UCSC faculty member at Kresge College, John Grinder. This course was my first formal introduction to Gestalt therapy. As well as the weekly seminars, there were private weekend and evening sessions with Richard at Dr. Robert Spitzer's house in Soquel, near Santa Cruz. Around this time Richard, who worked for Dr. Spitzer from Science and Behavior Books, was also asked to edit transcripts of Fritz Perls' Gestalt sessions at Cold Mountain, British Columbia and this experience helped inform Richard's Gestalt techniques.[3]

Another of Dr. Spitzer's authors was Virginia Satir. Richard was asked to tape Virginia's training group experiences. When Richard came back from these training sessions, he experimented with Virginia's methodology and techniques in small group sessions at UCSC and these experiences further contributed to the evolution of Richard's Gestalt technique. I attended some of these groups and, at these sessions, I learnt a range of techniques including posturing, caring language, "parts parties," and "family reconstructions." My guess is that the parts party was the precursor to the NLP six-step reframing model and parts integration techniques.

I was keen to participate in these groups: sometimes I was invited and sometimes I was not. It was in one of these training groups in late 1972 that I first met John Grinder. Group membership at these sessions varied with a core of frequent participants whose attendance spanned several years. The members that I recall as the most regular participants included Frank Pucelik, Devra Canter, Byron Lewis, Marilyn Moscowitz, David Gordon, Steve Gilligan, Paul Carter, Leslie Cameron, Judith DeLozier, and Robert Dilts. There were other participants but they were typically in groups that I did not attend.

The Gestalt workshops were intriguing. My involvement with these early groups continued regularly through 1974 and occasionally through 1977. My initial fascination was driven by my own personal development. At the time, I was carrying quite a bit of tension partly due to my experience in war and partly because of family dynamics. As the groups continued, my initial personal interest transitioned to a more professional one and I became a Gestalt therapy practitioner. I used the skills as a family counselor and later as a psychologist.

Gestalt was a lot of fun. It was even more powerful when we later learnt to gather information about the client using a questioning technique called the Meta Model and to use anchoring. A commonly used technique in Gestalt was "open chair" work where clients shuffled back and forth between chairs, conversing with feelings or imaginary people/parts of their personality that they would (in their imagination) place on the chair. The aim of open chair was to integrate the dissociated parts. Anchoring was a more efficient technique to achieve the same results; with anchoring the person did not have to shuffle between chairs and the mental and physical states of the person could instead be referenced and integrated by a touch, a sound, or an image.

Parts Party

The parts parties were fun. They provided an opportunity to be someone you aren't or, at least, someone you were not aware existed in you. Parts parties were like multiple open chair processes going on simultaneously. Instead of integrating two parts (as in the open chair process), with parts parties it was possible to integrate multiple parts. The client is referred to as the Star and the therapist as the Guide. The Star selects a number of famous men and women, drawn from diverse fields such as history, politics, or entertainment; each participant is then assigned a famous character to play. The Guide then instructs the participants to pretend they are at a cocktail party. Each participant's goal, as actors, is to use their character's attributes to develop coalitions among the players. This is accomplished by any means, including manipulation, seduction, persuasion, and threats, over a period of several hours.

During the process, the Guide occasionally instructs the party to freeze and then points out to the Star particular alliances or conflicts, using these to help the Star reflect on his/her own tendencies or behaviors. Over time the party's characters align, everybody has a group hug, and then goes home. The experience of the parts parties metaphor was significant for me as it provided exposure to the concept of multiple "parts" of a person. Today there are more elegant tools to explore this notion, but not many that are as much fun.

Both Gestalt therapy and the parts party, in my opinion, contributed to the development of the model of parts. Today I find the concept of parts dated; however, it was a useful evolutionary tool. There is the odd time when I ask a client to "go inside and ask the part" but more commonly I use techniques such as the swish technique, sub-modalities, or the time line to achieve my therapeutic goals. NLP techniques, such as six-step reframing and parts integration, I believe evolved from the parts party.

The Meta Model

The Meta Model was a milestone. As I understand it, it was the first of a number of models of what was to become neuro-linguistic programming. The Meta Model is a verbal questioning tool originally developed to enhance therapies where high quality information is needed. It is described fully in Bandler and Grinder's book *The Structure of Magic, Volume I*.[4] The Meta Model is a linguistic model that assists people to understand specific problems. Questions asked via the Meta Model encourage them to recover the information that is missing when they delete, distort, or generalize pieces of information (i.e., they use language violations).

Hypnosis in the Santa Cruz Mountains

In the hypnosis training in the Santa Cruz Mountains, we practiced deep trance identification using Milton Erickson, Virginia Satir, and Fritz Perls as models. The purpose was to experience some of their intuitions and behaviors for use in counseling and therapy work.

Personally, I found the hypnosis training very challenging, particularly the experiences that Dr. Erickson called "deep trance phenomena" including positive and negative hallucinations, time distortion, amnesia, and deep trance identification. These were all initially difficult for me but I persisted because I thought it important that I experience them myself – before I taught them. I also took it as a personal challenge to be able to control the things my unconscious was already doing, such as positive hallucinations and time distortion. I also learnt to see without the use of my contact lenses and to recover a memory of an automobile accident where I was unconscious for a period of time.

Learning hypnosis was great fun. It was a delight meeting Dr. Milton Erickson in Phoenix, Arizona and gaining first hand experience of how he worked with clients. Hypnosis put additional magic into my training in NLP.

Ongoing Development

My contributions to fostering the ongoing development of the NLP model and maintaining its integrity include the following:

The Spelling Strategy

In 1973, Robert Dilts and I were invited to conduct introductory NLP training courses in a number of Western/Mid-West states. Robert was traveling with his typewriter and, in his spare time, was developing the draft of *Neuro-Linguistic Programming, Volume I* in conjunction with the supervision of Richard and John.[5] One of our stops was Phoenix, Arizona. We stayed at the promoter's house and one day his 9-year-old daughter came home from school with some flash cards. She was having trouble spelling and the teacher had given her some words on the cards to take home and suggested she have a parent help her learn them. She tried to learn these but she lacked a systematic technique to do so, even with the help of her parents. I offered to help. I placed one of the cards in front of her and asked her to say the word and to indicate if she understood its meaning. She did. I then asked her to imagine seeing the word above the card. She could do this. I asked her to spell the word that she imagined. She could. I took away the flash card and 15 minutes later I asked her to spell the word that was on the flash card. I instructed that before spelling the word, she was to project the word on the wall in front of her and I watched to make sure she was focusing ahead to the wall. She was able to spell the word, just as though it was printed in clear text in front of her. Twenty minutes later

I asked her to project an entire sentence on the wall, make it different colors, and spell all the words in the sentence. The Spelling Strategy, through nuanced variations, can also accommodate more challenging spelling difficulties such as an inability to hold more than three syllables in consciousness.

I was acknowledged as a co-facilitator in *Neuro-Linguistic Programming, Volume I* because of the Spelling Strategy and the Outcome Sequitur.

Outcome Sequitur

In the early 1970s, I was conducting a training workshop on NLP and Business in Carmel, California. When I was teaching strategies as part of the course, I developed a strategy application that I called the "Outcome Sequitur" (which is described in *Neuro-Linguistic Programming, Volume I*). The technique is an effective mechanism for problem solving. Guided by a therapist or practitioner, a person describes their problem. The therapist establishes the problem state strategy and anchors it. Then the person is instructed to project and then associate into the future, and elicits what life is like having solved their problem. Next, the therapist establishes an anchor for the projected representational systems and then brings the person back to the present. The therapist then fires off the "old" and "new" anchors in such a way, placing the future anchor marginally first so as to integrate the desired outcome. In essence, the resulting strategy acquires a representation of the outcome of the strategy. The strategy then conforms to this new representation and operates to satisfy the desired goal. The outcome of the strategy becomes the starting point and the problem is dealt with more effectively.

I have written two books about NLP:

- *The Wild Days: NLP 1972 to 1981*: This is a first hand interpretation of the events and relationships created during the development of NLP.[6]

- *Happy Parents Happy Kids: Words and Actions for Parents and Kids*: This is a book on parenting using components of the NLP model to provide strategies for common parenting challenges. The book includes many practical exercises.[7]

I have also designed a computer program called LifeSet Meta Programs Survey. This is a 48-question assessment survey designed to elicit "meta programs" and hence to understand the drivers of people's behaviors.

The most important contribution that I have made is to maintain the integrity of the NLP model for over 30 years of my professional career, teaching worldwide. As one of the handful of people on the UCSC campus when NLP was evolving, I am in a unique position to understand its development and its power. All the participants have their recollections of events, perhaps distorted by personal wants and needs at the time; however, we can contribute a *mostly true* portrayal of our lives and experiences of NLP back then.

We also carry forward the spirit and adventure that is as much a part of NLP as any technique that was created. I am convinced that we are in the business of education and the evolution of the brain. In that context, there is also a personal/professional responsibility for us to insure that we preserve the quality of the original NLP model and contribute to its enhancement as the world changes.

Current Reflections

Current best practice now requires multi-dimensional skills and, at times, multi-level communication to be successful. A little history is a useful tool for ensuring solid and skillful comprehension of NLP techniques and their applications. For example, understanding the basics of anchoring and its evolution from the Gestalt sessions and the Meta Model can increase the effectiveness of practitioners when counseling or teaching.

It is a concern to me that NLP trainers think they can satisfactorily teach the Meta Model in a matter of a couple of hours. I argue that the Meta Model is a key tool of NLP and new students need to have a sound grasp of it to effectively utilize NLP. Some believe that the Meta Model is passé and is now superseded by more relevant information gathering techniques. I am not convinced. One of the most important tools that an NLP practitioner can have is the ability to ask the right question in the right way. I spend a lot of time on information gathering and a lot of the time reinforcing and correcting voice tone, predicate usage, sloppy posture, and calibrations to provide my students with sufficient skills to be able to efficiently gather relevant information. I have not found a satisfactory short cut to information gathering.

Some like to circumvent this process by suggesting that they do not need to know what the client needs; they will just trust their unconscious mind to guide them. Does the unconscious mind always know? How will a trainer, trusting the unconscious mind, know if it is right if the trainer has no external information to validate the mind's intuitive assessment? Some NLP instructors do not like to teach the Meta Model. They don't understand the grammar and they meet resistance from their students. The challenge, then, is to make it interesting, chunk the learning into understandable pieces, and put lots of stories and humor into it. Reflecting on their course content, many of my students tell me that the two most important things they learned in their training is the Meta Model and calibrations.

The hypnosis techniques we learnt in the 1970s seem crude by comparison to what we are doing now. However, fundamentally, they were the basis for more elegant techniques to follow. As with much of today's teaching of NLP, trainers in hypnosis also lack knowledge of how and why techniques work. Much of today's teaching is superficial; a situation sometimes evident to me when students have acquired some training from other organizations. They frequently lack the basic grounding to advance to more sophisticated techniques.

Since the early days, some of the originators of NLP have developed new models including Design Human Engineering, the New NLP, and NLP New Code. Some of these developments are exciting and they have opened the potential for using the brain more fully and for changing perception. Creating multiple timelines and belief systems can be fun and add to the power of NLP.

I remain, however, a firm believer in the value of the fundamentals. It is difficult to master the really slick stuff without core tools like the Meta Model, accessing cues, calibrations, anchoring, sub-modalities, and an understanding of how and why these are important. It is like going to a seller of new model cars and asking how the engine works. He responds, "We don't need to know that anymore, the car pretty much drives itself." Until it breaks down, of course, and then you are curious. How does this thing run? Modern cars might pretty much drive themselves these days, but the design engineers and the mechanics still need to understand the workings of the engine in order to innovate.

CHAPTER 3

The Early Days of NLP

Judith DeLozier

The early days of neuro-linguistic programming (NLP) were a time of transformation, exploration, discovery, expanded awareness, and a whole lot of youthful energy. I read recently that the reason history has to be rewritten so often is that it is never written correctly the first time. Probably the same will hold true here; some vital perspectives will be missing and the events behind the events will not be known.

NLP came into my life while I was one part each mom, student of religious studies, waitress, and NLPer. I was living with Frank Pucelik, Leslie Cameron Bandler, and others in a house in Scotts Valley, California. The owner of the home was a professor at the University of California at Santa Cruz (UCSC). He and his family were on sabbatical in England for a year.

On Wednesday evenings the NLP group would meet at the house to test new developments and explore possible emerging patterns. I had met Richard Bandler through Frank Pucelik some time earlier while living on campus at UCSC but I had no idea what he did or who he was. I did know that Frank and others were actively meeting and researching "something" of a psychological nature. This was long before NLP had a name, of course. At this time it was an emerging series of patterns.

Representational preferences were being explored in the limited number of meetings that I was able to participate in with the earliest group, as I worked on Wednesday nights. I remember discovering representational systems while looking into the eyes of Robert Dilts. We refer to this period as the time we fell in love – a deep connection of friendship formed which holds true to this day. I don't remember precisely where we were, but I believe it was a bench at the university. I did see those eye movements. I also experienced my first official trance with Robert, while modeling Milton Erickson. Yes, I did experience many unofficial trances along the way too.

Many people were involved in those early days: Stephen Gilligan, David Gordon, Mary Beth Meyers, Leslie Cameron Bandler, Frank Pucelik, and others mentioned by other authors in this volume. By this time I had the feeling that we were tapping into a very generative field. So the beginning of NLP, at least by the time I was on the scene, was a period infused with a sense of enhanced awareness, exploration, discovery, and excitement. The sense was that we were all a part of something that might change the world. This is my lasting impression from these early times.

While living at the house in Scotts Valley I met John Grinder. He offered me a manuscript copy of *The Structure of Magic* to read.[1] He later asked me what I thought about the manuscript. It was not easy going as reads go, but I felt that it offered a structure for understanding past experiences and also a way to evolve oneself. Gregory Bateson was very impressed with the book and ultimately created the support and introduction of Richard and John, which allowed for the time with Dr. Milton Erickson.

Gregory Bateson and Margaret Mead had spent time with Dr. Erickson before doing their trance work in Bali.[2] It was Gregory who said that there was an amazing guy who did amazing things and no one knew how he was doing it: a perfect place to focus attention for modeling. Later John Grinder and I married and NLP became a life path. All the while, most of those people involved in the early group were growing, experimenting, and traveling forward on their own journeys.

Other moments that really come back clearly are those related to the models – the people who gave so generously of their time and energy. This time and energy was given to us as young enthusiastic students of the mind. I remember Virginia Satir coming to our home in Ben Lomond, California. Virginia joined John and Richard at the house to model her work with family systems and the three of them collaborated to write the book, *Changing with Families*.[3]

I don't know that I fully appreciated Virginia at the time, but I did know that she was an awesome presence and a deeply aware person. In retrospect, the Satir postures were a kind of physical archetype which evoked memory from the muscle and helped set the stage for the later development of somatic syntax in NLP. Virginia was already an established icon in the field of family therapy. Through her awareness of the field and the development of her archetypical postures, she created a basis for more understanding of the somatic experience and "constellation" of connections between family members.

The next stellar punctuation experience was the opportunity to model Milton Erickson. Richard and John were originally introduced to Dr. Erickson by Gregory Bateson. Gregory read *The Structure of Magic*, was very impressed with the work, and pointed Richard and John towards Dr. Erickson as a person they might want to model. We had an opportunity to visit Dr. Erickson many times over the four years before his death. He was for me the most sophisticated communicator I had ever met. It was a joy and an honor to be present with him and to learn about the conscious/unconscious interface, and to have a foot in both worlds. This association over time produced the two volumes related to the hypnotic patterns, both linguistic and behavioral, of Dr. Erickson.[4]

My favorite story of Dr. Milton Erickson is a personal one. John and I were living together (this was the 1970s and early 1980s) and when I would call Dr. Erickson to make arrangements to visit, I would introduce myself as Judith DeLozier. Invariably he would respond with an, "I can't recognize you." I would persist and eventually say, "I am the Judith who lives with John Grinder." He would then say, "Oh, please come at such and such a time." This got to be tiresome so eventually I complained to John. His response was, "Just say that you are Judy Grinder." So the next time I did. Dr. Erickson said, "Come over immediately." When we arrived to visit him, we were met with flowers and a kiss under the Palo Verde tree. I am still ever grateful for his sense of direction and his sense of humor.

Throughout this time many of the original group continued to develop new theories and techniques and added many important books and models to the field of NLP. I feel that by 1980 John and Richard had begun to take different paths, both paths NLP, but different routes. In the mid 1980s John and I wrote *Turtles All the Way Down*[5] and set the stage for the beginning of the exploration into the second generation of NLP. By this time, institutes were evolving and people were beginning to apply and train in NLP around the world.

I suppose it is really those first few years that reflect the early history of NLP. It is important to say that there were people before me, and that John and Richard and others were responsible for setting the conceptual, analytical, and interactive frameworks that are still the basis of NLP that we all share today. I know those of you adding your thoughts to this volume will set that record straight and describe the other important early innovators of that time period.

This was a sort of modeling phase which, of course, led to the development of new techniques and a time of application began. It seemed that NLP was being applied to many areas – leadership, arts, education, and health. This was also a period when the focus of attention shifted from what was happening inside of one individual to what was happening in the spaces in between individuals. Thanks to Milton Erickson and Virginia Satir the idea of this amazing relational space began to have a more useful description in NLP. Today it is referred to as "the field." So that which was implicit from the beginning of NLP began to have a more explicit description.

Looking back over the years, even the very early days of discovery and excitement, I can recognize the basic foundations in the new generation NLP. The new explorers and creators being trained today have a wonderful and exciting journey ahead. Remember: the journey is the destination.

CHAPTER 4

Youth Services in Santa Cruz: The First NLP Community Testing Ground

David R. Wick

I moved to Boulder Creek in the Santa Cruz Mountains in 1970 with my then new wife. Our home had the resemblance of a castle nestled at the base of a hill, a stone's throw from the famous creek which we could hear through the trees. I was excited about living in the woods and being in an environment where we could embrace our evolving countercultural beliefs and lifestyle.

As I was completing my master's program in communications at San Jose State University, I was hired at the Santa Cruz Juvenile Hall as a counselor working in the boys' facility to secure their safety, keep them detained, provide programs and counseling, and offer an ear to listen. The living area was comfortable enough but the individual sleeping rooms were bare cinder-block walls with only a mattress on a cement platform. It was a significant challenge at times to discover what the real issues were when they were so frequently masked with a lot of bravado and acting out. I found that if I helped the boys blow steam in a safe way, and had the patience to sit and truly listen, the truth of the deeper pains would be revealed over time as their trust in me grew. I remember more than one young man saying to me, "No one has ever really listened to me, they just don't care."

Even after giving a boy my best shot at listening and using good counseling techniques, the feelings were better, but the challenging behavior often remained. I remember pondering, what is it that makes the difference for sustained change?

The Creation of Youth Services

During my three years working at the Hall, there were many boys and girls being logged in who I believed really had no business being there as they were brought in on what were then called "status offenses." This included runaway, beyond parental control, truancy, and other "light weight" youth-related problems. Time and again I saw that lack of communication and no one to really listen and guide them was a strong factor in creating the status offense, and that the answer was not being brought by police to the Juvenile Hall. But, there was no reliable alternative in Santa Cruz County. Given that Santa Cruz (and the surrounding areas) was a major mecca for young people, I was amazed and disturbed by the lack of creative resources to serve as an alternative pathway to teenage difficulties. I had also seen many young people develop a hard-life path and growing criminal action from what they learned when spending time in "Juvy." I believe this hardened self-identity was compounded by the occasional emotional and physical outburst which necessitated that we staff move into a physical restraint mode, with resulting isolation. This was hard to watch and be part of, and in many cases, it was a big waste of young lives and tax payers' money.

I was determined to do something about this horrible gap in options and started engaging in research and talking to a lot of people in the probation department, schools, psychologists, county mental health, and with kids on the street.

This was a time when the concept of Youth Service Bureaus (YSBs) was gaining interest and promising results in California. After a Santa Cruz County conference on youth in May 1974, which I helped to inspire and organize , the Santa Cruz Community Counseling Center (SCCCC) received state funds for a new position titled Primary Prevention Youth Counselor/Coordinator to work with young people and lay the foundation for a YSB. By this time I had a pretty good idea of the basic components and programs that were needed to create a diversion program, an alternative to the Juvenile Hall route for those engaged in status offenses. This would be a comprehensive approach that included personal and group counseling, working with the family, the schools, and include recreation and work resources. Having helped to create this opportunity I left the Juvenile Hall and was hired by SCCCC for this new position. This was very exciting, a dream come true, but there was no money to fund the program itself. The reality was that the responsibility and opportunity was on me to find funding and build the program from the ground up. This was a big challenge, but I knew in my heart that I could do it.

This became my first powerful experience of manifesting: holding a vision, bringing together talented and creative people, stitching together a coalition of organizations, leveraging influential relationships, and getting funds to make it a reality. I had already gotten support from the probation department, the schools, School Attendance Review Boards, Community Mental Health, and the Santa Cruz County Board of Supervisors. Thus I secured $17,000 in seed money to hire staff and set up offices in Santa Cruz and Watsonville.

Youth Services, our new name, was born with David Graas, Pat LeClair, and Carole Lopez as team members. We creatively laid out our office spaces in one of the old gingerbread style houses that SCCCC had on Water Street, directly across from the new county courtroom facility and office buildings. As part of the plan, we wanted to find volunteers who were skilled enough to help work with the young people and their families, and if possible, be trained to function in counselor roles. As fate would have it, many of our first volunteers came from the newly developing neuro-linguistic programming (NLP) student community that was evolving right next door at the University of California at Santa Cruz (UCSC). We came together like a hand in glove and did amazing things from the very beginning.

Finding Neuro-Linguistic Programming

My first connection with NLP was when I met Ken Block during a spiritual practice event in Ben Lomond in early 1974. It was from Ken that I learned about his involvement with John Grinder and Richard Bandler and an exciting new communication method that was known as Meta, later to become neuro-linguistic programming. I asked a lot of questions and was fascinated by the innovative thinking and methods of communication used in NLP. I was enthusiastic about the possibility of linking NLP with the youth program I was working hard to create. I could see some great potential in working with young people and, best of all, this was unique to Santa Cruz and way outside the box.

NLP: The Wild and Crazy People

As the program plans and goals we were developing at Youth Services began to be implemented, I wanted to make a more direct connection with NLP. Through Ken I started meeting other people in the program with John Grinder and Richard Bandler, who were among the first and second generation of students learning NLP. This included Ken, Frank Pucelik, Leslie Cameron, Peter Gaarn, Michael Patton, and others whose names I do not recall. There was a lot of activity going on at Kresge College at UCSC which seemed to be a hub of this new methodology. The more I heard, the more I knew that teaming up could provide pathways to the sustained behavioral change that I had puzzled about at Juvenile Hall.

My impression was that they were charting new territory in communications and human behavior, and that there were some pretty wild and crazy people involved. I found Frank, Leslie, and Ken to be very bright, inquisitive, full of ideas and energy, and deeply committed to what they were mastering through NLP. They each also had a lot of heart. I was excited about these high energy people with their open and creative worldview which was so aligned with mine. I also more deeply saw the potential benefits of NLP to the young people, their families, and the community organizations we started working with. I felt we could really move forward and have a positive impact on young lives – and so did they.

There was a lot of interesting activity taking place in the training with John and Richard and there was mention of me becoming part of the Meta group at Kresge College. I didn't quite understand all of the things they were doing, but I knew it was profound. When I heard that NLP was evolving from the great work of people such as Fritz Perls, Virginia Satir, Milton Erickson, and Gregory Bateson, I was very impressed. This melding was significant and mysterious, and sometimes challenging to grasp. At one time I was invited to join the NLP students at a home where there was a gathering with John and Richard. We had great discussions in this energized environment which was predominantly lit by candle light. People were clustered in small groupings which morphed and mingled with each other continuously and the evening was spiked with moments of uproarious laughter. Getting an insight into the new frontiers of communication that were opening up and being with these brilliant pioneers was thrilling and thought-provoking. I had no question that we were on the right track together.

Integrating NLP into Youth Services

As we talked with the NLP practitioners about working in Youth Services programs as volunteer counselors, I saw how everyone was keen because this would be an opportunity for them to apply the techniques and processes they were learning from John and Richard. This was a great resource and experiential gift for these NLP forerunners because they would acquire their Youth Services counseling experiences and then go back to the NLP program to analyze, discuss, and learn more from a real-life base. After attending our Youth Services training program, they plunged into experiment, testing out their emerging ideas and refining them in practice. Being aware of the responsibilities we carried, I also established counseling oversight by Pat LeClair who was a licensed marriage family and child therapist – and open minded.

The timing for becoming a testing ground for this innovative NLP practice was perfect. Here we were in Santa Cruz in the early 1970s, a hub for countercultural thinking, experimental lifestyles and new ideas, and with a brand new, leading edge university at UCSC on our doorstep. This was also a golden era for creative community programs in Santa Cruz, as awareness of the need to enhance the quality of life and the importance of environmental stewardship grew. This historic confluence provided an open atmosphere for NLP to be used in our programs, which was often quietly blended with other more traditional modalities. We recognized that this was a grand experiment because nobody knew how it would work with young people, their families and schools, but we were positive that we had a great combination of conventional and state-of-the-art methodologies.

Once we got up and running we had long discussions about NLP methods, and we created various planned and spontaneous training events during which Frank Pucelik, Leslie Cameron, and Ken Block would individually or collectively teach the rest of us about NLP so we would have a better understanding of what they were doing and perhaps bring it into our own work. These NLP forerunners were powerful, intelligent, outspoken, and establishment-irreverent at times. I recall being very attentive as I practiced mirroring behavior, watching people's eye movements, learned "the map is not the territory," and explored modeling and what a Meta Model was. They also provided training for all our volunteers who numbered around 30 at one point. I must admit that we men were very happy to have Leslie talk with us, about anything.

Did It Work?

After the training process our volunteers began working with the young people who were referred to Youth Services – working with them individually, with their families, with the schools, and other community and county organizations. The excitement of the NLP practitioners was high as significant results started occurring with the families and the young people they were guiding. NLP was becoming an important and powerful ingredient in our Youth Services work as it joined our other modalities. I was enthusiastic because of the alignment with one of my strong values: let's find what works, not what is based on good theory. We were getting results!

A number of documented results included:

- A young boy who was truant from school most of the spring semester and three weeks of the fall semester is now attending school regularly for the past three months.

- A girl who was living with an older man and considered a runaway and beyond parental control is now living with her parents, family communications are effective, and she has joined teen groups at the Young Women's Christian Association.

- A boy who spent four months in a California Youth Authority institution now has a better relationship with his parents, is working part-time, and his school attendance is good.

- A boy who was a truant, not attending school at all, started coming to the program for three hours of tutoring per day and going to school for half a day. He is still going to school and only coming to the program once a week for tutoring.

- A boy who was involved in petty theft and had poor school attendance is now working 30 hours per week, has not stolen anything in two months, and his grades have improved.

During the years 1975 and 1976, NLP became an integrated part of the Youth Services programs and in 1976, Ken Block was hired as the Primary Prevention Coordinator. The following are specific examples of this integration and the excellent results achieved:

1. In a proposal I wrote to the Santa Cruz County Drug Abuse Technical Advisory Committee – a proposal to create the Primary Prevention Coordinator position from State Office of Narcotics and Drug Abuse 409 Funds – I said:

> Initially the primary emphasis of this program will be on effective education. We hope to introduce alternative activities in the school systems and to supplement traditional curricula with affective education courses.
>
> This of course will be done in cooperation with each school we contact, and according to their needs. Specifically, we will begin by conducting workshops and training seminars, with students and with teachers and counselors, on communication skills (based primarily on Meta Model, the work developed by Bandler and Grinder), and on body awareness skills designed to promote mind/body/psyche integration; thereby helping an individual move from externally determined consciousness to internal self-awareness.

Two of the schools we worked with were Branciforte Junior High School and Rolling Hills Junior High School. Frank and Ken were the lead Youth Services representatives working with the students, teachers and staff. They got results as expressed by this letter from one of the school's principals:

Dear Mr. Wick,

I wish to state my gratitude for all the services that the Community Counseling Center – Youth Services – has given Branciforte Junior High School during the 1975/6 school year. Mr. Ken Block and Mr. Frank Pucelik have been working closely with several of our students this semester. These students have indicated a definite behavior pattern change that would allow them to function and cope with their academic, social, and personal lives and a greater level of self-understanding and maturity.

In 14 years of dealing with youngsters, I have never observed such definite behavior pattern changes in such a short period of time (6 weeks to 3 months). Therefore, I am writing this letter of commendation for the benefit of any individual persons or agencies that will be working with Youth Services in the near future. In my opinion there will be definite positive changes in the youngsters referred to this agency.

James Whiteley
Principal
Branciforte Junior High School

This and another letter from Santa Cruz City Schools are reproduced as Appendices 1 and 2.

2. The Primary Prevention Program Ken Block developed aimed to:

- Provide a Pilot Primary Prevention Program for the students, teachers, and parents of two secondary schools in Santa Cruz County.
- Give secondary school students tools to live more constructively in all the systems they are a part of – family, school, community, and peers – without the use of drugs or alcohol.

3. Another of the courses Ken created for students to take on a volun-
    tary basis was Peoplemaking. Unit goal 1 (the first of three goals)
    shows the presence of NLP under Section Goal II, "To enrich stu-
    dent's awareness of their present and possible models of the world"
    (through the theory and form of communication and language pat-
    terns) (see Appendix 3).

Epilogue

Today, Youth Services is the primary youth program in Santa Cruz
County serving 2,400 young people and family members per year with
a budget over $2 million. The mission remains "to provide culturally
relevant services to Santa Cruz County youth and families, in collaboration with other community organizations." The services are designed
to address the "developmental and emotional needs of our clients while
supporting them in creating and maintaining positive roles in their
communities" (see www.scccc.org/youth-services/youth-services).

I am proud of my contribution to move from a vision to a highly valued
organization with programs that are still genuinely making a difference
in people's lives and achieving the original goal of keeping kids out of
Juvenile Hall. There obviously have been many people and organizations that played very important roles in this co-creation. I thank you
all. I also know, without a doubt, that NLP and the first and second
generation students/practitioners of NLP were essential in making
foundational, innovative, and vital contributions which brought early
successes, respect, and support for Youth Services. In large part, this
ensured the growth and longevity of Youth Services which has benefited so many people over the last 38 years.

As my life moved along to San Francisco, San Mateo, and Ashland,
Oregon I did not keep contact with the NLP practices or practitioners,
but periodically heard about NLP in different fields. In Oregon, I met
a wonderful NLP Master Practitioner named Lindagail Campbell. She
renewed my attention in NLP. More recently Frank Pucelik reconnected
with me relative to this book, and I am delighted with our reunion. I
am also astounded at how far and wide NLP has evolved in so many
different organizations and industries worldwide.

I find that I continue to walk with the spirit of these creative days in Santa Cruz and to be moved by the vision of creating greater well-being in our world. I am now a father and grandfather; I've traveled to many countries; I've trained executives in major corporations; been a publisher; developed a closer relationship between Oregon and China; and served in the public diplomacy arena. I am currently bringing my 30 years of Peacebuilding through Business work with Pathways to Peace (PTP) to a new level. As a PTP Director and the Team Leader of the global Culture of Peace Initiative, which is related to the United Nation's International Day of Peace, I carry a broad, long view. Therefore, I pose both a question and a challenge to the NLP community all over the world.

The shift is on! Clearly great changes are taking place economically, socially, culturally, and politically everywhere, and I feel this time of change (perhaps transformation) is just heating up. How are you using your considerable NLP knowledge and skills to assist the shift in beneficial ways? And if you are not, how can you draw upon the local-global NLP community to become a positive force and make creative contributions that others cannot comprehend? What can you do for this, and future generations? You are needed!

> Few men are willing to brave the disapproval of their fellows, the censure of their colleagues, the wrath of their society. Moral courage is a rarer commodity than bravery in battle or great intelligence. Yet it is the one essential, vital quality for those who seek to change a world which yields most painfully to change.
>
> Robert F. Kennedy in 1966

CHAPTER 5

My Parts Party:
Early Dissociated State Therapy

Byron Lewis

It was a beautiful spring day in 1974. Although the drive over to Santa Cruz from my home in Los Gatos had taken me over scenic Highway 17 winding through the majestic redwoods of the Santa Cruz Mountains, then up onto the sprawling campus of the still nascent University of California at Santa Cruz (UCSC) campus, between the redwoods and the rolling meadow to the student housing, I was so shut down, I didn't see any of it. I was here to visit my friend, Leslie Cameron, who wanted me to meet a very interesting and powerful man, Frank Pucelik.[1]

I had recently participated with my wife in one of Richard Bandler's family therapy Gestalt groups. Leslie had brokered a special deal for my wife (who had been her best friend in high school) and me. We would be allowed to attend the eight-session workshop free as the "identified couple" for Richard to perform his Gestalt mastery on for the benefit of the other students. Although, in all outward appearances, his work with my wife and me worked miracles to mend our broken relationship, Leslie had seen through my façade and had invited me to her apartment at UCSC to work with just me, independently of my wife.

Using a technique I later learned was a revolutionary blend of Gestalt chair work, trance, and psycho-linguistics, Frank and Leslie guided me through a unique life-altering experience. I vaguely remember Leslie talking in one of my ears and Frank leading me through a fantasy in which I identified various "parts" and "resources" within me. The internal dance of images and feelings swirled as the party progressed, culminating in my slow "collapsing" of the images, thoughts, and feelings between my hands and drawing them back into myself as a powerful and *congruent* reorganized self. The moment is still with me as I pen these words; a sensation like being struck with a bolt of electricity, and a sudden clarity of thought and emotion I had never experienced before.

When I opened my eyes again, I remember that Frank invited me to step outside and report what I was aware of. It was profound. To this day, I remember the feel of the golden sunshine on my face, the meadow rolling down towards Santa Cruz in the distance below, the sound of the birds nearby, the rich scent of the pines, and the most profound sense of inner peace that I had known in many years.

That day led me to eventually return to UCSC (my now ex-father-in-law had once looked at me over the dinner table in his house after I told my wife's family of my goal to attend UCSC, and said, "Yes, but you have to be really *smart* to go there!") where I completed my undergraduate degree in psychology, which included two consecutive special studies courses under the guidance of Professor John Grinder. But I'm getting ahead of myself.

I left Los Gatos shortly thereafter, spent a year back in San Diego where I had grown up and completed another year at San Diego State before deciding to return to Santa Cruz and apply to UCSC. Of course, that year I was gone saw some of the most creative and generative work being accomplished by the inner core of the neuro-linguistic programming (NLP) founders. While I was not part of this group, I certainly benefited from their work upon my return. And it was during my time as a student at UCSC that I met and moved in with the woman who became my current wife. These were exciting times as I became more and more involved in the "late second generation" of NLPers.

UCSC Special Studies: Eric

As a student of psychology, I was afforded some leeway in my studies and chose to work directly with John Grinder who was still fairly new to the university. At the time, like many students, I was working nights having secured a job at the Santa Cruz juvenile detention facility. I would work all night, drive down the hill to Soquel for a quick breakfast, then off to classes at UC. It was kind of a schizophrenic period in my life, because I didn't have much sense of time or self. I would catch naps when I could, sometimes sleep in the evenings, drag myself to work, then start the grind again the next day. But I believe this craziness actually helped me remain open and responsive to what I was learning.

One of my projects focused on observing and codifying how a young, blind high school student, Eric, navigated around without sight. I still have the old reel-to-reel video recordings of our sessions together, where Eric demonstrated how he could identify the number and placement of chairs in a room, simply by clapping his hands a few times, and how he described the internal "map" he made in order to move about without bumping into obstacles. In the last dramatic session he describes what he "sees" when holding a series of photographs, and the audience is left to ponder just how this sightless individual is able to describe the essence of each photo without the use of his eyes.

Alba Road

Yes, these were exciting times, and I was encouraged by my mentors to feel free of the normal limits of academic exploration. Early on I was invited to attend the most dynamic and revolutionary workshop series I could imagine. Held in a forest in the mountains, we would gather once a week to explore, experiment, and grow using the rapidly expanding arsenal of techniques coming out of the inner circle of NLP. I remember sitting in awe as Richard Bandler and John Grinder would describe one or another technique and then put us into various groups to "play" with the techniques.

I have a vague memory of members of their "inner circle," people like Steve Gilligan, David Gordon, Leslie Bandler, Judith DeLozier, Paul Carter, and others milling around and observing us as we worked on each other. One night in particular stands out as a great representation of the kind of creative work we were doing.

I had been paired off with Terry McClendon. Our task that night involved using hypnosis, but I don't recall the specific task. I remember Terry describing an experience he'd had a few years earlier, where he was in a terrible accident on a winding mountain road. While he could remember everything leading up to the accident, including losing control of his car which slammed into a tree, he had amnesia for everything after the accident. We decided that I would work with him to try to uncover that memory.

I recall putting him into a deep trance using "hand levitation." (Terry and I were both good trance subjects. I, in particular, was so easy that whenever Richard needed a subject for a demonstration, he would say, "Can I have a volunteer," and look at me. My hand would already be inching up towards my face!) After establishing a "safety fallback" where he was allowed to not remember anything that was too painful or unpleasant, I led him in trance through the moment-by-moment description of what he had described just before the accident.

I had him "see" the curving road and wet pavement, had him "feel" the steering wheel, had him "hear" the squeal of the tires on the road as he lost control. And then, in a moment of inspiration, I said, "and then you *HIT THE TREE!*" as I slammed my fist down on the table next to us.

Terry jumped physically but remained in his trance. His neck tilted at an odd angle, as if he had been knocked out. (He later confirmed that he had been knocked out.) Slowly, over the next half hour or so, he recited bits and pieces of his memory of the events following the impact. He remembered a person arriving at the scene and yelling for someone to call for an ambulance. He remembered some of the conversation between the medics in the ambulance. He remembered the week he was in the hospital, the friends who came to visit him and what they talked about. Finally, again, giving him "permission" to bring back into his conscious awareness only that which was not threatening or too uncomfortable, I brought him out of the trance. What a remarkable experience for us both!

Alba Road Revisited

Around this time, I began to get invited to work with various "clients" who either showed up at or were invited to John and Richard's place halfway up the winding Alba Road in the Santa Cruz Mountains.

I vividly remember answering the phone and hearing John say, "Hey, Byron, if you're free, I've got someone up here who needs some work." Oh, yes, a chance to run up to Alba Road and work with one of John's clients while he and Richard pounded out one of their books! What an opportunity!

I would jump in my old rusting blue VW and, leaving my soon-to-be wife Marcia in Soquel, drive through Ben Lomond and up Alba to their place. Richard and John had a long coffee table with a typewriter at either end. Sometimes they would both be working on a different section or chapter of a book at the same time. If one or the other would get "stuck" they would just trade places and keep working. An amazing process to observe.

I would show up, and John would come out and say something like, "OK, Byron, here's the deal. This guy wants to do X, and he has all the resources to do it, but he keeps failing. Put him in a trance and acquaint him with some of these resources." After a few minutes working with the client in their "therapy room," I would go out and "report" to John who would give me a new set of instructions. This would go on for about an hour or so, until John was convinced the client had received what he had come for. John would enter the room and "test" him to be sure the change had taken hold, then would "excuse" me with a thanks and return to his work. I think I grew more during some of those experiences than anything else.[2]

The Exorcism

I was so excited about what I was learning that I told everybody I knew. The folks I worked with were always being regaled by my stories of the workshops and techniques we were working with. Marcia's roommate had gotten married and moved out, and I set up a therapy room in our house in Soquel and was seeing clients interested in experiencing some of these techniques and exploring the limits to their personal growth. So it was no surprise when one of my co-workers showed up on our doorstep one afternoon asking to speak with me. A devout Catholic, she told me that she was convinced she was possessed by a demon which had taken control over her soul and was making her think "terrible thoughts." She was concerned that it was going to eventually make her do things she did not want to do. She had been on her way to see her priest and was going to ask him to "exorcize" the demon. On the way, however, she started thinking about some of the stories I had shared and decided to ask for my advice first.

I told her that I would be willing to assist her to confront her demon and would help her galvanize all her resources to come to terms with what was going on inside her. The deal was that, if she did not feel the session had worked, she would go directly to her priest for the exorcism. She agreed.

For the next half hour or so, I worked with her in a mild trance to identify the parts of herself that were objecting to or were afraid of the "demon." She created several powerful images of these parts, gave them voices and rehearsed their concerns and how they could confront the demon. Then, using one of the key concepts of NLP at that time where *the symptom becomes a resource*, I carefully "reframed" the demon into an "aspect" of her personality that might actually be trying to "help" her achieve something, and told her that all she had to do was gather up her empowered parts and, when she was ready, imagine it sitting across from her. She agreed to try this.

I was hardly prepared for what happened next. As she formed the image of the demon sitting across from her, she suddenly let out a blood-curdling scream that lasted for several moments. (I later found out that Marcia, much to my relief, had gone out to do "damage control" with several neighbors who had come running over to find out who was being murdered!) Once she had regained control of herself, I took her calmly through the standard dissociated state therapy (DST) processes of reframing and resource building and ultimately re-integrated the parts. As she put her hands together in the integration gesture I had learned years before from Frank Pucelik, and slowly drew her new integrated "self" back into herself, she began to sob with relief. When she had composed herself, she said the "voice in her head" had stopped for the first time in many months.

She felt a sense of calm bliss and said she did not think she needed to see the priest after all. Over the year or so after our session, I regularly saw her at work, and she frequently thanked me for the session, saying that she had regained her sense of happiness and well-being lost during her "possession."[3]

M.E.T.A. Institute

I graduated with my Bachelor of Arts in Psychology from UCSC in the spring of 1977, and Marcia and I were wed in August. I began to teach various classes with Terry McClendon and we talked about writing a book, which seemed to be fashionable back then. Marcia took some hypnosis classes from Leslie who had married Richard. I remember helping them stuff envelopes with brochures advertising their workshops to help pay for some of Marcia's classes. A year came and went, and then I got a call from Frank. He invited us to come down to San Diego to meet with him and learn more about his new organization.

Of course, we went. When we arrived, Frank showed us around the house-converted-to-institute and introduced us to some of the folks he had working for him, including Marilyn Moskowitz, Steve Lorei, and Jeff Paris. At the time, Frank was the director of the San Diego branch of M.E.T.A. which also included Paul Carter and Steve Gilligan as trainers. He talked about how he had created a partnership with Hedges Capers of the San Diego Institute for Transactional Analysis (SDITA) and would be offering advanced master's-level college degrees through International College. This was exactly what I was looking for: here was an opportunity to get my Master's in Marriage, Family and Child Counseling while studying with my original mentor, Frank, with a focus on the most exciting therapeutic change technology available, NLP.

Within three months, we had relocated and I was enrolled in International College and taking classes at SDITA and the M.E.T.A. Institute. This was another exciting time. My classmates included Carol Martin, Lisa Chiara, a retired teacher named Jim, Jack Bingham, and several others. The coursework at Frank's M.E.T.A. Institute eventually formed the basis of my master's thesis, "Meta Principles of Communication and Change: A Model for a Process Theory of Personality," which Frank and I later refined and published as the book, *Magic Demystified: A Pragmatic Guide to Communication and Change.*[4]

M.E.T.A. International

Following graduation in 1979, Marcia and I decided we were tired of the southern California rat race and decided to relocate to Eugene, Oregon, where I hung up my shingle as a counselor. Frank had meanwhile moved to Oklahoma where he launched M.E.T.A. International.

He hired me and together we put on a series of one-day workshops in various locations in the Northwest that resulted in a six-session once-a-month NLP workshop series that I taught in Portland, Seattle, and Vancouver, BC. I continued to work with Frank on various projects, including the publication of *Magic Demystified* through to the end of about 1983, when Marcia and I decided to move back to Santa Cruz.

Substance Abuse Treatment

In 1985 we took a big plunge and went to work for the US Army in Germany (USEURA). That was my introduction to work in the field of substance abuse counseling, and as a result of my earlier experiences – with few restrictions other than the mantra, "If what you're doing isn't working, change what you're doing" – I flourished. Starting as a counselor at one of the local community counseling centers and working with soldiers, their spouses, and civilians associated with the army, I soon found myself promoted and eventually ended up as a Supervisory Counseling Psychologist and Clinical Director of one of the army's largest outpatient counseling centers in Europe.

During this time, I linked up with another mentor, Jim Ronan, and began to research and apply cognitive behavioral therapy (CBT, a very comfortable adjunct to the Meta Model) and techniques of relapse prevention (anchors, cues, and changing internal dialogue) to my work with soldiers and their families. With Jim, I helped to set up a comprehensive training program for counselors that drew from and utilized my experiences with NLP, the Meta Model, CBT, and relapse prevention. The program was eventually adopted by V Corps as the substance abuse treatment training standard.[5]

We left Germany in 1990. I continued to work in the field of substance abuse treatment and prevention and penned my second book, *Sobriety Demystified: Getting Clean and Sober with NLP and CBT*, which was published in 1996. In keeping with my previous pattern of growth, I was again promoted from a counselor at a Monterey County Health Department outpatient program to that program's Director, and then went into management and on to become a Senior Departmental Administrative Analyst in charge of the substance abuse prevention and treatment contract programs for the county of Santa Cruz, from which I retired in 2004.

Postscript

One of the most remarkable aspects of people like Richard, John, Frank, and all the other brilliant early NLPers was their ability to accomplish what always appeared implausible or even impossible. There was this attitude that something had never been successfully done before simply because it hadn't been tried or tried *this* way. In describing the brilliance of Steve Jobs in his recent biography, author Walter Isaacson talks about how he created a "reality distortion field" around himself. Quoting Debi Coleman, one of Jobs' Mac team managers: "It was a self-fulfilling distortion. You did the impossible, because you didn't realize it was impossible."[6] That effect imbued everything we did back then, and, to a certain extent, I think it is still alive and well in some NLP circles.

I recently looked up NLP on Wikipedia and was not surprised, but a little disappointed, at the amount of press dedicated to research discrediting some of the basic precepts of NLP, such as representational systems and accessing cues. While there is a growing body of work that provides scientific evidence for the efficacy of NLP, there are still a significant number of practitioners who are not particularly concerned about proving this. Here is how that mindset might work: in the generative and nearly boundary-less processes of the early creators of NLP, the models developed appeared to be based more on *what works* rather than *what can be proved.*

While accessing cues, for example, failed to pass the scrutiny of established scientific testing, what is remarkable is just how important they were in making the student or practitioner *pay exquisite attention* to the subject. This close scrutiny enabled the observer to actually become more aware of multiple processes happening as the subject went through the processes of remembering past experiences or generating new ideas.

So, if I thought I observed a "visual accessing cue," then checked by *pacing* with visual representational processes (posture, tone, words, etc.) and it *worked*, then I really don't care that it hasn't been scientifically proven that the accessing cue exists. The possibility that, in my attempt to observe it, I am doing something different than if I wasn't trying to observe it and I am doing something that helps me better communicate with and/or guide the subject towards a desirable outcome, is more important anyway. I'm not saying that I would go out now and teach accessing cues as scientifically validated behaviors that can be observed. I might teach, however, that learning the lexicon of representational systems, including accessing cues, can broaden your ability to map a subject's internal processes and open you to experiences that can assist you in the processes of communication. And that is the point.

PART 2

Introduction to Part 2

John Grinder

In this section of *The Origins of Neuro-Linguistic Programming*, I have the pleasure of presenting my personal article alongside a poem by Joyce Michaelson and three articles in the voices of Steve Gilligan, James Eicher, and Robert Dilts.

I take it, as co-author of *Origins*, that I have the prerogative to edit what the authors in this section have written. At the same time, this requirement is to be balanced with the strategy that Frank and I have adopted for the presentation of the history in *The Origins of Neuro-Linguistic Programming*. More specifically, the strategy that we pursue here is to rely on the intelligence of the readers to assimilate the representations by different authors that diverge in significant ways and, through some multi-angulation of these divergent descriptions from distinct perceptual positions, to arrive at their own understanding of what occurred.

I have resolved the tension between editing the submitted articles and leaving the voices that these authors have presented their experiences in intact by simply not editing the articles.

While there are descriptions and statements made in these articles with which I most definitely disagree, this is not the forum to resolve them. With a clear appreciation that well intentioned, intelligent people can reproduce memories that significantly diverge from one another when describing common events, I have respected this principle by refusing to edit the articles, but rather leaving these written records of what they have chosen to present in their original voices.

The Love Song of NLP

Joyce Michaelson

(with apologies to T.S. Eliot)

Let us go then, you and I,
where the redwoods spread out against the sky,
Like a stoner etherized while lying a green field.
Let us go through 1970s Santa Cruz
Where revolution (inner and outer) were news,
and students gathered to be healed.
Where restless nights in Gestalt groups led by Grinder
Who showed us how to help, not hinder
and led us to an overwhelming question:

Oh, this was his declaratory:
"The map is not the territory!"

In the room the students came
Working to have their minds reframed

And in time we learned the Meta Model,
the kind of questions that do not coddle,
but challenged deletions, nominalizations and distortion,
linguistic, sensory and thought contortion.

In the room with Richard and John,
we created the NLP salon.

And matching breathing, creating rapport,
we went on for more and more.
Shifting contexts, changing meaning,
Visual, auditory, kinesthetic screening,
Accessing cues, anchoring, reframing,
Modeling excellence was where we were aiming.
Watching eye movements, left or right glance,
We discovered we were all in a trance.

How, then, could we presume
to really know what happens in a room?

Surprising ourselves with what we knew,
Unconscious and conscious mind merge: a coup!

Joyce Michaelson lives in Santa Cruz, California, where she practices psychotherapy and is deeply involved in theatre and the art of acting.

CHAPTER 6

The Middle of Know Where:
My Early Days in NLP

Stephen Gilligan

1974 was quite a year for me. I dropped out of the University of California at Santa Cruz (UCSC) in January, moving back to San Francisco to continue my high school legacy of sex, drugs, and rock 'n' roll. I landed a job with my cronies on the midnight shift in a steel factory in the middle of the Oakland ghettos. The main reason that a 19-year-old, pony-tailed hippy kid and his VW bus safely escaped that neighborhood each night was the factory's location right across the street from a black Muslim bakery, where bow-tied members stood outside keeping watch over things. All praise due to Allah!

This life path clearly wasn't a happy one, and my dark interior featured an internal dialogue that intoned, "I don't want to live this life! I don't want to live this life!" My conscious mind thought this meant I was supposed to kill myself. I struggled to resist, aided by the counter-inductions of early Catholic trances ("It's a sin to kill yourself!") and the thought that perhaps the 49ers (football team) might someday win the Super Bowl and I would miss it! But the internal dialogue intensified, leading me to secure enough drugs to die. I went to my parents' home when they weren't around, sat on the kitchen floor, and decided to no longer resist the voice. Fully convinced that this meant suicide, I was therefore shocked to experience a deep energy explode within me, erupting as I threw the drugs down and began to sob a long sob, the first cry since I was young boy determined to never break down when my father hit me. As the tears subsided, an image twirled outwards from deep inside, unfolding a picture of the Santa Cruz campus. And then it was quite clear: that voice was a deep voice of integrity, pointing out that the life I was leading was not my path, that my path was something else. The emergent image indicated that deeper path involved returning to UCSC.

This was a significant step in the long and winding road of learning to listen to the creative unconscious wisdom that moves through each of us. What I learned in my early days with neuro-linguistic programming (NLP) was how to distrust and dissolve the conscious maps that would distract from that deeper listening, so that a more interesting and creative life could be realized. The near-suicidal experience was a sort of a death and rebirth process, where the old skin of my childhood self was shed to allow the emergence of a new identity. In retrospect, this event began my NLP journey.

The next day, I called the university and told them I wanted to re-enroll. They said that the following day was the registration deadline for the next quarter (starting in two weeks), so I hopped in my VW van, drove the 70 miles down the coast to Santa Cruz, and took care of the paperwork.[1] Perusing the course options, I somehow selected two strange sounding but intriguing courses. The first was Steps to an Ecology of Mind, taught by some fellow named Gregory Bateson. The second was Political Economy of the United States, co-taught by a young assistant professor by the name of John Grinder. This class advocated the overthrow of the United States government by any means possible, and seemed like the sort of course that any self-respecting Santa Cruz student would take at the time. So on the first day back in school in spring 1974 I met Gregory Bateson, and on the second I connected with John Grinder.

It was a happening time in Santa Cruz, and these courses fired my imagination. Grinder's presence instantly elevated my state of consciousness. With a twinkle in his eye and a spring to his step, he talked about change and creating new possibilities, all the while engaging with his students as if they were intelligent beings who had something to contribute. He mentioned to me that he was collaborating with a Gestalt therapist by the name of Richard Bandler, a skinny, long-haired mountain outlaw type. They were holding groups twice a week in a house rented (as I remember) by Frank Pucelik, Leslie Cameron, and

Judith DeLozier. I joined both groups, thus beginning an odyssey of deep trance-formation and beyond.[2]

The main people that I remember in those 1974–1977 groups included Judy and Leslie, as well as Jim Eicher, Joyce Michaelson, Patrick and Terry Rooney, and Trevelyan Houck. I lived with Frank Pucelik and Paul Carter during much of that time, and they were actively in the mix as well. David Gordon and Terry McClendon were in the earlier groups, and Robert Dilts came in around 1976, if I remember correctly. That community, including Bandler and Grinder, was a group of merry pranksters that spent seemingly every waking moment exploring, reading, experimenting, creating and, most of all, having fun. We roared through the Meta Model and then the Milton Model, trying out every possible communication pattern we could dream of – on ourselves, each other, waitresses in restaurants, professors in classes, people at bus stops, and so on. The Marx Brothers movies – that's Groucho, not Karl – offered excellent models of possible ways of being. We were young, intensely curious, and determined to "go where no man or woman had gone before."

A central forum for the early groups were the evening groups led by Bandler and Grinder. They were small groups, perhaps 12–15 people, mostly UCSC students. Each meeting was about three hours or so with a relatively straightforward structure. The question would be raised as to who wanted to make deep personal changes that evening, and volunteers would be directed to different individual rooms. In the initial groups, a single Meta-Model distinction – for example, challenging deletions – would be introduced to the remaining students. Each volunteer would be joined by two of these students, who would enthusiastically badger the volunteer with that single Meta-Model question. Not surprisingly, this would go only so far, the interrogation working itself into a feverish pitch until the door swung open and Richard Bandler would appear, standing like a gunslinger from the Wild West. The volunteer was obviously primed for something (anything!), and Bandler would make a quick intervention that would typically elicit a massive change process. (We were not quite consciously aware of response potential at that time.) I especially remember how Bandler's tough exterior would soften as a person opened up, and how he skillfully guided them to an integration.

After 90 minutes or so, the groups would re-adjourn to the main room and conversation about what had happened would ensue. In the initial year or so, I remember Bandler as the front man, while Grinder would more observe and meta-comment on the process. This shifted over time into a more symmetrical teaching role. In the last 30–45 minutes, Bandler would go on a rave about (and mostly against) psychotherapy – about the limitations of all maps, how they were nominalizations that trapped people inside theories and away from direct observation and relational connection. Bandler spoke at times like an inspirational preacher and his raves lit a passionate fire within this young psychology student. They invited me to see through maps and look more to the effects of a map on a given experiential process. They emphasized a process of sensory connection and getting feedback, but also one of living beyond maps. This latter notion of a "world beyond words" was being fed by many other influences in my life at that time – Carlos Castenada, Allan Watts, the Grateful Dead, Ram Dass, meditation, LSD, John C. Lilly, John Coltrane, and G. Spencer-Brown, to name a few. But for those few precious years, the Bandler and Grinder groups were the core contexts for this exploration.

The challenging of maps had two noteworthy levels in those early days. First, a main purpose of the Meta Model was to develop a more complete mapping of experience. The idea, of course, was that the deletions, distortions, and generalizations made (typically without awareness) in a representational process resulted in an impoverished map that led to limited choices. The implication of the Meta Model was that developing more complete and less distorted maps would allowed better choices and thus superior experience and performance. This is one of the significant contributions of the Meta Model (and NLP in general) to a number of different conversational domains.

But a second, equally prominent, emphasis of the early days was learning to navigate without fixed maps; that is, to learn at an unconscious level. As I soon discovered in doing trance work, a hypnotic induction is a set of communications that de-frames or dissolves fixed maps, thereby allowing new experiences unhindered by the map bias. From this naturalistic view, virtually my entire time spent with Bandler and Grinder was a hypnotic induction – the core spirit guiding the work was dissolving all fixed views (in ourselves and others), so that both laughter and significant new realities could emerge.

To me, the revolutionary spirit of early NLP came from a beautiful combination of these two levels of (1) learning without maps (i.e., unconscious learning) and (2) learning via maps improved by meta-modeling principles. The former provided a deep well of original ideas and possibilities, while the latter offered a means to refine and for-malize these possibilities into teachable and replicable models. In my view, subsequent generations of NLP relied too heavily on the latter and ignored the former, leading too often to an industry of "building better mousetraps."

I remained interested in both, especially the infinite creativity of uncon-scious learning. This was in no small part fueled by my encounters with Milton Erickson, easily the most gifted communication artist I have ever met. As I remember, Gregory Bateson, who lived on the same property in the Santa Cruz Mountains as did Bandler and Grinder, was deeply impressed with the *Structure of Magic, Volume I*,[3] and suggested that if Richard and John really wanted to know something about com-munication, they should go study the "great purple one" in the Arizona desert. (Erickson was color blind, only "enjoying" the color purple, and thus wore only purple in his later years.) Bateson and Erickson had been friends for over 50 years, beginning when Bateson and Margaret Mead consulted with the already legendary hypnotherapist, Milton Erickson, before they went to Bali to study trance rituals.

Richard and John went to visit Erickson in late 1974, I believe, for three or four days. When they came back with stories, tapes, and books, my cosmic egg cracked open. Fritz Perls and Virginia Satir had been the prominent wizards of the initial Meta-Model focus, but adding Erickson to the mix was like introducing imaginary numbers into a pri-mary math equation of adding numbers. Whatever it was, it was (and remains) something of mysterious and melodious beauty! I remember this inner space opening up, and a silent voice said, "This is why you're here." Dramatic, yes, but quite meaningful for a 19-year-old kid!

Actually, Erickson so skillfully and consistently violated virtually every Meta-Model rule that it required the development of the "Milton Model," a sort of inverted pattern of the former. These complementary models suggested different ways to communicate with the conscious and unconscious minds. Whereas skillful communication with the conscious mind was helped when a fuller linguistic map was developed (via the Meta Model), effective communication with the unconscious occurred via Meta-Model violations (ambiguities, generalities, deletions, etc.) that invited the listener to perform their own "trance-derivational" search, resulting in a creative unconscious elaboration. This movement into a dual-mind model opened up infinitely more possibilities of experimental communication, and the pleasure of ever deeper discoveries.

By this time, Paul Carter and I had started teaching student-directed seminars at UCSC, under a never before used provision that allowed students to teach courses under faculty sponsorship. Grinder (as well as Bateson) was more than happy to provide such sponsorship, and we designed and taught courses around NLP-related topics. Next to the staid atmosphere of most university courses, they were a big hit. So much so that one day the provost called us into his office and complained about reports that students were having intense learning experiences in the classroom. He pointed out that this sort of thing wasn't allowed under university guidelines. We returned to the classroom and solemnly broke the news that the provost had decreed that meaningful experiences were not to be allowed in a classroom setting, and so if students felt an experience coming on, they would have to leave the classroom immediately and go outside to have it. In the revolutionary hey-day of mid-1970s Santa Cruz, the students were predictably outraged and defied the order in every way possible.

Following Richard and John's lead, Paul and I began to offer evening courses, especially for those interested in the "deep learning experiences not allowed within university guidelines." After several years, we had four weekly evening courses of 20-person student groups where we explored various experiments in consciousness, especially featuring trance work. Much of this was experimental, guided by the principle that identity and reality are constructed, and thus many different possible realities and possible identity states could and should be created in order to go beyond arbitrary limits and fixed beliefs.

For example, we had secured a large psychiatric textbook from the Napa psychiatric hospital where John and Richard had been invited to train the psychiatric residents. We would go through and identify the psychiatric disorders that seemed like apt descriptions of various student behavioral patterns, then have those students step into a trance identity that included these symptoms, then have other students help them find a "cure" by transforming the symptom into a resource. Needless to say, it was all good fun, with a few notable exceptions, like the time we suggested to a huge, muscular guy who was so sweet and shy that he take on the trance identity of Idi Amin, the infamous Ugandan mass killer. No formal trance induction was needed, for upon hearing the assignment, this fellow immediately became enraged that anybody would suggest he was capable of such a thing. As nimble young men, we were skilled at running and ducking when needed.

Our fascination with Erickson's work led us to scour all available literature on hypnosis. In one of the hypnosis journals we came across research by a Russian psychologist by the name of Vladimir Raikov. He had been having hypnotized subjects "deep trance identify" with famous artists, such as Rembrandt, and then painting pictures while in that identification trance. Results showed a superior performance when in the trance identity, a finding that stimulated our curiosity in many ways. It led to the suggestion, I believe by Grinder, that I do a deep trance identification with Milton Erickson. It was still a month or so before I was to meet Erickson personally, but I had been living and breathing his work rather intensely.

The first identification experience occurred at Bandler's place, and Richard and John were both there. Right before the experiment, one of them ran over to invite Bateson to observe. With Bateson sitting in his awkward fashion in the chair next to me, John performed the induction. To say the least, it was a deep trance. However, upon opening my eyes to interact with Bateson, the trance identity began to waver, no doubt given my anchors to Bateson as my teacher. So I went back inside and asked my unconscious to help me to utilize all available resources and patterns to successfully enter Erickson's consciousness. This time, when I opened my eyes, I found myself deeply absorbed in the eyeglasses that Bateson was nervously fidgeting with in his hands. They were the most interesting eyeglasses I had ever seen, and the hands holding them were the most fascinating channels of connection to "my old friend Bateson," who was shimmering like a quantum wave in my peripheral field. I began to talk with Bateson (through the glasses, of course), who after a short period jumped up and ran out of the room. Apparently I had disclosed information private to him and Erickson!

Even more interesting than this humorous side note were the experiential learnings gained in the creative trance state. I had anticipated that Erickson's internal state was filled with very fast, clever thinking, the fastest gun in the west. To my astonishment, I experienced something radically different in the identification trance. First, there was no internal dialogue whatsoever, everything inside was completely quiet. Second, when I opened my eyes, it was readily apparent that *everybody was already in a deep trance.* There was no need whatsoever to "hypnotize" anybody, to "do anything" to get them into trance, as their unconscious was already in deep trance. The only thing that was needed was to speak directly (or rather, metaphorically) to the creative unconscious that was already fully active and absorbed. I doubt I ever would have gained these learnings from a "conscious mind" state, and the values they have provided are immeasurable.

I had ample opportunity to practice and explore trance from this new state. Paul, Frank, and I had stereo systems with Erickson's hypnotic voice being piped into the rooms throughout our house. I worked out of an old purple wheelchair we had found at a garage sale. All I needed to do was sit in that chair, clasp my hands together in a certain way (like Erickson), close my eyes for a moment and, *voila!* It was an exhilarating and amazing state: anything related to trance and communicating with the unconscious, I could intuitively trust myself to do, discovering many surprising learnings in the process. For example, moving from the "Steve" trance to the "Milton" trance taught me that most of our lives are lived within the rigid boundaries of fairly arbitrary "identification trances" that we inherit or randomly develop, and yet it is possible to step out of these arbitrary conditionings and live from a freer, more generative space.

This experience of Erickson's "no content" internal state was confirmed when I interviewed him about his working strategy some months later. I came in with pencil and paper, determined to model the great wizard. Secure in my early NLP belief that all consciousness could be reduced to sequences of three representational systems (visual, auditory, kinesthetic), I asked Erickson if I could inquire about his working state.

"Go right ahead," he said.

"Do you have internal dialogue when you're working?" I asked.

"No," he straightforwardly answered. I checked that category off on the list.

"Well, then," I continued, "do you make a lot of visual pictures?"

"No," he responded again. And I crossed off another category.

"Well, you must have a lot of kinesthetic sensations then," I insisted, growing a bit worried in my Carlos Castaneda role.

"No," he answered with equal measure.

I was at the end of my known world, like a sailor ready to sail off the flat earth. "Well, then, what do you do when you're working?"

"*I don't know*," he said, with a soft intensity. "All I know is that I have an unconscious mind and they have an unconscious mind, and we're both sitting in the same room together. And therefore, *trance is inevitable!*"

I began slowly to write down those last three words, but somehow before I could finish, I was too deeply entranced.

"I don't know *HOW trance will happen.* I don't know *WHEN trance will happen.* I don't know *WHY trance will happen.* And so I'm very curious to discover just how, when, and why it does happen now!

"Now I know that sounds ridiculous," he continued, "but *it works!*"

I slowly wrote down on my notepad, "IT WORKS!"

Like most Erickson tales, this interaction was funny yet also suggestive of a deeper point: *it is possible to think, learn, and act at different levels of attention and consciousness.* The first order attention of the conscious mind can track and be attached to various content, but the second order attention of the creative unconscious can operate from a more generative level. Again, this dual level was a primary feature of the early NLP community, allowing an ever changing set of content to emerge.

Predictably, attunement to the creative unconscious seemed to weaken considerably as NLP began to emerge on an international level in the late 1970s. Primary attention was given to fixed content, such as accessing cues and representational systems, and competition grew among who had the fastest seven-step model for this or that. While such fixed-content models can be helpful tools in certain application contexts, primary attention to their content typically results in confusing the maps as the territory, while also favoring the development of technocrats over creative thinkers. Such an outcome is ironic, given that the initial base for NLP was precisely the opposite. The original groups rarely seemed to get caught for long in "fixed content" positions; perhaps we were too busy laughing to get rigid. Something about the movement between multiple maps and multiple positions seemed intrinsic to that early spirit, and it kept the music unfolding like a beautiful jazz improvisation.

Part of the issue here is the relation of the reader to the map. Maps can be read and used as literal texts or poetic metaphors. This distinction is reflected in the difference between a "sign" and a "symbol." A *sign* may be described as something that has a context-invariant meaning; for example, a red light at a traffic stop does (and should) mean the same thing to all drivers. A *symbol*, however, has multiple, contradictory meanings, many of which are not consciously available. This, of course, is the distinction between the conscious and creative unconscious minds. The conscious mind operates from a fixed referent point, while the peripheral field of the unconscious allows a fluid movement of multiple positions. The point is that the same map can be read as a sign or a symbol. In the pre-NLP world of the mid-1970s, patterns were definitely engaged as metaphorical symbols.

The ecological and creative prominence of maps as metaphors was shared not only by Grinder and Bandler, but also by Erickson and Bateson. Bateson emphasized the idea of double or multiple description as a core requirement for an ecological map, while Erickson would equivalently emphasize that "people come into therapy because they are rigid, and your job is to help them get un-rigid!" In other words, limitations develop when one rigidly adheres to a fixed map, and new possibilities open when multiple maps are developed.

This principle played out in both their teaching approaches. Bateson might open a lecture with an example from biology, then move without explanation to a story from literature, then to another about cybernetics, and so forth. At the end of the lecture, he would not tie the stories together. Instead, he would typically "harrumph" his archetypal British harrumph, wipe the chalk from his hands onto his pants and shirt, and then ramble off, leaving behind a wake of students in curious learning trances.

Similarly, Erickson would often start a teaching session by meaningfully asking, "What do you want to learn today?" I quickly learned that if there was anything whatsoever you were curious about, it was a good time to speak your mind and then buckle your seat belt. He would immediately turn to some poor soul and launch into a hypnotic demonstration, replete with multiple levels of metaphors. At some point you would recognize that he was also now working with another student and then another, all with parallel hypnotic phenomena and cascades of metaphorical stories. This would typically go on for who knows how many hours of clock time (certainly not my Irish consciousness!), whereupon he would pause and ask with a twinkle in his eye,

"Any other questions?" Of course, most people wondered what the first question was; but there was no mistaking that many answers had been developed.

This use of metaphor seemed a higher level than the mere isomorphic mapping of content proposed in some of the metaphor models. Each metaphor contained a particular pattern that, in itself, was interesting (and could be regarded as isomorphic). But the relation of the different metaphors provided a deeper pattern, like all the different parts of jazz improvisation fitting together into a deeper whole. And perhaps more interesting, each metaphor could simultaneously carry multiple contradictory meanings, raising the number of possible meanings exponentially. It was no wonder that arguments would break out outside of Erickson's office regarding exactly to whom he had been communicating, and what the "real point" of the communications had been.

It reminds me of the story of the teenage kid who walked into the Toronto Hilton honeymoon suite of John Lennon and Yoko Ono during their marriage "love-in" in 1969. Wading through the multitudes gathered in the suite, the youngster approached Lennon with a tape recorder and asked, "Mr. Lennon, would it be alright if I asked you a few questions?"

"Yeah, sure," Lennon kindly responded.

"They say," continued the young man, "that there are many hidden meanings in the Beatles' songs. What do you say to that?"

"I completely agree with them," Lennon replied. "Usually, about six months after we release an album, I sit down and listen to it. And I'm totally amazed by how many meanings I hear in the songs that I didn't know were there. And I wrote the songs!" He further elaborated that this was true in all art: it was a communicational metaphor that carried multiple, contradictory meanings, many of which are not consciously available.

This was my experience of the early days of NLP. It was a wonderful band of gypsies that was playing a new type of music. The songs (i.e., maps, books, lectures) that arose were not intended as "truth," but as interesting metaphors that might temporarily offer new ways of seeing and acting in the world. Once the content map proved useful, it was no longer useful, because the engagement with it shifted the whole space, requiring new maps. At a more meaningful level, those early days suggested a way of meta-learning, letting go of fixed positions and maps and learning to learn as creative improvisation. The experiences with Bandler and Grinder, combined with Bateson and Erickson, illuminated a way to live life as a great journey of consciousness.

I left Santa Cruz in 1977, moving over the hill to Stanford to do my graduate work in psychology. I continued my close connection with Erickson until his death in 1980, but not so much with the Santa Cruz world of NLP. Partly this was due to graduate school commitments, partly to the schism that developed between Erickson and Bateson, but mostly to a need to sort out and integrate all that I had absorbed in Santa Cruz. While the base of my experience was tremendously positive, the underbelly of 1970s NLP included an arrogant, "take no prisoners" contempt for all "outsiders" in which anybody and anything was fair game for ridicule. This antagonistic attitude seemed to deepen as NLP moved to an international level, culminating in a mid-1980s cacophony of lawsuits, criminal charges, bad mouthing, and other unpleasantries. The principle that the "map is not the territory" seemed altogether forgotten in such events, and NLP suffered as a result.

Examining corresponding processes in my own life was part of a soul-searching I engaged in during this period, no doubt prompted by Erickson's influence. I was inspired by his dedication to operating at the highest level of technical craft and generative thinking while enjoying every moment thoroughly. Especially impressive was how his exceptional way of working included such creative playfulness, all the while operating from the highest ethical levels of respect and generosity for every person. This combination of extraordinary creativity, effectiveness, and ethical integrity challenged me to grow and change in many ways, a process still in motion.

My work evolved into the post-Ericksonian approaches of self-relations and generative self. These models presuppose that "reality" is constructed through conditioned filters operating at different levels, for example, the conscious and unconscious minds. Since these mental filters are constructed (i.e., they have no fixed or innate structure) they can be deconstructed and reconstructed in countless ways, each giving rise to a different reality. This encourages exploration of those constructions that enable the most generative processes (and dissolution of those that don't), with special emphasis on the feedback loops between the minds that create a tertiary level of "generative self." When the two minds are operating in harmony at their highest levels, the result is art, creativity, genius, and transformation.

Over the last 15 years or so, I have gradually re-connected with parts of the NLP world. Robert Dilts and I have shared a professional collaboration (and personal friendship) that has been extremely rich and rewarding. I teach for various NLP institutes and have some good friends in the field. Of course, you cannot speak about NLP in the singular anymore, as there are many different modes and forms. Not surprisingly, I favor those that insist upon the presence of the creative unconscious in any modeling or application process. The New Code developed by Grinder and DeLozier, and further elaborated by Grinder and Bostic-St. Clair, is a clear example of this, as is the NLP University work of Dilts and DeLozier. While there are significant differences, these approaches maintain the generative spirit of early NLP while advancing the theory, applications, and ethical base in significant ways.

What the early days of NLP represent for me now are examples of the infinite possibilities of creative learning and consciousness. As Bob Dylan sang, "He not busy being born is busy dying." These births – past, present, and future – are wonders to behold. Who could possibly ask for anything more?

CHAPTER 7

Commentary on
"The Middle of Know Where"

John Grinder

In his presentation, "The Middle of Know Where," Gilligan offers a humorous and touching narrative of his collision with NLP and the circle of people who either informed it (in particular, Bateson and Erickson) or those whose activities pivoted around it – the co-creators, Bandler, Pucelik, and myself and the shifting band of people involved in its initial testing and development. His style in this article captures much of the feel that I remember from those days.

Gilligan is clear about memory and its shortfalls, as he comments in his first footnote:

> I have done my best to accurately recall events, including dates, people involved, etc. Memory is undeniably a constructive process always in revision, so my apologies for any significant distortions or deletions.

While I may have distinct memories of some of the experiences that Gilligan describes, and even questions about the classification that he uses, these are mere quibbles compared to his excellent ability to capture something of the spirit of the original days.

Gilligan writes:

> a main purpose of the Meta-Model was to develop a more complete mapping of experience. The idea, of course, was that the deletions, distortions, and generalizations made (typically without awareness) in a representational process resulted in an impoverished map that led to limited choices.

Here Gilligan refers to the three so-called universals of human modeling – deletion, distortion, and generalization – that were the currency
of the era in presentations by Bandler, Pucelik, and myself. There are,
as a well-known English playwright of some centuries ago succinctly
stated, *inventions that return to plague the inventor*. Here is one such:
these so-called universals of human modeling.

Consider what is being proposed here, and ask yourself: *What is the
relationship among these three putative universals?*

What emerges as an answer to this question from me personally is:

> *What were they thinking to have made this preposterous proposal?*

How does a generalization emerge? Let's say that we have two things
– two experiences – and we wish to make a generalization about those
two experiences. How are we to proceed? Well, obviously, each experience is unique in some ways and if there is any coherent basis for a
generalization across these two experiences, it will be found in those
elements that they share, what they have in common.

How is this to be achieved? By the ignoring of the differences between
these two experiences and an unwavering focus on their commonal-
ities. But, hang on, the term *ignoring* as used in the last sentence is a
surrogate for deletion – one ignores something by deleting that thing
from his or her attention. So, clearly the relationship between deletion
and generalization is one of process, and the resulting generalization is
itself the consequence of the application of the process of deletion. You
achieve a generalization by deleting the class of elements not shared
by the two experiences and focus your attention on those areas where
they overlap.

Now, consider *distortion* and its relationship to the pair deletion/gen-
eralization. At least under the conventional meaning of *distortion,* the
act of deleting an element in the description of some event in order to
achieve a generalization would certainly constitute a distortion of the
description of that event. In a court of law, for example, such an action

would be considered a distortion of the evidentiary base of whatever action the court was hearing.

I regard this proposal – the three putative universals of human modeling: distortion, deletion, and generalization – as incoherent at best and will be happy to see it deleted from further discussion. The situation is epistemologically hopeless with respect to this proposal. The interested reader is invited to review the current successor to this proposal – the epistemology offered in Bostic-St. Clair and Grinder's *Whispering in the Wind*.[1] Gilligan's report is accurate for what was on offer at the time – my apologies!

Gilligan comments:

> But a second, equally prominent, emphasis of the early days was learning to navigate without fixed maps; that is, to learn at an unconscious level. As I soon discovered in doing trance work, a hypnotic induction is a set of communications that de-frames or dissolves fixed maps, thereby allowing new experiences unhindered by the map bias. From this naturalistic view, virtually my entire time spent with Bandler and Grinder was a hypnotic induction – the core spirit guiding the work was dissolving all fixed views (in ourselves and others), so that both laughter and significant new realities could emerge.

Compare this description with what Dilts and Eicher offer later in this book about the time and the impact of the various practices on them – the tension between these three descriptions is rich stuff indeed. Again, I rely on the interest and intelligence of the reader to work out some coherent overall version of the events referenced by all three of these authors, which are wildly different in the consequences, the selection of elements reported and their significance.

I am sympathetic to Gilligan's commentary. I will comment that I would prefer that he had made clear what the term *fixed maps* refers to. At points in his narrative, Gilligan seems to be singling out consciously perceived maps (the first sentence of the extract above) as the referent of *fixed maps*; at others (re-read the last sentence in that same extract), it seems to include any internal maps. In any case, I would add that he is accurate that much of the tasking, the insane testing of the patterning, the extraordinarily strange exercises that we created, had as its subtext the challenging and dissolving (to use Gilligan's term) of these fixed maps.

I add that my experience continues to be that both conscious, explicit maps and unconscious implicit or tacit maps are equally dangerous with respect to serving as obstacles to new experience.

What Gilligan's narrative doesn't mention is that it is difficult in the extreme, under the assumption that you succeed in dissolving such maps at time X to avoid the development of new maps at X plus some lapse of time. Gilligan uses the phrase, *and significant new realities could emerge*. The maps of these new realities themselves become an obstacle to fresh experience and will, in their turn, have to be dissolved if the explorer is to remain alert and accessible to, in turn, each of these new realities.

Gilligan writes:

> To me, the revolutionary spirit of early NLP came from a beautiful combination of these two levels of (1) learning without maps (i.e., unconscious learning) and (2) learning via maps improved by meta-modeling principles. The former provided a deep well of original ideas and possibilities, while the latter offered a means to refine and formalize these possibilities into teachable and replicable models. In my view, subsequent generations of NLP relied too heavily on the latter and ignored the former, leading too often to an industry of "building better mousetraps."

Well said! I would add that, as in my comment above, *the creation of teachable and replicable models* itself constitutes precisely such a danger – the danger that the creator will start to believe in his own creations and thereby accept a set of fixed maps rather than dissolve them in favor of further explanation.

I wish, in particular, to endorse Gilligan's "better mousetrap" comment. This is the same development that he refers to as the activity that had occurred and was continuing to occur at the point that Gilligan chose to leave NLP altogether. There is further evidence of the accuracy of Gilligan's observation. How many NLP trained people have actually ever modeled anyone? How productive has the most radical part of NLP modeling been? How is it that in book after book in the NLP realm there is a constant repetitive presentation of the same patterning or trivial variations on some classic pattern from this era? If modeling is not an example of drinking from the deep well of the *creative unconscious* (Gilligan's term), I don't know what would be. Gilligan's own special form of hypnosis is, in my opinion, a fine example of the blending of his own personal modeling of Erickson and the particular qualities that make Gilligan Gilligan!

Gilligan writes:

> This movement into a dual-mind model opened up infinitely more possibilities ...

I would suggest a different wording here – *dual mind* – not really, from my point of view. A coordination of the two hemispheres, each with their own specialty, working as a team would be my preference. Indeed, Bateson was fond of frustrating the new age types that so frequently found their way to him by insisting that creativity was NEITHER a property of the non-dominant hemisphere nor of unconscious processes, but rather the natural consequence of the irreducible tension between the two. I add that the art of living well consists in some significant measure to learning to coordinate these two great processes (conscious and unconscious; or if you prefer, the dominant and the non-dominant hemispheres) and especially *when* each is to assume the lead on any particular experience.

Gilligan offers an excellent description of the beginning his official deep trance identification with Erickson, with a form close to NLP modeling but using videos and auditory tapes as the input material as opposed to direct access to the genius him or herself.

> ... when I opened my eyes, I found myself deeply absorbed in the eyeglasses that Bateson was nervously fidgeting with in his

hands. They were the most interesting eyeglasses I had ever seen, and the hands holding them were the most fascinating channels of connection to "my old friend Bateson," who was shimmering like a quantum wave in my peripheral field. I began to talk with Bateson (through the glasses, of course), who after a short period jumped up and ran out of the room. Apparently I had disclosed information private to him and Erickson!

These limited materials (the video tapes and audio tapes) gave Gilligan a running start on his actual modeling of Erickson who he was to meet about a month after this reported experience. Note that this form allows the modeler to assimilate the patterns of the model. What it lacks is the third of the essential elements in the structure of a pattern – namely, the answer to the question:

Under what specific circumstances/conditions does the genius elect to use pattern X as opposed to pattern Y?

As the materials available to Gilligan at the time consisted entirely of video (single camera capture) and audio tapes of Erickson working and the imitative behaviors offered by Bandler, Pucelik, and myself, it was missing precisely the information necessary to answer this last question effectively. Since the camera (single perceptual position) was focused either on Erickson (the majority of the time) or on the client, but never simultaneously on both, the relationship between the response by the client (the most significant of the conditions and Erickson's selection of which pattern he would apply next) and what Erickson chose to do next is missing. Gilligan went on to add this dimension of the modeling to his learning a month later when he made contact with Erickson.

Obviously, Gilligan's ability to emulate Erickson had already reached the point where it was developed enough to spook Bateson. I remember watching Bateson closely during this encounter as I was concerned about his reaction. He reacted precisely as Gilligan records it. Concerned by his state and dramatic exit, with a nod to Bandler to monitor Gilligan until I returned (as I had done the induction, I carried the responsibility to ensure a successful and safe exit for Gilligan from his severely altered state), I followed quickly on Bateson's heels and found him standing in the driveway between the house that we had been working in and his own residence (all at 1000 Alba Road), mumbling softly to himself. I waited patiently until he acknowledged my presence whereupon I asked some appropriately vague question about his perceptions of Gilligan. He paused a lengthy lapse of time and then said:

"That was the clearest case of possession I have ever witnessed."

It may well be that Gilligan, as he comments, disclosed some private piece of information. If so, I was not privy to it. By the way, if you are looking for a brilliant example of how solutions emerge from unconscious processes, study well how Gilligan made the shift from the wavering profound altered state that he has achieved to the complete and unremitting focus on the most fascinating pair of glasses (and hands) that ever existed.

Bandler and I were impressed with Gilligan's uptake, especially given the limited selection of materials available to him and thus we decided to arrange a meeting between the master and Gilligan. We took him on our next visit to Phoenix to meet with Erickson. I select and offer two descriptions among a host of memories regarding this encounter.

Gilligan had somewhere purchased a small statue of an owl – he had heard stories from us about the extraordinary clutter of small statues and carvings that filled shelves on two of the three walls of Erickson's working house. When we arrived with Gilligan, as was the custom, Betty Erickson showed us graciously out to the working house. As we awaited Erickson's arrival, I noticed Gilligan fiddling around with this small statue of an owl. I asked him what he intended to do with it and he said that he had brought it along as a gift for Erickson. I suggested that he seat himself in Erickson's chair and determine by observation where he might place the owl amidst the extraordinary clutter on the shelves so that it would be visible from that vantage point. Gilligan selected and subsequently placed the owl in a position such that most (but not all) of it was just visible from Erickson's chair.

Erickson entered the room and assumed his usual position. The meeting did not have an auspicious beginning as Gilligan had decided to demonstrate his competency by a display of Ericksonian patterns as Erickson himself. This was not entirely acceptable to Erickson, who began to tell a series of stories about pathological young men who would knock him (Erickson) off the sidewalk and into the gutter. It did not take many of these metaphors for Gilligan to get the point and he made the appropriate adjustments, again acting as the young 20+ year old man he was at the time. The remainder of the visit was filled with exquisite demonstrations and exchanges rich in their depth and scope.

Some hours later, Erickson was tired and offered non-verbal signals that he was about to retire. Gilligan seized on the opportunity to ask Erickson respectfully whether he had noticed anything different in the room from the last time he was in it. Without missing a beat and without any glance at the figure Gilligan had half hidden between an ironwood sculpture. Erickson looked directly at Gilligan and said:

"I don't give a hoot about such things!"

Game, match, and set!

I also found Gilligan's comments about the turn that NLP took in the late 70s both accurate and one of the most significant (the activities that he cites as the factor for his leaving the circus).

I appreciated, in particular, his sensitivity to this spirit in his comment:

> ... primary attention to their content [fixed-content models] typically results in confusing the maps as the territory, while also favoring the development of technocrats over creative thinkers. Such an outcome is ironic, given that the initial base for NLP was precisely the opposite. The original groups rarely seemed to get caught for long in "fixed content" positions; perhaps we were too busy laughing to get rigid. Something about the movement between multiple maps and multiple positions seemed intrinsic to that early spirit, and it kept the music unfolding like a beautiful jazz improvisation.

Gilligan is here describing an important turning point in the development of the field of NLP. I find myself in complete agreement with his observation. At the time Gilligan indicates, there was a movement away from the raw trial-and-error, exploratory spirit of the beginning days and far too much focus on coding and the coding of already coded patterning of what had already been discovered. Further, while there are significant differences between us about some of the details of these events, I sense a deep agreement about the ultimate reference point – the processes of the unconscious. His response to this left brain corruption was to leave the field and strike out on his own – with fine consequences – while my response was the creation of the New Code of NLP. As he comments:

> ... I favor those that insist upon the presence of the creative unconscious in any modeling or application process. The New Code developed by Grinder and Delozier, and further elaborated by Grinder and Bostic-St. Clair, is a clear example of this ...

The reader is invited to use such a comment to determine whether any particular form of intervention putatively called NLP can, indeed, be considered to be a form of NLP congruent with the origins of the field or, indeed, is simply an attempt by someone to ride on the coat-tails of a previous success by using the same name (NLP) and whose proposed patterning and behavior is wholly incongruent with this spirit of exploration.

Remember, for terms such as *generation* (a fundamentally biological concept) to be taken seriously as an accurate label, it will be important for the reader to judge whether inheritance is present. That is to say, for something to be the next generation, there has to be some key characteristics that are inherited from the claimed source and previous patterning of what it claims to be the next generation of. This applies with equal force to the era of NLP under scrutiny in this book as well as present claims in the field of NLP.

Gilligan has captured one such key characteristic in his narrative. Calling something by a name will not make it so – it requires a deeper and far more congruent action than simply naming it so. And calling it what it is not, no matter how frequently, will not change that!

He characterizes the differences between the early groups and the turn that NLP took in the late 70s as follows:

> The original groups rarely seemed to get caught for long in "fixed content" positions; perhaps we were too busy laughing to get rigid. Something about the movement between multiple maps and multiple positions seemed intrinsic to that early spirit, and it kept the music unfolding like a beautiful jazz improvisation.

This difference between the early groups and what occurred in the late 70s seems to me to still be a valid comment about the quality of what passes for NLP in many parts of the world.

CHAPTER 8

"It's a Fresh Wind that Blows against the Empire"[1]

James Eicher

This is my attempt to convey the color of the times and feeling of origin that accompanies something amazing, that to this day influences millions of people, without the majority of them being aware of it whatsoever.

There are times in your life where you hear something, or feel something, or see something that offers a vantage of significance that twists your mind in an unthinkably novel way. Since I was a small boy these experiences have always been marked by a slight chill, a shiver that momentarily shifts me from the present to some other time and space. In the spring of 1974 there was …

A Voice of Significance

JM said: "You really have to meet to Grinder and Bandler. They are really on to something."

"What is it?"

"They have this Meta Model."

"What's a Meta Model?"

"They offer workshops you can go to."

"I'm going to be gone for the summer."

"Then sign up for one when you're back in the fall."

I shook off the chill and did.

Prologue: Context

Then, the social and physical landscape fueled so much change.

California, early 1970s: Esalen, Encounter Groups, T-Groups, Erhard Seminar Training, Here Comes Everybody, including us. There were many simultaneous social, technological, economic, and political *permutations* (a word I had never heard until 1973, now a part of my day-to-day vocabulary). There is nothing like being involved in a period of great discovery and integration. This was Northern California and the San Francisco Bay area from the early to the late 1970s: the seeds of change were all around us, minds open to new ways of seeing, building, integrating: Apple, Atari, Amdahl, and more. It was just the beginning.

I had started at the University of California at Santa Cruz (UCSC), Kresge College, in the fall of 1973. The UCSC campus was still relatively new, less than 10 years old. The original faculty was amazing: outside-the-box thinkers from all over academia, with concentrations from the best public and private schools, foreign and domestic. Norman O. Brown, author of *Life against Death* and *Love's Body* was there,[2] and, of course, Gregory Bateson.

As you first encountered the sprawling 2,500 acre campus, the hot rolling meadows gave way to cool, towering redwoods in a near-digital switch of terrain, as if you'd walked out of a bright, dry desert into a dark, cool cave. Deep into the woods, a musky smell of another, primordial time permeated, the acoustics that of a medieval cathedral.

Those of us interested in psychology, counseling, self-understanding, and self-disclosure were young by any standard and disproportionately well-read in the area of clinical psychology. This was the focus of many, but not all, of the students at Kresge College in 1973, creating some tension at the college between the "touchy-feely" clan and those interested in "proper" academic pursuits.

For better or worse, our affinity group was familiar with Rollo May, Carl Rodgers, Freud, Melanie Klein, Alexander Lowen, Fritz Perls, R. D. Laing, Jung, Joseph Campbell, Virginia Satir – the *People* magazine stars of the psychointelligensia. In retrospect, this near obsession with Self might have been disturbing to our parents and teachers. Or perhaps it was just a way to cope with them.

We were recently post-Vietnam, not yet wading in Watergate cynicism, a generation still on social adrenaline; so much energy for making changes, so much hope, narcissistically drunk with a sense that our numbers had changed the world. But at that time, we had a notion, false or not, that we needed to change ourselves "inside," so the "outside" stuff we had helped to "correct" for the past 10 years would not be repeated. We needed to rethink ourselves, or it would happen over and over again. We had focused on the system "out there"; now we wanted to focus on the system "in here." It was the "me" decade.

With this context as the blue screen of my 18-year-old self, I enrolled in a workshop with John Grinder and Richard Bandler, to begin the fall of 1974. Had JM issued me with an invitation to some kind of cult? I realized soon after beginning that this was the anti-cult, that JohnandRichard (one word) were *systematic anarchists of the mind*.

Part 1: The Family Ballet or "What, Specifically?"

By the time I had heard of John Grinder and Richard Bandler in the spring of 1974, John, Richard, and Frank Pucelik had been working together for about a year. John's background was in transformational linguistics developed by Noam Chomsky at MIT. He had recently received his PhD in Linguistics from the University of California at San Diego and had published, with Suzette Haden Elgin, the best-selling *Guide to Transformational Grammar*.[3] Prior to that he had been a Green Beret, but that is a story for another time and place. Richard had already earned attention by editing Fritz Perls' *The Gestalt Approach and Eyewitness to Therapy* for Science and Behavior Books in Palo Alto, California.[4] Frank had just transferred into UCSC from a Community College in San Diego. He was studying psychology and had recently spent four years in the military including a year in the jungles of Vietnam. He was a Navy medical person transferred to and serving with the Marine Corps for two of his four years in the service. During his four years of college before he transferred to UCSC, he was actively studying every system of change he could find (sensitivity training, encounter groups, Gestalt, co-counseling, psychodrama, Rogerian, transactional analysis) trying to rebuild a personality mostly decimated by his time in Southeast Asia.

I had met and briefly worked with John in the spring of 1974, before beginning one of JohnandRichard's training seminars in the fall. John conducted a Gestalt seminar with some of the Kresge College students. John and I hit it off in the brief seminar and have been friends ever since.

At the first training seminar of the school year in the fall of 1974, I met Richard Bandler. Richard is one of those people who always seem much older that they are, overly self-confident and self-aware. He talked in a clipped voice that sounded somewhat familiar but I couldn't place it. Richard looked like Dennis Hopper in *Easy Rider*. John was cool with minimal affect. He looked like a dark-haired Peter Frampton in a trench coat, complete with a Sherman in his hand. He was on the cold side of cool, sort of a James Dean with a PhD.

About 25 of us sat on the floor of the cabin-style house in the redwoods on Graham Hill Road. Pardon the pun, but there was magic in the air, even though the first Grinder and Bandler book, *The Structure of Magic, Volume I*, was not yet published.[5] We had no proof that there was a there, there. No evidence that anything meaningful or long lasting was going to happen. Still, the air crackled. Something was happening. I imagined it was like going to a rock concert in the early Fillmore days, listening to an unknown band, say, Jefferson Airplane or The Byrds, and thinking: I think these guys are going to go somewhere.

One by one, Richard went around the room and asked each one of us:

"What are you aware of, *right now* ...?"

It was a simple question, but I felt that there must be something to the simplicity. It made me nervous. I felt that if I answered it I would reveal something deep and dark about myself – in front of this group of mostly strangers – that had never come into my consciousness before. As is it turns out, I was sort of right.

"What are you aware of, *right now* ...?"

As Richard asked the question, John would hand out either a gray, red, or green "card" (actually a torn portion of construction paper), or some combination thereof, to each of us. This added to the sense of someone knowing something about us that we didn't know ourselves. This was exactly the point.

"So what was I aware of right now?" I said out loud to myself: I'm 19, I'm in my second year of college (barely), and the only thing I am really aware of is whether me or anyone else I was interested in was still a virgin. Thinking and awareness from the waist up were necessary evils to pass classes, but please, don't ask me in front of all these other Carl Rogers in training. Please, no self-disclosure.

One by one they handed out different colored cards, or portions of different colored cards, paired people up randomly, rotated the pairings and gave each pair a problem to solve. Here was the problem (it was the same each time):

"You each have to think of something you are aware of in the room right now. Each person has three chances to guess what the other is thinking about. The pair [they called the pairs 'dyads'] that guesses the correct answer raises their hands immediately and shows everyone their cards."

The paired individuals with the same card combinations, for example, all red, half-red and half-gray, gray, green and red thirds, and so on, always solved the problem first, over and over. How they could quickly guess what a stranger was aware of seemed, well, a bit creepy. JohnandRichard challenged us to figure out the pattern, carefully distinguishing between answering "why" and discovering a pattern.

Our explanation needed to be in form of describing a pattern, akin to breaking a secret or code, not a rationale beginning with the phrase:

"I think the reason is …" If we began that way, we would be mocked or made fun of in some humorous way. We were not encouraged to offer a single cause to *any* problem that was put to us. The solution needed to be a series of linked connection points, with clear relationships drawn between multiple causal points and the connectedness of their effects. I didn't know it at the time, but this was part of our training in cybernetic thinking as an approach to problem solving, and the influence of Gregory Bateson and Ross Ashby on the work of JohnandRichard.

When it came to my turn to answer, I said something like the following: "I am aware that you are asking me 'What am I aware of?' in this strange staccato tone of voice. It sounds really weird. I am thinking I am saying something about myself that reveals something I myself am not aware of."

They gave me a green card with no other colors. I recall that I was the only one that got a 100% green piece of card stock. Everyone else had gotten red, gray, or some combination thereof, some with a portion of green. But I was the only one who got completely green card stock. I didn't know whether to be happy or terrified.

I noticed a mutual glance between them as John handed me the green card, a nod and a wink between the unit that was JohnandRichard. They were always synchronized in thought, word, and movement, often finishing each other's sentences, even their jokes, never having to look at one another for a visual cue. Like a well-rehearsed comedy team or band. They were so in sync, so mutually orchestrated without direction that it was unsettling. It was part of their personal power. Finishing each other's sentences, placing people and objects in purposeful positions without discussion, predicting behavioral results, an uncanny seduction.

About one hour into the workshop we took a break and JohnandRichard took me aside into a small anti-room in the house. The meaning of the cards wasn't yet revealed. They sat on the left and right side of me, mouth towards my ear, each taking turns talking, a pattern that was to become familiar to all of us at a later date. They said to me:

John: "You're just like us …"

Richard: "… do exactly what we do."

"What…?" I asked.

"Just copy us," they said in unison.

They got up and returned to the large room and the workshop continued.

A few seminars later, it was revealed that the "problem" we were trying to solve was uncovering the favored sensory or *representational systems* each person used to make "sense" out of the world. The premise was that cognitive style was not "random." Individuals do have consistent preferences *and* the words you use are also not random: they can reveal much about your cognitive style. Your cognitive style is your map, but not your territory. We were also learning what later became known as "meta-cognition" or thinking about thinking.

The verbal clue to preferences that JohnandRichard discovered are the predicates; that is, the verbs, adjectives, and adverbs that individuals use in speech and writing. This is a core concept of what became neuro-linguistic programming (NLP). In the early days we referred to them as "rep systems," that each of us had behavioral and cognitive learning "styles" or preferences. It was shortly to become the VAK (visual, audi-tory, and kinesthetic) model.

The explanatory power was immediate and had what is called in psy-chology "face validity." My personal and simultaneous gift/curse of being extremely auditory (the meaning of the green card stock; the red, visual; the gray, kinesthetic) became apparent: I could pick up a lan-guage by hearing it, but I had difficulty with written text. I could play music by ear, but not read and retain musical notation. Anything that involved words, I was a star; math, a struggle. The payoff of learning this early was that I could learn to become what I was not, overcome my limitations, a key premise of what was to become NLP.

It continued week after week, a different question to learn, a different and, after a while, predictable set of responses that followed, each one a portion of the Meta Model.

"I want you to remember a time when ..."

"I can't."

"What stops you?"

"What?"

"What stops you?"

"Well, I think what stops me is this feeling of being stuck."

"Stuck, how, specifically?"

"Stuck that I can't do it."

"What stops you?"

"Well, I think I would fail."

"What would happen if you did fail?"

"Well, this just is how I talk."

"What would happen if you changed the way you talked?"

"I don't know."

"How do you know you don't know?"

"What? Say again."

"How do you know you don't know?"

"I don't know."

"Guess!" yelled Richard.

"That's a new one ..." I said to myself.

"I think it's not part of my beliefs."

"Beliefs about what, specifically?" continued Richard.

"This is an intrusion ..." I thought to myself.

"Who was intruding about what, specifically?" I heard myself saying to myself. Shit, the Meta Model was becoming second nature in spite of any hesitation I had. That was the "desired outcome" I found out later.

The language was abrupt, even in a clinical setting. Each question or Meta Model "violation" peeling the language onion of my day-to-day discourse, uncovering the layers of meaning that lay beneath the vernacular of everyday discourse. Everyday conversation was good for buying things at the grocery store, but not in the context of learning and therapeutic change where individuals tended to cover up or block, consciously or unconsciously, emotionally charged experiences.

The Structure of Magic, Volume I, which focused on the Meta Model and verbal skills, was not available, but the manuscripts were being printed. We would get a copy of the Sacred Text in a couple of weeks. The straightforward philosophical premise of both the *Magic* and "Milty" (*The Patterns of the Hypnotic Techniques of Milton H. Erickson*)[6] series of books was taken from Alfred Korzybski's *Science and Sanity*, especially his key phrasing "the map is not the territory."[7] If natural language is a model of experience (i.e., a map or description of experience and not the experience or territory itself), then the language patterns in *The Structure of Magic, Volume I*, describing efficient, direct therapeutic obstruction and intervention, were a *model* of natural language, or a "Meta Model."

Not being an automatic true believer and being skeptical at the time of what was essentially "best practices" process modeling (the term "best practice" had not been coined yet), I went and read/watched videos, listened to audiotapes of Perls, Satir, and other therapists they had mentioned such as Frank Farrelly. Sure enough, the Meta Model questions were in the texts and on the tapes.

I realized that Perls, Satir, and others used these questions and techniques, but far less systematically. The distillation of the questions linked to the linguistic categories of transformational syntax integrated theory and practice, ideas and pragmatics. The integration had the effect of uncovering the identified problem of an individual much, much faster.

As the weeks continued, different patterns of family therapy were added, each session building on the prior one. After the introduction and emphasis on learning the linguistic Meta Model patterns – deletion, semantic ill-formedness, nominalizations – and what we now knew as representational systems, we were introduced to family system tools and techniques, chiefly the non-verbal patterns found in Virginia Satir's *Peoplemaking*.[8]

We would go through a series of demonstrations, role practice, and critique. John and Richard would "sculpt" us in one of the four Satir postures (Blaming, Placating, Super Reasonable, and Irrelevant) and provide us with a scenario to act out; kind of family counseling improv.

"OK, one of you get in this posture, one of you get in this posture, one of you in this posture and one of you cycles through all four postures."

They would begin:

"Here's the situation: you are to plan a family picnic. Mary, you're the mom. You're a blaming witch. Everything anyone does in this family is wrong and not up to your standards. You use a lot of universal quantifiers when you talk. 'You never ... you always ...' Stuff like that.

"Tom, you're the dad, and you're a completely clueless flake who punts on every decision. You're an irrelevant fifth wheel. You alternately blame, placate, and are super reasonably analytical when there is conflict, and then you just exit the room. You use all the Meta Model violations in your speech.

"Leslie, you're the daughter and the youngest, about 10. You concede to anyone who looks at you cross-eyed. You hate conflict and would placate the devil. You are always having your feelings crushed.

"And Patrick, you're the son and older, about 12 or 13. You spend your days and nights analyzing the most trivial things, think you are smarter than everyone your age, and like to use big, super reasonable nominalizations like 'boredom' and 'rejection' and explain the 'reasons why' people do things."

It would start out with each of us in an assigned posture and roles and a simple instruction: "You have to decide where to go on a family picnic ... stay in your roles as long as you can."

The four would begin:

Mary to Tom: "You can't do anything right, even planning a picnic."

Leslie to Mary: "Stop blaming dad."

Patrick to all: "This is just ridiculous. Let's be calm and think together."

Tom to all: "Well, I'm upset. I don't know what to do. Poor me, but Tom's right, let's think about this. What are we trying to do? Oh, I give up. Let's stay home."

We would watch and listen. JohnorRichard or both would pause the scenario or family "ballet" and ask each person what they were aware of and how they felt. Then ask questions like: "Was it difficult to stay in the role or easy?" In the large group we would debrief, discuss what we observed, and so on.

And so it continued over the months. During this time about five or six of us got into an old van each week, driving to and from Graham Hill Road, excitedly trying to figure out the patterns, how they fit together, how we could use them, and what effect they had on our lives.

Part 2: Bateson Sighting

Like the words you hear and never forget, there are people you see for the first time and never forget, like some lost member of your extended intellectual and spiritual family that you have been on a quest for: Neo, Obi-Wan Kenobi, Chuck Norris …

MC was my resident assistant for our building at Kresge College. We called them "Proctors" at the time. I can't remember why. It led to a lot of medically related jokes. MC and I were out on the balcony in the spring of 1974, looking into the main college quad.

"Who is that tall guy walking in the middle of quad?" I asked.

Fast forward to today: the figure looked like Gandalf in *The Lord of Rings*, but with shorter hair.

"That's Gregory Bateson," said MC.

"Who?" I asked.

"Gregory Bateson. Ever hear of the double-bind theory of schizophrenia?"

"No. Yes! That's talked about in R. D. Laing's Self and Others. *Do they know each other?"*

"They're friends," stated MC. "Have you heard of Margaret Mead?" she asked.

"Of course." Now her I had heard of.

"That's her ex-husband."

"No shit?" I asked.

"No shit," she said.

"So what does this have to do with me?"

MC looked at me squarely in the eyes: "With your interests in psychology and behavioral science, you need to know as much about him and about everything he knows as possible."

"Why?"

"It will be obvious."

Another chill to shake off; we never spoke about it again.

Much has been written over the years about Gregory Bateson, about him, his ideas, and his continuing influence in ecology, evolution, anthropology, cybernetics, and the behavioral sciences. In this section I want to call out my observations on some of Bateson's influences on both JohnandRichard and me.

Bateson served not only as a powerful intellectual influence on John and Richard; he was, in my opinion, at least as powerful a professional influence. I believe the intellectual and conceptual influences are clear: thinking of behavior as a system of interactions, using cybernetic modeling to characterize families and organizations; the anthropological approach to observation and understanding, as opposed to psychology's more traditional experimental/laboratory paradigm. Even phrases and tools, such a logical typing, "the difference that makes a difference," and most notably, turning the concept/term of framing and reframing – a term Bateson had coined – into a lasting NLP tool.

Bateson, through endorsements to his peers, gave JohnandRichard a whole new level of credibility they did not have in the clinical community. Yes, they were becoming wildly successful and in demand, but there was soon an exponential jump. The next influence was the personal introduction to Dr. Milton H. Erickson, which gave JohnandRichard the next platform of material and basis for combining tools into early NLP. Finally, Bateson sponsored a workshop in the early days, inviting many of his peers and friends. In this workshop Bateson introduced and showcased them. They were "on" that night and blew the skeptics away. Other opportunities manifested as a result. It was the beginning of the beginning.

I started out, after my epiphany on the balcony of Kresge College, to read *Steps to an Ecology of Mind*[9] – many, many, many times. I then started to audit Gregory's *Steps to an Ecology of Mind* class, befriended his executive assistant, JVS, and hung out around his campus office as much as possible, unashamedly "sponging" as much as I could.

In the spring quarter of 1976, I formally took Gregory's *Steps to an Ecology of Mind* class. After taking *Steps* I asked Gregory to sponsor me for a grant on communication and interaction through the university. Although I was not awarded the grant, the opportunity to work with Gregory and receive his guidance and mentoring continued.

That summer I organized, with other interested students, an informal seminar group to meet at Gregory's house in Ben Lomond. About every other week a number of us would meet at his and Lois Bateson's house and discuss anthropology, evolution, the double bind, and anything else that seemed appropriate to the discussion. One day at a seminar I recall both R. D. Laing and Margaret Mead calling on the phone and speaking with Gregory.

The following academic year Gregory asked me to be his teaching assistant for his *Steps* class. It was arguably the high point of my academic career. Not only did it afford me more mentoring and insight, we also had – as best as someone my age could have with someone of that experience and stature – formed an informal relationship. I felt comfortable asking him all kinds of questions: So what was it really like doing the groundbreaking work in Palo Alto? What were Jay (Haley), John (Weakland), and Don (Jackson) really like? What role did they have? What's Ronnie (Laing) like? What do you think of his ideas, his use of existentialism in theories of behavior and psychopathology? What about Margaret (Mead), her ideas? I'd ask and he would tell me.

Gregory had to travel for one of *Steps* classes when I was his teaching assistant and would miss it. He asked me to lecture in his stead. I was greatly flattered, but thought no one would come to class since "the master" was not going to be there. Gregory said I could select the topic, but he wanted to go over it with me before I delivered it. We met for lunch at a restaurant on Mission Boulevard in Santa Cruz and talked for a while. I said I wanted to talk about the relationship between cybernetics and morality during the class. To my surprise, he thought it was an excellent topic to discuss and felt I was "getting" what he was trying to convey to others. Most of his students came to class the day I lectured.

The last time I saw Gregory I was on my way to Esalen in Big Sur in 1978. I was asked to speak at one of their informal (i.e., not yet in the catalogue) sessions on NLP. Gregory, who was in residence at Esalen at the time, was there and I was looking forward to seeing him. However, he was headed out to give a lecture that day and I saw him driving out of the entrance to Esalen as I was driving in. We waved to each other as we passed by.

Part 3: Something about Tomato Plants, But It's All a Bit Fuzzy

Back to 1975: JohnandRichard had been "away." I didn't know where away was, but I noticed a marked shift in behavior. Gone were the staccato clips of Fritz Perls' Gestalt delivery, the body sculpting shifts into Satir postures. Questions of Meta Model violations were replaced by delivery of the violations, but in a storytelling format, somewhat mumbled, with JohnandRichard occasionally holding one hand against the left side of his face … or was it the right side … nobody really *knows* … or was it *nose* … but you can start from *scratch* … That's right! We were going to the State of Arizona, without leaving the room.

In the 1930s and 1940s, Gregory Bateson and Margaret Mead had studied trance phenomena in the culture of certain tribes in Bali, Indonesia. They published a classic anthropology book on the subject, *Balinese Character*.[10] A key individual who served as a consultant to them on trance phenomena was the medical doctor and hypnotherapist Dr. Milton H. Erickson.

Early in the development of the Meta Model, Bateson introduced JohnandRichard to Dr. Erickson. Dr. Erickson was shown a pre-publication copy of *The Structure of Magic, Volume I* and, along with Virginia Satir and Gregory Bateson, endorsed the series. Gregory, who contributed so much to JohnandRichard, had now given them the next set of behaviors they explicitly modeled and patterned.

Dr. Erickson (or "Milty" as he became known to us) was highly respected in his field. Whereas hypnosis was largely associated was charlatanism, parlor tricks, and snake oil, Dr. Erickson was highly respected by the medical profession. Professionals who in general did not "believe" in hypnosis would admit that Dr. Erickson "knew how to do something profound that the rest of us do not know how to do or really under-stand how it works." This was the sentiment under which we, the student groups, studied the work of Dr. Erickson.

Again, a group of about 25 of us sat on the floor of the same cabin-style house in the redwoods on Graham Hill Road. Richard looked at me and said:

"Tomato plants, can, Jim, *learn new things ...*"

I stared, looking at them.

"Yes, I guess they can ..." I said.

They laughed their synchronous laugh.

"Everything we've taught you up to now is wrong ..." said John.

"It's a lie ..." said Richard.

"Is this the part where I ask for my money back?" I asked myself.

One after another they continued:

"... And as you're sitting there ..."

"... in complete (or was it *incomplete*?) bewilderment ..."

"... you can begin to enjoy the difference between now and then ..."

"... then and now ..."

"... knowing ..." they said in unsettling unison ...

"... that you can ..."

"... and *will* ..."

"... learn new things ..." and they drifted off to silence.

Not a word was spoken, nothing stirred. I don't recall how the silence was broken.

"Tomato plants?" I said to myself sometime later. I wasn't sure when. Or where.

As with learning the Meta Model, we were given different linguistic patterns to try on each other, observe the reaction, and report to JohnandRichard and the larger group. The language patterns were those Dr. Erickson used to induce various trance states in his clients. JohnandRichard were beginning to cluster the inductions into linguistic patterns, again using portions of transformational syntax to label and describe. Now, instead of distilling and modeling the verbal and non-verbal behavior of Fritz Perls and Virginia Satir into teachable formats, they were distilling and labeling Dr. Erickson's verbal and non-verbal behavior in a similar way. Thus the series *Patterns of the Hypnotic Techniques of Milton H. Erickson* was born.

Again, it continued week after week, but not a different question to ask – gone was the intrusive probing of the Meta Model. We had a different *declarative* phrase to learn. We were instructed to use representational system language to describe to the other person what we saw, heard, and felt, peppering phrases that, consciously or unconsciously, I can't really recall, JohnandRichard had been using.

Pairing up, we each began:

"… And now you are beginning to feel …"

"Feel, what, specifically?" I reflexively asked myself.

"… those feelings you experience when you see …"

"… and hear …"

"… unprecedented opportunity …"

"… knocking at the door of …"

"Did someone just knock on the door of the Graham Hill Road house?" I asked myself.

"… what it is you need to change and grow …"

After a simple "induction" we were to observe the reaction of the other person. Indeed, some did "drift off" into a kind of state I had previously associated with guided meditation, but much, much faster, and it seemed for some, deeper; that is, less aware of his or her surroundings. We really didn't ask "why" anything at this point, it was not part of the ritual. Just do, learn, and pattern.

With the exception of recognizing the use of representational system predicates, this sounded like a mishmash of deletions, unspecified verbs and nouns, and nominalizations. This is what I found out I was supposed to be hearing – and *systematically* using – to verbally induce an altered state of awareness. After first just "modeling" Dr. Erickson – that is, literally imitating his words, intonation, facial gestures, speech cadence and volume – then JohnandRichard started "chunking" or categorizing Dr. Erickson's trance language into transformational syntax-labeled clusters.

The blinding flash of the obvious, so to speak, was that Dr. Erickson was using language systematically in the opposite way that JohnandRichard had formulated the Perls and Satir patterns for the Meta Model. Perls would ask for specificity and to be "in the now" or the moment, not in the past or the future. Erickson was giving his clients verbally non-specific direction to allow the client themselves to complete their thinking and internal problem solving in a trance state.

Dr. Erickson would guide the process of a client's thinking, but not necessarily the content. If there was a specific clinical issue he wanted to address, he would use metaphor rather than direct comment. How did this translate into what became known as the "Milty Model"? Let's do a comparison (see table overleaf).

The modeling of Dr. Erickson's hypnotic language – using transformational syntax categories – clarified and expedited learning Dr. Erickson's techniques, much as it had learning Perls' and Satir's.

There were a few shifts going on at this time in the development of "pre-NLP." The first was the rapid inclusion of behavioral patterns that were not a part of anyone one else's pre-existing work, but instead patterns John and Richard noticed and integrated.

Convinced there had to be some consistent non-verbal indicator of representational systems, John and Richard were watching, and discovered, that the lateral and vertical eye movements people used when asked a question in conversation were not "random," but analogous to representational system predicates. Eye movements to retrieve memories, problem solve, and so on generally occur at constituent structure breaks in language, usually accompanied by a vocalized pause such as "hmm, let's see" or "umm." JohnandRichard ascertained that the eye movements indicated internal "accessing" of visual, auditory, and kinesthetic information.

Comparison of the Meta Model and Milty Model

Statement	Meta Model	Milty Model	Comments
It's bothering me …	What, specifically, is bothering you?	I'm noticing something may be bothering you …	In the Meta Model, you ask the client to specify the unspecified noun, "it"
			In the Milty Model, you declaratively comment on the client's general state, allowing them to imagine the source of the state. You intentionally offer up an unspecified verb and noun ("bothering" and "something")
It …	What's "it"?	And that you can picture …	Again you ask the client to specify the noun "it"
			You suggest creating an unspecified representational system opportunity – visual – as a way to connect his or her feelings and the source of his or her discomfort
This feeling …	What feeling?	That feeling that you feel when your unconscious mind realizes there's no need to blame …	The client has offered the therapist a verb, but an *unspecified* verb; you ask the client to specify, etc.
			You close or "loop" the connection back to the original feeling, with a suggestion to problem solve the issue by stating the verb "blame" without a specified object

The second shift was the expanded inclusion of language, metaphors, and research from other branches of psychology. Research as to the different neurological and cognitive functioning of the cerebral hemispheres had been going on for decades but had exploded due to the availability of new equipment that facilitated the testing of healthy subjects.

It seemed to John and Richard that the so called "dominant" (left cerebral hemisphere in most people) was the seat of syntax and by extension the "conscious" Meta Model mind, and the so-called "nondominant" (right cerebral hemisphere in most people) was the seat of metaphor and meaning, or the "unconscious" Milty Model mind.

At this time John and Richard included the concepts of cognitive psychologist George Miller, author of the article "The Magical Number Seven, Plus or Minus Two."[11] John had known Dr. Miller prior to teaching at UCSC. Specifically, the term "chunking" became integrated into the early NLP lexicon, as well as the basic feedback model of TOTE found in his book with Eugene Galanter and Karl Pribram, *Plans and the Structure of Behavior*.[12] And so, with the introduction of accessing cues, the use of the conscious and unconscious mind analogy, chunking, and TOTE, the bridge to NLP was created.

Finally, there was a palpable "philosophical" shift away from the very directive Gestalt/Meta Model approach to client problem solving to a more indirect approach that involved either inducing trance states or directing clients to problem solve "reflectively" without divulging the exact content or nature of the problem. As time marched on this approach is evident in all aspects of NLP to this day. The two volumes of *The Structure of Magic*, the *Patterns* books, and the single volume *Changing with Families* round out the pre-NLP period and the shift to the future.[13]

Part 4: Through the Corpus Callosum – From the Meta Model to the Milty Model: The Birth of NLP

Often the delivery processes and mechanisms are unknown to the individuals that deliver them. As the Meta Model and Milty Model began to become popular, people were not asking how to become better at Perls than Perls, or better at Erickson than Erickson, or better at Satir than Satir. Instead they began to ask: How can I become more like JohnandRichard? How can I successfully model the modelers and their "magic"?

Not lost on JohnandRichard, they, and in turn, we, began to describe what we were doing to model the excellence of others. But it needed a name. One spring day in the quad of Kresge College, John and I ran into each other on the way to a class.

John: "I have to tell you something."

Me: *"Go for it!"*

John: "Richard and I figured out what we're going to call this stuff we're doing ... neuro-linguistic programming or NLP. What do you think?"

In the summer of 1976, the seminars moved from the Graham Hill Road house to a house near the Santa Cruz campus on Continental Street that my college girlfriend, JB, and my best friend, MS, shared. (MS was later to manage and produce many of Richard Bandler's seminars after Richard went out on his own.) There were more leaders in the mix in addition to John, Richard, and Frank. Judith DeLozier was involved and helping to co-author the second volume of the *Patterns* series. So were Leslie Cameron, Bob Dilts, and Steve Gilligan. Bob was beginning to pattern the patterns and help describe NLP. Steve, passionate and gifted in hypnosis, continued to explore Erickson. Leslie focused on family and couples patterns and Virginia's work.

John and Richard had introduced the practice of anchoring, another of their rapid applications of a concept – in this case, classical conditioning – into the mix of NLP tools and techniques, combined with representational systems, accessing cues, and now reframing.

Framing and reframing was a term Bateson had coined in his 1955 article "A Theory of Play and Fantasy."[14] It was made famous through University of California at Berkeley sociologist Erving Goffman's *Frame*

Analysis.[15] It was also discussed by Paul Watzlawick, Janet Beavin-Bavelas, and Don Jackson in *Pragmatics of Human Communication*,[16] a book that described much of Bateson's Palo Alto years.

John and Richard took the concept of reframing and "operationalized" it like they had done with many concepts. They created steps, integrating, threading, and layering it in with the Milty Model, accessing cues, and now new terms to describe what they were doing that became an umbrella for much of NLP and lives on today in pop culture: developing rapport and trust as the foundation for effective human interaction and change.

In order to develop rapport and trust you needed to *pace* or match the communication style – defined as the sensory preferences of an individual. Next, you practiced *leading* or communicating – consciously or unconsciously – the desired outcomes needed for the person to change. The quickest way to do this was to intentionally and consciously *mirror* the verbal and non-verbal behavior of another.

The rapid combining and "packaging" of behavioral technology continued. Accessing sensory experience, developing rapport and trust, mirroring, pacing, leading, anchoring, reframing, future pacing, personal ecology, and so on became the vocabulary of the new field of what was JohnandRichard and friends.

As students, we were learning modeling; that is, we directly imitated the mannerisms, tone, accent, and movement of the people we were studying. It was method acting for the clinically inclined, similar to indigenous tribes who mimic the patterns of behavior of the prey they are going to hunt in order to learn about how they behave, so as to anticipate their moves and be a more effective hunter. The prey, in this case, was the human subject in question: the client. Tactically it was a way of standing in the other person's shoes, to learn their perspective, to get out of our heads, and understand the point of view/model of the world that was his or hers.

Throughout this time JohnandRichard, sometimes in opposition to their public disdain of conventional psychological research, wanted to know if someone else had done something similar. For whatever reason, they would ask me to check into it. Accessing cues – any other research? Double inductions – anything about attention and simultaneous speech and the effects on memory or cognitive processing? Linguistics – anything about sensory preferences in language?

As I looked into these areas, there were others with similar pursuits, not as a clinical application, but to test a hypothesis. Part of the results of my exploring these requests is included in a paper I published in the spring of 1977 in the journal *Papers in Linguistics*, titled "Linguistics and the Problem of Serial Order."[17] The article was part of my senior thesis in linguistics for the University of California.

NLP, as what JohnandRichard were doing was now known, circa 1977, was so feverishly popular at the time that some of the early students, myself included, were asked to conduct seminars and offer lectures. The clinical and education population was hungry for anything NLP. I knew something was up as early as the fall of 1976 when I was John's teaching assistant for his Introduction to Transformational Syntax course at UCSC. I ended up teaching a large portion of the course as JohnandRichard were away much of the time. They were becoming the "it" team of the clinical world.

After graduation in 1977, Bob Dilts and I teamed up for a time to teach NLP. Then I started teaching workshops through UCSC Extension in 1978. As NLP Comprehensive was beginning, Steve Andreas (formerly John Stevens) and Connirae Andreas were putting together what would become the NLP classic *Frogs into Princes*.[18]

While traveling cross country in the summer of 1978 with my post-college girlfriend, BD, we stayed with Steve and Connirae in Boulder, Colorado. On the floor of the room we were staying in was the raw audio transcription of what was to become *Frogs*. Steve asked me to help with some editing and to return in the fall to conduct some NLP seminars. *Frogs* came out in 1979, as did Daniel Goleman's *Psychology Today* article "People who Read People,"[19] which brought NLP to national and international attention.

From small seminars in the redwoods to national media, here we were.

From Families to Organizations: My Personal and Professional Journey

For the first 18 months after graduating from UCSC in the spring of 1977 I conducted NLP seminars around the Western United States. During this time I considered my interests and options regarding NLP and its applications. In parallel with the development of the Meta and Milty Models and NLP, Kresge College was host to other applications of psychology and communication. At the time, many professors and consultants visited Kresge who came from the background of group and team development, and what later became known as the field of organization development. Among them was Philip Slater, author of *The Pursuit of Loneliness* and *Earthwalk* (also a Bateson inspired book).[20]

In the fall of 1979 I returned to Los Angeles where my family lived and started working for a large corporation in their training and development department. My intention at this point was to apply the early days and nascent NLP to corporate training and organization development. After four years of corporate experience I completed the first draft of *Making the Message Clear* (which I believe was the first book on the application of NLP to business). I gave it to John and Judith DeLozier to consider publishing. After adding a couple of chapters and revising a few sections, I sent it out for potential endorsement. This was about 1986 and NLP was extremely popular at the time and had transcended the clinical world, entering the worlds of business and self-help psychology.

Through the "six degrees of separation" of others, I sent the book to Paul Hersey, who with Ken Blanchard had developed situational leadership, arguably the most widely used management training methodology worldwide. I also sent the book to Robert Lorber, at the time co-author, with Ken Blanchard, of the best-selling *Putting the One Minute Manager to Work*.[21] To my very pleasant and shocked surprise, both agreed to endorse *Message*. John and I finished up the editing, he wrote the Preface and *Message* was published in 1987.[22]

At the same time in the early 1970s as John and Richard were developing NLP in the San Francisco Bay area, down in southern California, in San Diego, John Jones and Bill Pfeiffer had established University Associates. They were assembling what became standard approaches to improving leadership, team, and organization performance in the business world. Like John and Richard, they wanted to take theory and turn it into practice, but for public and private organizations. They created the "structured experience" of taking business and organization theory and turning it into repeatable, scalable, and easy-to-use tools. It was a wild success.

Shortly after publishing *Message*, I was looking to create business tools and contacted the co-founder of Organization Design and Development (now known as HRDQ), Rollin Glaser, to see if he would be interested in reading *Message*. To my happy surprise he had already read it, liked it, and wondered if I would be interested in teaming up with the same John Jones to write and publish a series of NLP-related assessments. John Jones had recently teamed up with Bill Bearley and created a series of best-selling assessments for business in the 1980s, and now I was going to work with them.

After I picked myself up off the floor, I enthusiastically thanked Rollin and contacted John. We created and published with Bill the *Neurolinguistic Communication Profile* and *Rapport: Matching and Mirroring Communication*.[23] I had been now "thrice" blessed: not only did I have JohnandRichard as mentors and friends in my teenage and 20-something years, I had been Gregory's teaching assistant and recipient of his guidance and wisdom. Now, in the world of organization development, John Jones offered me direction and coaching.

Over the years I have continued to apply NLP to business in the form of papers and recently the ebooks, *Rapport-Based Selling* and *No Need for Conflict!*[24] I continue to use the tools to facilitate teams and improve organization performance. In retrospect, I see that the systems and family basis of pre-NLP was indeed the foundation of my understanding of how business groups fail, function, and change and is the source of my career to this day.

As I reflect on what I learned at the "meta" level, as JohnandRichard would say – beyond the obvious tools and techniques, which, at the end of the day, are just that, tools and techniques – for me, the ethics were good.

So, what every parent would want their college kids to know:

- Look for patterns, they are always there.

- Challenge all my assumptions.

- Change, Jim, can be good.

- Use *all* my senses, even the ones I am not aware of.

- Understand the world from another's perspective, not mine.

- Listen more, talk less; if I do talk, ask questions.

- Everyone is doing the best job they can given the limitations of their beliefs.

- My job is to get people to use the best of themselves to get better, to improve.

- Everyone has a chance; if something didn't work, it's because of my limitations, not the other person's.

- I am ultimately accountable for and own the outcomes of my choices. All of them.

CHAPTER 9

Commentary on "It's a Fresh Wind that Blows against the Empire"

John Grinder

I thoroughly enjoyed Eicher's ability to set the context for his later remarks (in his Prologue) – he reveals himself with honesty, dry wit, and outrageous humor and sets a fine (and to me, quite accurate) cultural context – both quite reminiscent of Gilligan's opening remarks. A reader seeking a richer feel for the era would be well advised to consider these two quite distinct but parallel descriptions of the context in which the creation of NLP occurred.

Eicher offers a detailed (and remarkably accurate) description of the substance and style with which Bandler and I conducted seminars. I invite trainers purporting to train NLP patterning to decode this description with an eye to the design of training – in particular, the inductive approach to learning. Interestingly, I have an already published an account of precisely this event (in Bostic-St. Clair and Grinder's *Whispering in the Wind*)[1] – I urge the interested reader to place these two descriptions side by side to appreciate the multiple perceptual positions occupied by the designers of the event (myself and Bandler) and how it was experienced by someone on the other side of the loop. There are differences and I find them instructive as pointers to deeper aspects of what occurred back then. Eicher is correct to recognize (albeit at a time well past the actual events involved) the influences of both Gregory Bateson and W. Ross Ashby in the approach that Bandler and I used during those training seminars. The dialogues that Eicher reconstitutes have to my ear both the ring of authenticity and an air of the absurd – one that permeated nearly all our activities in those days.

Eicher writes:

> Convinced there had to be some consistent non-verbal indi-
> cator of representational systems, John and Richard were
> watching, and discovered, that the lateral and vertical eye
> movements people used when asked a question in conversa-
> tion were not "random," and analogous to representational
> system predicates.

Convinced there had to be some consistent non-verbal indicator ... I am flattered by Eicher's statement that Bandler and I had successfully created
the illusion in the perceptions of Eicher (and, presumably, some of the
other people involved in these explorations) that we knew what the
hell we were doing. I certainly didn't!

What, from my point of view, actually happened is described in
Whispering in the Wind. In particular, with respect to the calibration
points (visually, the eye movements and, auditorily, the predicates and
voice quality shifts) was not nearly as well organized and systematic
as Eicher proposes. The actual discovery sequence which occurred in
1973/74 was initially that of the predicates. Remember, the first model
we had created was a linguistically based model, the Meta Model, and
Bandler and I remained alert to cues issuing from that class of behavior, followed by the eye movements.

The narrative of these two discoveries, offered in *Whispering in the
Wind*, describes an entirely fortuitous incident that allowed Bandler
and myself to work out how the predicates unconsciously selected and
used by a person reveal the representational system activated at the
time of the formulation of the intention to speak and the actual speech
act itself. The reader is invited to compare my description of the events
in the group that occurred during that discovery process with the portrayal of the same event offered by Eicher in his article.

It is interesting to note the exchange that occurred between Bandler
and myself about a week after we had worked out the significance of
the predicates. What had happened was that in this intervening period
of time, during which we were separated, the coding of the predicates
that we had already accomplished had created a calibration reference

point. We knew that the presence of a specified representational system predicate signaled the activation of a particular representational system and the corresponding portion of the cortex. This calibration reference point was, therefore, a stable marker in face-to-face exchanges. Once we had that reference point, noticing that the person's eye movements were systematic was relatively trivial – hence, the highly coded exchange between Bandler and myself upon meeting one another after this period of separation.[2]

Richard: "Hey, what's happening?"
John: "Hey, you know as well as I do!"
Richard: "So, you've seen it?"
John: "How could anyone miss it!"

While this exchange is fabricated, it is typical of the close rapport that existed between the two of us during this era. What may not be as clear is that the last response by me (with the usual arrogance that seems characteristic of our attitude in those days), is incomplete. It would better have been:

How could anyone who had already worked out predicates as a stable reference point in calibrating face-to-face encounters miss it (the systematic movements of the eyes associated with those reference points).

I have three comments here:

1. Eicher is accurate in characterizing this discovery of predicates and eye movements as an original contribution by Bandler and myself to the patterning of NLP. Up to that point in the creation of NLP, our work had nearly exclusively pivoted around the modeling (unconscious assimilation) of patterning from models already exhibiting those patterns; perhaps not as systematically as we made them but the patterns were there and often marked a major shift in the experience of the clients involved. Our task was to unconsciously assimilate those patterns, test them rigorously in contexts parallel to the ones we had observed the models using them in, and then generalize the patterns to additional contexts. In this case, we discovered something loose and running free in the

world, in people's everyday experiences – not a limited data set by observing a model of excellence. When generalized back into the context of change work, these markers of unconscious selection and utilization of representational systems proved to be excellent leverage points in creating contexts in which the clients we worked with could develop the choices that they were seeking.

2. To this day, I have the impression that representational systems are a significantly underused and underexplored pattern in the set of NLP patterns. I suspect that this was an accidental consequence of the development of anchoring, shortly after we had found representational systems and their calibration points. We did experiment during this short period, after representational systems had been coded and prior to anchoring emerging as a full-on set of formats for application in the context of change. I mention one such case.

We were working at 1000 Alba Road at the time when a man in his late thirties showed up as a client seeking help. The case involved a peculiar situation where the man had become almost confined to his house. The client stated that he was afraid to leave home as he had to urinate frequently and he did not want to put himself in a situation where he had to urinate but had no access to a toilet.

My memory is that this was one of the clients with whom we used students as filters to test patterns (in this case, rapport, Meta Model, and representational systems) – in particular, I remember David Gordon working in this capacity. David was given the task of establishing rapport with the man, ferreting out the issue – what was to be changed – via the Meta Model and noting representational systems preferences and sequences, and then reporting to me.

David did a fine job and when he reported back with me to determine what intervention to make, he mentioned that the man's eye movements were systematically at variance with his predicates. More specifically, his eyes went to the down right position whenever (or nearly whenever) he used visual predicates and, inversely, when he used kinesthetic predicates, his eyes went above the horizon, in what is the typical movements for visualization. I was intrigued and had David demonstrate what he had detected. A series of provocations and my own calibrations easily confirmed that David was correct; there was a systematic reversal of the typical relationship between predicates and eye movements for the visual and kinesthetic systems. While I had seen lots of variations on the standard eye movements, I had never seen a crossed system such as the one that this client was exhibiting.

As was typical when I uncovered an unusual case – and this one certainly qualified – I proceeded conservatively. I was certain that some form of anchoring and/or Ericksonian patterning would succeed in assisting this client in getting what he had come for. Therefore, the game was, what is the minimum intervention that would succeed with such an unusual case, always being alert to the possibility that there was a new and fascinating pattern behind what we were observing? I instructed David to return to the client and through the exaggerated use of his own eye movements and predicates, he was to carry on a conversation (content was irrelevant) in which he first matched the peculiar pattern he had detected (eye movements associated with the opposite set of predicates) and focusing on visual and kinesthetic predicates, the entire time sustaining a high grade of rapport. After a period of time (five minutes, say) he was to start to mix these unusual cross-over signals with the standard ones, so that over the next period of the conversation he was to move from the mixed presentation to one in which there was congruence between the predicates used and the eye movements demonstrated. He was further instructed, during this graded incremental movement to the standard relationship between eye movements and predicates, to leave space for the client to respond and, critically, to note whether the client was following this pacing and leading presentation. If the client followed his lead, he was to continue until the client's eye movements and predicates matched; if the client was not following his lead, he was to move back to matching what the client was doing and then, by smaller incremental steps, lead him to the standard signals. David accepted the task and returned to the client. Some time later (my memory is less than an hour), David returned to report that the pacing and leading strategy had succeeded and the client was presently demonstrating the standard match between eye movements and predicates. These two key reference points were now aligned.

When I entered the room, it was immediately obvious that something of consequence had occurred: the client looked significantly different. The excess muscular tension that had marked his physiology was gone, his voice had dropped to a deeper tonality and had a new rhythmic quality to it. I asked him immediately whether he wanted to pee – his response was classic. He looked surprised by this (what-seemed-to-him-in-his-new-state) odd invitation and then laughed as he realized that it had been something approaching two hours since he had last relieved himself. I was satisfied. A follow-up phone call with him revealed that he was free of the concerns about urination and finding a toilet, his relationship with his girlfriend had taken a new and positive turn, and ...

To this day, I have little appreciation of what actually happened: How had the calibration of a mismatch between the two primary (at the time) reference points in calibration for representational systems, followed by a simple pace and lead, carried the day with this client? Of course, I can speculate, but I refuse as such speculations are little more than an exercise in erecting filters that may well interfere with my ability to discover what is lying beneath this peculiar presentation when I next encounter such a case. The point of this example is to alert the reader to unexplored aspects of the set of classic patterns called representational systems, and with some good fortune, it will provoke the reader to explore this largely uncharted territory.

3. I call the reader's attention to the overall form of this case as an example of one set of choices about how to proceed when faced with an unusual case – one that is unprecedented in your experience. Tread carefully, as such cases both come infrequently and may well contain a gem of a pattern buried beneath the surface markers of calibration. This careful handling of unusual cases actually led Bandler and myself to practice with some of the more wild examples of clients that showed up in our *impossibles* practice to

take the time at the front of work with them to train them to be capable of on-demand amnesia.

With such a client so trained, we could apply a pattern, or set of patterns, observe the consequences, use amnesia to remove the effective intervention, and then use a distinct pattern, or set of patterns, to determine whether we could make a second, third (and so on) intervention using these alternative patterns and sets of patterns.

Again, to this day, I am unable to decide what such a use of amnesia, and the subsequent retesting of patterning that it afforded us, represents epistemologically. Did we actually succeed in removing active traces of the first, second, and so on interventions? Is this actually a viable method of conducting research? In the cases where the client demonstrated marked reactions – such as a phobia – it certainly was convincing at the time. Such a radical program requires careful evaluation. There may well be ways to answer this question with the newer forms of instrumentation to determine what precisely is going on with amnesia, and its possible use as a research tool.

Eicher writes:

> And so, with introduction of accessing cues, the use of the conscious and unconscious mind analogy, chunking, and TOTE, the bridge to NLP was created.

I take it that the "bridge" Eicher refers to here is between a portion of academic psychology and what we were doing in NLP at the time. I had spent one academic year as a Guest Researcher at George Miller's lab at Rockefeller University in New York City (1969–70) and had great respect for Miller's work. While the original transformational model developed by Chomsky in 1957 had been replaced/advanced by the time I got to Rockefeller, I noted that Miller was the only researcher (to the best of my knowledge) who had succeeded in operationalizing any of the key concepts in Chomsky's work for actual detectable consequences. Chomsky had never claimed a "psychological reality" for the abstract formal work in syntax that he had pioneered. Miller blew right past this caveat and succeeded in finding, for example, longer processing times for sentences that differed only in the number of postulated transformations connecting Deep Structure with Surface Structure. One of Miller's enduring contributions was the article *The Magical Number 7+ or –2*, a paper published in 1956 and still today is one of the most cited articles published in the field of psychology.[3]

Several further comments here:

Eicher mentions the TOTE (Test Operate Test Exit) model as part of this putative bridge. It is useful to recognize that the TOTE itself is a reaction to a battle that was occurring in psychology and more generally in the intellectual environment of the era. Chomsky's work (and especially his critique of Skinner's *Verbal Behavior*)[4] impacted psychology and ultimately, over the next decades, liberated psychology from the grip of Behaviorism (the form that Positivism took in this era in psychology). One consequence of his astonishing precise critique was (not immediately but inexorably) the discarding of the central explanatory concept of Behavioristic psychology – the stimulus–response relationship (S–R) – as the core of learning and performance. Thus, the psychology of the era was left devoid of any core explanatory device for its domain. If not the S–R model, what is there to explain all this behavior?

The answer emerged in 1960 with the publication, as Eicher correctly notes, of the book *The Plans and Structure of Behavior* by Miller and two associates, Eugene Galanter and Karl Pribram.[5] In this book, they offer an alternative to the S–R arc; it is a sound cybernetic replacement, the TOTE. Consistent with the requirement of any cybernetic model, the TOTE contained a closed loop system in which the consequences of an action are fed back to the generating device – the simplest form of feedback.

Eicher's inclusion of the TOTE in his comment puzzles me, as the TOTE is simply an abstract explanatory device in the theory of psychology. Given that the original model in NLP, the Meta Model, itself (even in its name) contains logical levels in a hierarchy of logical inclusion (the natural ordering of human languages), the TOTE is certainly far more compatible with the NLP patterning than the S–R arc. However, it is not itself an NLP pattern. There are no applications of the TOTE in any applied process pattern that is not already contained in NLP patterning itself. It is a theoretical classificatory notion that filled a historical gap left with the demise of the S–R arc. In what sense, then, is the TOTE part of NLP?

I mention in passing that during this era, and consistently since, I have refused the classification of NLP as a part of academic psychology. Academic psychology, at least as practiced in the United States, is the study of the average performance and activities of people given certain tasks – a statistical approach to the study of human behavior. This was and remains the domain of psychology. NLP, in contrast, is the study of one of the extremes of human performance – the patterning of genius, the patterning of the most advanced performers available. Thus, NLP and psychology are easily distinguished by two variables: the domain of study (average performance in psychology and excellence in performance in NLP) and the methodology applied. Given this distinction as the object of study, it is not difficult to conclude that the tools appropriate for one of these, academic psychology, form a statistical approach in which the aggregation of the performances of the subjects in isolated and typically artificial contexts (experiments) occur and a host of methods for determining the average – from the simple division of the cumulative performance by the total number of subjects yields the average. There are, of course, far more sophisticated measures and methods that can be applied to these performances, testing for the range of variation and the independence of the various variables under scrutiny.

However, all of these measures involve aggregation with operations that identify the average of the distribution as the fundamental act of analysis. The study of the extremes of human behavior called excellence is sharply distinguished from such data manipulations – it is the difference between statistics and algebra. One is a set of operations defined over a distribution; the other is a working out of the precise patterning of a single (in this case) equation. How is it that statistics is an inappropriate tool for algebra? Simple enough, there is no average solution to an algebraic equation (although there can be sets of (not averaged) solutions to some of the more complex algebraic expressions). This logical type distinction seems not to be available to most of the, no doubt well-intended, researchers subjecting various NLP patterns extracted from the original NLP modeling to their particular statistically based methodology. If they performed the same operations on logic, formal systems, or even algebra, they would conclude that the patterning in these disciplines does not exist.

The reader, cognizant of the fact that the original models, both in the sense of the geniuses involved and the consequences of the application of the NLP modeling techniques, are rooted in the therapeutic practice of the era, might object that perhaps my remarks are accurate for academic psychology but fail to see how they apply to clinical practice. This split between the rat-runners and the warm supportive therapists in clinical practice is legendary.

Consider a therapeutic application. An agent of change is confronted with a real human being who has come to secure choice in contexts where they experience little or no choice in their life. Now suppose that this encounter is occurring in Zagreb or Boston or ... Apparently fortunately for the agent of change, the local psychologists have determined through statistical sampling that 67% of the population of Zagreb or Boston (wherever) unconsciously select visual processing as their preferred mode of processing information and experience. Cool, so how can this agent of change use this statistically based (and let's assume accurate) information in his or her work with this client?

Well, if this is the state of knowledge about representational system preferences for the population of which this client is a member, they will choose to match the most likely case – they will make the operating assumption that this client unconsciously prefers visual processing. It is the best guess. The problem, of course, is the classic category error – the fact that 67% of the population of which this client is a member makes this the best guess available. Let's further suppose that this agent of change appreciates the importance of communicating with this client so as to establish rapport and to provide an effective way to exchange information. The agent of change will therefore bias her or his behavior towards those aspects of communication that appeal to the preference for visual communication.

So, whatever happens, the agent of change will be effective (at least to a point in the encounter we are describing) two out of three times. Indeed, rapport will develop and the exchange of information will occur effectively. For the other 33% of the population, well too bad! They simply do not fit the statistical profile. Surely, you will say, the calibration abilities of the agents of change will allow them to detect that there is a mismatch between this particular client and the agent of change's choice to follow the statistically best guess. One would hope so although, ...

So, what did the agent of change gain from the use of the statistical analysis about the unconscious preferences of the population of the local area? Nothing, or worse, a non-sensory based guess that erected a filter to noticing and responding preferentially to those aspects of behavior on the part of the client that signaled a visual processing preference.

The attribution of some characteristic that occurs in the set constructed from a sampled population to a member of that set is a category error of the first rank. It just doesn't work. A statistical approach to clinical work offers nothing of value and represents an example of the left brain pathology of treating categories as opposed to the actual people directly in front of you. Compare the elegance and effectiveness of using the various calibration points available to single preferences – the eye movements and the predicates, for example – with the above scenario.

So, to return to the original question: Eicher proposes that some bridge was made between academic psychology and NLP, or what he refers to as pre-NLP. It is difficult to know how to appreciate what he is proposing. What is he pointing at with the term "pre-NLP"? By this point, the modeling of Perls, Satir, and the initial stages of modeling Erickson had already been completed and we were deeply into testing the patterns that we had coded (including accessing cues and predicates, conscious and unconscious processes, and chunking – the basis of the meta model. Surely, unique contribution of NLP modeling and its use in modeling and coding the initial patterning of NLP indicates that, with or without the actual name NLP, the technology was fully operational.

CHAPTER 10

My Early History with NLP

Robert Dilts

My journey with NLP began in September 1975, before there was actually formally such a thing as NLP. The name *neuro-linguistic programming* emerged in the spring of 1976. It was inspired in part by the field of *neurolinguistics* – an area of study, predating NLP, whose purpose was to explore the neurological basis of language.[1] NLP founders Bandler and Grinder coined the name in order to distinguish what they were doing from traditional psychology, psychotherapy, and hypnosis (as well as from the field of neurolinguistics).[2] My own path to NLP, however, did not come as a direct result of the study of any of these fields.

I grew up in the San Francisco Bay Area in the 1950s, 60s and 70s. This was a time of great change in the world, much of which was focused in that particular part of Northern California. The culture in which I spent my youth was a cornerstone for such phenomena as the hippies, the rise of rock 'n' roll music, protests against the Vietnam War, psychedelic drugs, sexual freedom, feminism, gay rights, environmental awareness, the human potential movement, and the launching of the technology revolution in Silicon Valley. Change, new ideas, innovation, and a revolutionary spirit were a natural, everyday part of the reality in which I came of age.

In 1973, I arrived at the University of California at Santa Cruz (UCSC), an hour or so drive over the coastal mountains from the Bay area. UCSC was a highly progressive experimental school; a real reflection of the idealism of California in the 1960s.[3] It was completely co-ed (including the bathrooms) and there were no official grades. You either passed or there was no record. So it was not even possible to fail a class. Prior to that I had gone to a Catholic, all boys, college prep high school and was ready for a change. UCSC at that time was about as opposite an environment as you could get from my education up to that point.

Some people struggled with the lack of structure, but I was like a fish in water. One thing I had learned from my college prep experience was how to be disciplined, and this really served me at UCSC. Someone who was self-motivated and disciplined could really take advantage of the opportunities and freedom the environment provided.

Given the heavy emphasis on science I had in my high school years, I decided to go in the other direction and started off as an arts major. UCSC encouraged interdisciplinary studies, however, and I was interested in everything. That first year, I also took classes in psychobiology, economics, cultural anthropology, and computer programming (back in the days when you had to use boxes of punch cards and the computer took up a whole building).

I switched back to "hard" science in my second year, immersing myself in physics and calculus. It was during this period that I developed a deep appreciation of the work of Albert Einstein. Interestingly enough, I was born in 1955 in the same hospital in Princeton, New Jersey where Einstein was passing the last weeks of his life. I was coming as he was going. Perhaps there was some exchange in the field between us, because I have always felt a close connection with his thoughts and values, and he is the subject of one of my books on *Strategies of Genius*.[4]

During this time, I kept a connection with my artistic side as well by doing an independent study in animation. This taught me how to really look at the whole world of movement from a very different perspective. Breaking down each second of time into 32 discrete images led to quite an altered state of perception. This probably made it easier for me to observe very subtle non-verbal behaviors later on.

A typical young person of my times, I was searching for myself and became attracted to more social and philosophical topics. Thus, in my junior year at UCSC I decided to switch to being a politics major. As part of my study of politics, I decided that it would be important to know something about language and linguistics. My older brother,

Michael, was a graduate linguistics student at Harvard at the time and encouraged me to look into that area of study as well.

As a result, I walked into a beginning linguistics class on that fateful day in September 1975. It was a large lecture course with over 200 students taught by a professor named John Grinder. Needless to say, Grinder was unlike any other other college professor I had ever met. In his mid-thirties at the time, John was dynamic, charismatic, physically vital and powerful, confident, curious, and indisputably intelligent and talented.

A member of several United States Special Forces military groups in the early 1960s, Grinder had returned to the academic world to study linguistics in the latter part of the decade and, like many others of that generation, had transformed to become a committed proponent of the counterculture. He had a reputation as a "radical" professor. He would bring students into faculty meetings because he thought they should have some say in decisions that influenced them. At one point, he organized a group of students to lie down across one of the local freeways in protest of the Vietnam War.

He demonstrated little tolerance for the bureaucracy of academia. One of the first things he said to the students in the beginning linguistics class was that if anyone was there just because they needed the course as a requirement, to come up and see him after class. He said that he would sign the necessary paperwork for them to get credit for the class right away because he didn't want people who felt they were required to attend but did not want to be in the class. He thought that was unproductive and unnecessary. I was immediately struck and impressed by his commitment to congruence and his willingness to bypass bureaucratic rigidity.

More surprises were in store. John and a mysterious cohort named Richard Bandler had just finished their first publication, *The Structure of Magic, Volume I*.[5] This book outlined a dozen key language patterns, called the Meta Model, that he and Bandler had modeled from highly successful psychotherapists, such as Fritz Perls (Gestalt therapy) and Virginia Satir (family therapy). The idea of the book, and thus its name, was that what seemed to be "magical" results achieved by these experts could be described and transferred to others through a process of modeling their deeper structure. Their notion was that the power of language came from its form rather than its content.

According to Bandler and Grinder, effective therapists acted as if they listened for certain categories of language and asked predictable questions rather than getting caught up in the details and drama of their clients' specific words. These questions helped people to address certain generalizations, deletions, and distortions that arose in their verbal descriptions of life events. This, in turn, supported them to achieve a fuller representation of their experiences, widen their mental model of the world, and perceive more choices, especially in situations of pain or distress. As Virginia Satir wrote in her introduction to this seminal work: "What Richard Bandler and John Grinder have done is to watch the process of change over time and to distill from it the patterns of the *how* process."

It was on a Thursday, our first full class period, that John taught the Meta Model language patterns, all in one two-hour chunk. It was the first immediately practical thing I had ever learned in school. Even though I had no training as a therapist, and had not even taken a class in psychology, I found to my astonishment that I was able to ask questions as if I were an experienced psychotherapist. I discovered that by asking a few well-chosen questions, family members, classmates, friends, and even casual acquaintances experienced valuable insights and breakthroughs. It became clear that recognizing a few fundamental language patterns and knowing the right questions to ask gave one incredible power to stimulate change and growth.

It soon also became obvious, however, that knowledge of language alone was not enough. By the next class period, on the following Tuesday, about half the class arrived depressed, dejected, and forlorn. They had alienated their lovers, teachers, and friends, cutting them to pieces with their Meta Model questioning, which came across more like an interrogation or inquisition than a mutual exploration. Shortly after that, Grinder and Bandler began to emphasize the importance of rapport.

I had developed a natural skill for mirroring. From the time I was a child, this had been an intuitive pattern in my behavior. As is visible in home videos from when I was very young, I would constantly mirror key behaviors of those around me; this is a key element in establishing rapport and gave me an advantage in using the Meta Model.

I found what I was learning in that class from Grinder to be novel, exhilarating, and powerful. There was a growing feeling among a number of members of the class, which was encouraged by John, that we could "change the world" with the Meta Model. I immediately began to apply the Meta Model language patterns to the Socratic Dialogues that I was studying in a political philosophy class and wrote a paper on it (published later in *Applications of NLP*[6]). I showed how the Socratic method of dialectic systematically challenged assumptions by questioning language patterns known in the Meta Model as *modal operators of necessity* – words like "should," "must," "need to" – and *universal quantifiers* – words such as "always," "every time," "never," "only," etc.

At that time, John and Richard had basically only used the Meta Model for therapeutic purposes, so to apply it to politics was new and innovative. John found this interesting. He had co-taught some courses on politics and had even written a book on Marxist economics.

Grinder and Bandler were also beginning their exploration into the impact and implications of the sensory representational systems (visual, auditory, kinesthetic, etc.) on consciousness. I remember coming up to John after class to discuss my work on the Socratic Dialogues and the Meta Model. I was surprised but pleased to hear him pronounce me one of the few auditory persons in the class (as opposed to visual or kinesthetic), which put me into the same category that he considered himself, Bandler, Bateson, and Erickson. According to Grinder, people "with ears" only made up about 10% of the population.

One of my next projects was to make a similar analysis of Gregory Bateson's "metalogues" from his book *Steps to an Ecology of Mind*.[7] Bateson (1904–1980) was an anthropologist and social scientist whose ideas and theories significantly influenced fields as varied as cybernetics, linguistics, communication theory, psychiatry, and systemic psychotherapy. Bateson chose the term "metalogue," a clear reference to the Socratic Dialogues, to describe his own conversational method to "think about thinking" and challenge assumptions.

Bateson had an incredible ability to recognize order and pattern in the universe. He emphasized that it was more important to focus on the interactions and *relationships* between the elements in a system, rather than the particular elements themselves. The hypothesis was that Bateson's metalogues intuitively applied the Meta Model language patterns to systematically address other types of verbal categories than the Socratic Dialogues – in particular *nominalizations*, which are words (such as "communication," "thought," "freedom," etc.) that turn actions, ongoing processes, and relationships into "things." This intuition proved to be correct.

Grinder and Bandler had shown Bateson, who was also teaching at UCSC at the time, the manuscript of *The Structure of Magic*. Bateson was impressed with the work, and wrote in a preface, "John Grinder and Richard Bandler have done something similar to what my colleagues and I attempted fifteen years ago. They have tools which we did not have – or did not see how to use. They have succeeded in making linguistics into a base for theory and simultaneously into a tool for therapy ... making explicit the syntax of how people avoid change, and, therefore, how to assist them in changing."[8]

It was after reading *The Structure of Magic* that Bateson made arrangements for Bandler and Grinder to meet Milton Erickson (1902–1980), a long-time colleague and friend of Bateson's, to see if they could create a similar model of the complex communication patterns used by Erickson in his hypnotic and therapeutic work. This led to some of the most seminal work in NLP.

Bateson had first met Erickson in the 1930s when he and his wife at the time, well-known anthropologist Margaret Mead, were doing research on trance dancing in Bali.[9] They were interested in getting background information on hypnosis and trance. They were introduced to Erickson through a common friend, the renowned writer Aldous Huxley (author of *Brave New World* and *The Doors of Perception*).

In the fall of 1975, Bandler and Grinder were deeply into their study of Erickson, traveling down to Phoenix, Arizona on a regular basis in order to observe and model Erickson. After one such trip, I remember John coming into class and excitedly saying, "Everything you know is wrong." Their experience with Erickson had led them to completely rethink their view on the Meta Model. John's comment (a humorous reference to an album by a popular comedy group of the time called The Firesign Theater) reflected his and Bandler's realization that, rather than asking questions and challenging the assumptions of his clients, Erickson used the Meta Model patterns in reverse. He purposely used language to create generalizations, deletions, and distortions as part of his hypnotic work. They called this approach, along with Erickson's use of metaphor, presupposition, and embedded suggestion, "the Milton Model" and published the results in their next book, *Patterns of the Hypnotic Techniques of Milton H. Erickson, M.D.*[10] Like Satir and Bateson, Erickson found the work impressive. As he wrote in his preface, "[I]t is a much better explanation of how I work than I, myself, can give."

It was around this time that I got my first glimpse of Richard Bandler, who made a guest appearance at John's linguistics class. Twenty-five years old at that time, Richard was thin and gaunt, with long hair and a goatee. He was clearly brilliant and equally intense. He seemed unafraid to try anything and confident to the point of appearing arrogant. He had an aloof, almost otherworldly expression, and a way of looking at people that gave one the feeling he was seeing through you. His stare and attitude could also become menacing if he felt crossed, manipulated, or disrespected. These qualities in combination produced a type of Svengali aura; one that belied a deep sensitivity, compassion, and a sense of playfulness and humor equal to that of the best stand-up comedian. (To this day when I want to laugh deeply, I put on a video of Bandler giving a seminar.)

Bandler's visit climaxed with him and Grinder doing a double induction on the whole class of 200 students. While Grinder spoke about Erickson and his language patterns at the front of the class, Bandler walked to the back of the lecture hall, speaking at the same time and cadence as Grinder, making suggestions that we would all have many surprises, insights, and discoveries in our dreams that night.

The next class I had with Grinder at UCSC was Syntax 100. This was in early 1976 and was a much smaller class of about 20 people. Bandler and Grinder's *Patterns of the Hypnotic Techniques of Milton H. Erickson, M.D., Volume I* had just come out and they were moving at full speed in their research on the connection between language and the various representational systems. I have never been more excited about holding a book in my hands as when I received *Patterns I* in the mail. It seemed like a great wisdom was contained in this book and that it would change my life (which in many ways it did).

In the class, John was teaching about the generative power and influence of language on perception. The class was fascinating and intense, producing new insights and discoveries every day. I recall one day someone asking a question, and John stopped the whole class and said, "I just want to point out here that no one in human history has asked that question before." It struck me that what he was saying was true. John's point was that the use of language was leading us into new areas of perception and consciousness. It felt like the territory into which we were moving was truly groundbreaking.

John would give us assignments like taking one Meta Model pattern and focusing on listening for and questioning just that language category for a whole week. We were then to notice how it shifted our consciousness and attention.

One day, John gave us the assignment to notice something that we had not paid much attention to before, give it a name, and observe how our experience of it changed. After class, I went up to him to get a little more clarification about what he meant and to get an example. As I was thinking about my question, my eyes looked to the side. He said, "Well, what about that?" I said, "What?" He responded, "Your eyes just looked off to the side."

As soon as I became aware of the movement, I remember being cognizant that I had "gone inside" and had been thinking about something that was just below my conscious awareness. I gave this phenomenon the name of something like "unconscious cuing." From that moment, it was as if scales had fallen from my eyes and I suddenly became aware of all the things people did unconsciously to cue themselves: blinking their eyes, touching their faces, looking to different locations, making little gestures, noises, facial expressions, and so on.

I observed everything from people clicking their tongues to blinking their eyes to snapping their fingers to looking up and looking down and sideways when they did it. I watched people in the library studying, noticing when their eyes shifted in different directions. I remember the excitement of making, noting, and reporting my observations of these largely unconscious cues, especially the eye movements. John seemed pleased with these observations and gave me more specific assignments with respect to observing various cues, including eye movements and their links to the various sensory representational systems.[11]

It was about this time that John started inviting me up to the "Meta" group meetings on Alba Road in the hills of Ben Lomond. I wasn't really involved in the "Meta" group until seven or eight months after I first met John. I think John wanted to sort of keep me as his own experiment at first, as a type of "sorcerer's apprentice." So I didn't have much interaction with Richard and most of the other "Meta" group members until the spring of 1976.

As group leaders, Bandler and Grinder perfectly captured the revolutionary spirit of the times. Their method of teaching was completely "heuristic," meaning to lead with experience. Their philosophy was act first – start with sensory experience – and then "digitalize" it (i.e., describe it in words). They instilled in us the confidence that we could do anything and change anything.

One of their ways of modeling Erickson, for example, was to reproduce with us everything that Erickson had done with his clients. Once they could do it themselves and then teach us to do it, they were certain that they had the pattern explicitly identified. Their mode of teaching was also very immediate and experiential. They would do something, point to one of us, give us a few instructions, and we would go and immediately repeat it with someone else. We would then come back and reflect with them on what had happened; what had worked and what hadn't.

The next step was to see if we could achieve the same result without needing to induce a trance state. This is how many of the original NLP techniques were developed.

One of the strategies that they taught us was how to generate an even greater amount of learning and choice from every experience or life situation. We were instructed to review the events of the day and identify the significant choice points. We were to reflect on the choices we had made at those points and whether they were successful or unsuccessful in reaching our desired outcome. For each choice point, we were to imagine three alternative ways we could have responded, other than the way that we did (whether or not what we did was successful). In our imagination, we were to then project the results and consequences of each alternative and imagine what it would be like to have actually made this choice by stepping into the experience and fully living it somatically in imagination.

The object of this exercise was not to find the "best way" to respond to a particular situation. Rather it was simply to get in the habit of creating more and more choices. Doing this exercise regularly created the possibility of getting three times as much experience per day as we would have by simply recording what happened that day in memory. This type of exercise, plus the constant focus on process as opposed to content, accelerated our ability to learn from what we were doing tremendously. By the time I was 23 years old I was teaching new things to experienced therapists who had been working with clients longer than I had been alive.

Many strange and wonderful things would go on in those groups at that time. I'm sure to some it would seem like a circus. We tried out every hypnotic phenomenon, including positive and negative hallucinations, catalepsy, deep trance identification, age regression, post-hypnotic suggestions, and projection into the future. It was not an uncommon experience, for example, to see somebody fully age regressed to 2 years old, crawling around and acting like a child as a means to enhance his or her ability to learn a language. We experimented with everything from extrasensory perception to creating, and then reversing, phobias. We also explored strategies for naturally recreating all types of altered states of consciousness, including those typically induced by drugs.[12] The world was wide open back then and everything seemed possible. We sometimes humorously referred to it as the "Academy of Space," and we were the "space cadets."

The core members of the "Meta" group that I remember most vividly from that time were Frank Pucelik, Judith DeLozier, Leslie Cameron, David Gordon, Stephen Gilligan, Jim Eicher, Byron Lewis, and Terrence McClendon; many of whom went on to make significant contributions to the field as trainers and authors (and a number of whom have remained close colleagues and friends). Judy and I, for example, have been partners at NLP University held at UCSC for the past 20 years and have co-authored a number of books together, including *The Encyclopedia of Systemic NLP* (2000) and *NLP II: The Next Generation* (2010).[13] Steve Gilligan and I co-teach seminars around the world on topics such as Love in the Face of Violence, The Evolution of Consciousness, Generative Coaching and The Hero's Journey, the subject of a recent book that we wrote together.[14]

While many people who attended the weekly groups were caught up in the drama of their own personal change, the mystique of Bandler and Grinder, the "magic" of hypnosis, or getting the steps of some technique right, this core group was interested in the deeper aspects of what we were doing and experiencing. There was strong rapport between us centered around our common passion for what we were learning and discovering. I vividly remember sitting with Judith DeLozier during one of Bandler and Grinder's weekly evening group meetings and looking into each other's eyes as we asked each other questions and noticing the spontaneous eye movements in different directions.

In those days, Bandler and Grinder encouraged us to keep a "meta book" which was a notebook, similar to those kept by Leonardo da Vinci, cataloging our thoughts, ideas, and observations. I still have a couple of my early "meta books," which are fascinating to look back over from time to time. I remember feeling that these distinctions and patterns were so basic, so pervasive, and so powerful that it was hard to believe that people like Aristotle had not already discovered them centuries earlier.

At the young age of 21 I had the vision that some day these observations and ideas would be spread all over the world and, in my dream, I would be traveling the world, teaching them to healers, teachers, and leaders from every nation. In retrospect, this was quite a prophetic vision, as this is exactly what I am doing today.

As I recall, Bandler and Grinder were charging people something outrageously inexpensive like $25 per month to attend a group meeting one night a week in those early days. I was a "poor starving student," however, and didn't have any money. So they let me come in exchange for being a sort of personal secretary. I did a number of things from organizing file cabinets to handling certain correspondence. I can remember writing the first letter they sent out to people when they decided they wanted to go out on the road and do workshops, primarily on hypnosis. I believe they were hiring themselves out for $200 a day for the both of them.

In those days, in addition to taking on the "impossible" clients of the local psychiatric institutions, Bandler and Grinder were always working on some type of creative scheme to become "millionaires by Christmas." One of them was to market placebos. A placebo is a "sham drug" that has no inherent medical value, such as a sugar pill or an injection of salt water, but which can trigger a dramatic improvement in symptoms in some patients under the right conditions. Placebos, in fact, have been demonstrated to influence a variety of symptoms including pain, anxiety, psychosis, high blood pressure, arthritis, angina pectoris, and even cancer.

Bandler and Grinder were convinced that the placebo effect was a result of a type of "neuro-linguistic programming." They believed that there was immense healing potential in the body that could be released via particular neuro-linguistic processes. Their refreshingly audacious idea was to sell fake pills under the label "Placebo" and be very up front about the data on the placebo effect. There would be a booklet that came with the bottle which would clearly state that these pills had no pharmacologically active ingredients, but list the statistics on placebos. They would say, "Placebos don't work for everybody, but they may

WORK FOR YOU!" They would then show the various degrees of effect that placebos had on particular symptoms.

One of my jobs was to collect the necessary research on placebos. I was surprised to discover that, since every drug that is put into the marketplace must be tested against a placebo, there is a large amount of clinical evidence about their effects. An examination of this data reveals sometimes startling facts about placebos. Studies on their effects across a wide range of different symptoms, for example, have shown that, on average, placebos will work as effectively as active drugs 35–40% of the time.[15] In the case of certain powerful pain medications, such as morphine, placebos were shown to work as well as actual morphine more than 50% of the time.[16]

It was even going to be necessary to post warnings about possible side effects of placebos. In one study, for example, women with breast cancer were given placebo chemotherapy. Astonishingly, one third of the women who received the placebo chemotherapy lost all of their hair!

Grinder and Bandler figured that their placebo idea would stir up a lot of controversy and thus publicity. In the middle of the expected hubbub they planned to release "Placebo Plus," which would have "20% more inactive ingredients in each capsule" and "Designer Placebo" which was based on research (repeated a number of times) showing that certain representational characteristics of placebos influenced the placebo effect. For example, small, shiny, red, expensive placebos stimulated greater healing potential than larger, fatter, powdery, cheap-looking white pills that left dust on your fingers. Bandler and Grinder also planned a "time release" placebo that would last longer over time.

As I recall, there was supposedly a Texas millionaire who was ready and willing to provide the financial backing for their scheme. Apparently, however, they were prevented from proceeding by the US Food and Drug Administration; perhaps because the government agency was fearful of the impact it might have on the drug industry.

Be that as it may, this research on placebos opened a doorway to my own understanding of the healing potential of the human psyche and the human body which has been a key theme of my work ever since – especially the healing potential of belief. This background also provided the foundation and inspiration for the remarkable recovery of my mother from metastatic breast cancer in 1982 and was the basis for my book *Beliefs: Pathways to Health and Well-Being*.[17]

In addition to attending the "Meta" group meetings and working for Bandler and Grinder, I continued to take classes with John at UCSC including *Pragmatics of Human Communication*. During this time, he and Bandler were working intensely with Virginia Satir (1916–1989), completing the second volume of *The Structure of Magic* and the book *Changing With Families*, co-authored with Virginia.[18] A key element of this work was the notion of *internal "parts."*

I was into the more scientific and rigorous aspects of NLP at the time and found myself struggling with the notion of a "part" of a person. It seemed to me to be more abstract than the more directly observable distinctions such as eye movements, representational systems, synesthesias, and strategies. I remember having a meeting with John Grinder at his office, trying to explain my dilemma with the notion of "parts" and saying something like, "I am sure it is a useful idea, but a part of me just doesn't get ..." At that moment, John broke out laughing. Obviously, the "part of me" that did not get what "parts" were all about *was* a "part."

It was in that moment that I understood that NLP was fundamentally about the structure of "subjective experience" rather than objective observation. The notion of "parts" was a particular map of a shared subjective experience that was clearly a type of "neuro-linguistic program."

Bandler and Grinder's work with Virginia Satir and their exploration of parts also led to the *principle of positive intention*. Simply put, the principle states that at some level all behavior is (or at one time was) "positively intended." Another way to say it is that all behavior serves (or at one time served) a "positive purpose" – i.e., every "neuro-linguistic program" emerges and lasts because it serves some type of adaptive function.

While I liked the principle, at first it seemed mostly like a nice philosophical idea. Like everything else in NLP, however, it eventually became a very personal experience that changed my life. It did not come in a flash of blinding light as to St. Paul on the road to Damascus. It was subtler. But the moment that I deeply realized all of my behaviors had some type of positive intention, even if I did not immediately recognize what it was, something shifted inside of me that led to a deep trust in my own being; that somehow, as Einstein proposed, "the universe is a friendly place" at its core. Even today the principle of positive intention seems to me to be the most spiritual principle in NLP.

Many of the other foundational NLP techniques were beginning to emerge at this time including anchoring, changing personal history, future pacing, and the new behavior generator. We were also deeply into the exploration of synesthesia patterns (an overlapping of the senses called "fuzzy functions" in *The Structure of Magic, Volume II*) and cognitive strategies. I remember John Grinder saying that some day we would be able to map out the strategies and synesthesia patterns of the world's geniuses and teach them to our children. I found this a deeply inspiring notion and it planted the seed for my own future work on the strategies of geniuses such as Disney, Mozart, Einstein, Leonardo da Vinci, Freud, and Tesla.

In October of 1976, I wrote an outline for perhaps the first paper written specifically on neuro-linguistic programming for a class I was taking on The Neurophysiology of Experience. I defined NLP in the following way:

> Neuro-linguistic programming (NLP) was developed as a means to explore and analyze complex human behavior. It is a cybernetic approach, as opposed to causal, linear, or statistical methods, utilizing the phenomena of language and perception to look for the "differences that make a difference" in the way that human beings organize their experience. Specifically: (a) distinctions people make about their internal experience (i.e., mental images, feelings, internal dialogue, etc.); (b) strategies people use to make sense of their experience; (c) strategies people use to access and communicate stored

perceptual information; and (d) how these distinctions and patterns can be integrated to understand, promote, and contribute to the human processes of change, choice, and learning.

Being a cybernetic model, the structure of NLP is generative: it has the ability to predict to a certain degree and find alternatives to specific behaviors as well as the ability to describe those already elicited. NLP has also what might be called an "open" structure in that the structure itself may change or expand in accordance with its own findings.

This still seems to me to be a legitimate definition of what NLP, at its foundation, is all about.

That same year, I made my first trip to Phoenix, Arizona to see Milton Erickson. Even though I had no degree or professional experience, Erickson kindly agreed to let me visit at the request of John Grinder. I had drawn a pencil portrait of Erickson from a photo on one of his books and gave it to John as a present. John took it as an unconscious request to him on my part to see Erickson and immediately called and set up an appointment for me to go visit the venerable old man in Phoenix. John sent along the portrait as well as a gift to Erickson.

Grinder and Bandler had just finished the second volume of *Patterns of the Hypnotic Techniques of Milton H. Erickson, M.D.* and gave me a copy of the manuscript to bring to Dr. Erickson.[19]

I was a college student with little money and Dr. and Mrs Erickson kindly offered to let me stay in their guesthouse. I roomed there with another young college student – Jeff Zeig, who later founded and still runs the Erickson Foundation. The friendship we began there has continued for over 35 years.

I had, of course, heard all about Erickson's genius from Grinder and Bandler and had read everything by him and about him that I could get my hands on. Naturally, I was in absolute awe of him. I was immediately struck, however, by the deep humanity, humility, and generosity that he and Mrs Erickson showed to me and the others around them.

Erickson also immediately exhibited his famous sense of humor. When I was first introduced to him, I handed him the portrait that I had drawn of him and brought him from Grinder as a gift. He looked at it, handed it to Mrs Erickson and said with a twinkle in his eye, "Betty, why don't you file this in the circular filing cabinet" (meaning the garbage can). Then he glanced at me with a sly grin to see how I would respond. I laughed and said it was his and he was free to do whatever he wanted with it. I saw later that it was displayed prominently along with other gifts that Dr. Erickson had received.

At the end of the first day, he turned to me with that same knowing smile and said, "And now do you know that I am nothing like what Grinder and Bandler said I was?" I laughed again and said that I had already known that and this was why I had wanted to come down and see what he was really like for myself.

On this first visit, I was there for three days. Most of the time Jeff and I were the only people with Dr. Erickson during the day. I think he must have taken a liking to us because he seemed to be in rare form. He treated us more like we were his sons than visitors.

Towards the end of the stay, Erickson showed us a card that his daughter Roxanna had sent him. On the front of the card was a cartoon of a little man standing on an asteroid out in the middle of the universe. He was looking around in wonder at all of the stars and planets surrounding him. The caption read, "When you think about how vast and mysterious the universe is, doesn't it make you feel kind of small and insignificant?" When you opened the card, the inside quipped, "Me neither."

To me, this characterized so much of what Erickson stood for. He had the ability to face the unknown and the uncertain, embrace the awe and mystery of life, and remain confident and fully present because he knew he was part of that awe and mystery. As he put it:

> It is important to have a sense of security; a sense of readiness; a full knowledge that, come what may, you can meet it and handle it – and enjoy doing it.

161

> It's also nice learning to come up against the situation that you can't handle – and then later think it over and realize that, too, was a learning that is useful in many, many different ways. It allows you to assess your strength. It also allows you to discover the areas in which you need to use some more of your own security, which rests within yourself …

> Reacting to the good and the bad, and dealing with it adequately – that's the real joy in life.[20]

Erickson's approach to life is a classic example of the power of "not knowing." When those of us fortunate enough to be in the "Meta" group would go to see Erickson, we were, of course, full of questions for him. We would ask questions along the lines of, "If you use this particular approach with a person who has that particular type of issue, will it produce a certain result?" Erickson would invariably reply, "I don't know." We would ask, "Will it work to use this process to address that problem?" Again, Erickson would respond, "I don't know." We ended up with pages and pages in our notebooks saying, "He doesn't know. He doesn't know. He doesn't know."

It wasn't that he was trying to be evasive, however. It was that he did not operate from a lot of beliefs and assumptions. Each situation was unique to him; each person was "one of a kind" and his relationship with that person was also unique. So when asked about the probability of a particular outcome, Erickson would always say, "I don't know. I really don't know." And then he would add, *"But I am very curious to discover what is possible."* The state of not knowing combined with curiosity is the essence of generative change.

As a result of this, I never took notes during my time with Erickson. I knew that what I received from him would not be something in a notebook, but rather something in my unconscious. I would frequently only realize weeks or months later what I had absorbed from being with him. As with all great teachers, what I learned from Erickson came mostly from his way of being. The acceptance, affection, generosity, and sponsorship Erickson showed me is something that I deeply appreciated and have attempted to share with my own clients as a part of the legacy I received from him.

In the fall of 1976, I also attended Gregory Bateson's Ecology of Mind class at UCSC. I can say unequivocally that Bateson had the greatest depth and scope of thought of anyone I have ever known. His lectures would cover topics ranging from communication theory, to Balinese art, to Maxwell's equations for electromagnetic fields, to schizophrenia, to genetic deformities in beetles' legs. His talks, however, were never a disjointed collection of thoughts or jumbled group of ideas as the diversity of topics might suggest. Bateson's version of cybernetics and systems theory was able to tap into the deeper structure, or "pattern which connects," all of these topics into a single fascinating weave of life and existence.

Reflecting back, attending Bateson's class was one of the most transformative experiences of my life. I would sit in his class, listening to his deep voice and distinctive Cambridge accent, which sounded to me like the voice of universal wisdom. For me, he was, and remains, a type of "spiritual guide." Thoughts, ideas, and revelations would flow into my mind, some relating to his lecture and some from completely other areas of my life, education, and experience. Usually they came so quickly I couldn't write them down fast enough.

My second class under Bateson was a student-directed seminar entitled Studies in Schizophrenia. Typical of the emphasis on experiential leaning, one of the requirements of the class was to spend at least six hours a week with someone diagnosed as psychotic or schizophrenic. I volunteered at a local locked-ward private mental hospital that provided only "chemotherapy" for their patients. I also volunteered at a place called the Soteria House that had the opposite philosophy and offered no drug treatment for patients but only emotional support by untrained volunteers.

Bateson had proposed that psychosis was less a result of individual genetic and chemical disturbances than it was a response to pathologies in the larger family and social systems in which it occurred. As I interacted with the various patients in both of these institutions, the stigmas and myths of psychosis disappeared and very quickly the veracity of Bateson's view became clear. The importance of viewing the "identified patient" or problem in the context of the larger system in which it is occurring is a learning that I have taken with me through the rest of my career.

The importance of the relationship between the individual and the larger system became frightfully clear to me one day when I was getting ready to leave the private hospital. I arrived at the locked door and said I was ready to leave. The staff at the door had changed shifts while I had been there, however, and no one recognized me. As a volunteer, I had no official badge or documentation. They thought I was a mental patient and were not going to let me out. When I tried to explain that I was a volunteer, they just nodded, saying, "Sure, sure, of course you are." Nothing I said would convince them to let me out. Fortunately, another staff member came by who recognized me, otherwise I might have been there an uncomfortably long time. It occurred to me that the locked door, and who decided who was crazy, was as much a part of the conditions creating insanity as the symptoms of the individual patients.[21] Bateson's proposal that double binds are a critical co-factor in producing either "insanity" or "genius" has also been a concept that I have continued to contemplate and explore these last 35 years.

One of Bateson's most important and powerful distinctions was that of "logical types" and "logical levels" of learning and change. The notion of *logical levels* refers to the fact that all processes and phenomena are created by the *relationships* between other processes and phenomena. By making the relationship between two variables a variable for a second relationship one creates another logical level. For example, we use differences in lightness and darkness on a piece of paper to make an "image"; when we compare two images to find differences, we have jumped to the next logical level of process. Similarly, when two hydrogen atoms and an oxygen atom unite, the water made from their combination is no longer just a mixture of individual hydrogen and oxygen atoms but is rather its own new entity, a different logical type. In the same way, learning to learn is a different logical level than learning.

Bateson applied the notions of logical types and logical levels to many aspects of behavior and to biology. He contended, for instance, that a tissue that is made up of a group of cells is a different logical type than the individual cells – the characteristics of a brain are not the same as a brain cell. The individual brain cell cannot "think" like the brain can. The two can, however, affect each other through indirect feedback – that is, the functioning and connections of the overall brain can influence the behavior of a single brain cell and the activity of a single brain cell contributes to the overall functioning of the brain. Indeed, a cell may be said to affect itself through the rest of the brain structure.

To Bateson, logical typing was a "law of nature," not simply an intellectual theory. In his view, our brain structure, language, and social systems form natural hierarchies or levels of processes of these types. Bateson believed that most problems and pathologies emerged as a result of the confusion of logical types and levels, and the failure to perceive and respect the discontinuities between them. Urging us to seek the "differences that made a difference," Bateson emphasized that, "The major problems in the world are the result of the difference between how nature works and how people think."

As a student in his Ecology of Mind class, Bateson instilled in me the importance of considering logical types and levels in all aspects of life and experience. And, because I was exposed to these ideas at the same time as I was becoming involved in NLP, Bateson's approach has always been an integral part of my understanding of NLP. His distinctions about different logical types and levels of learning seemed of particularly profound significance.[22]

I vividly remember discussing the power of Bateson's notions of logical levels and logical types with a participant on an NLP course that I was teaching in Oslo, Norway in 1986. The person was also familiar with Bateson's work and we were reflecting on the deep importance of logical types and levels of learning. We both agreed, however, that these ideas had not been applied as fully and pragmatically as they could be. I recall saying, "Yes, someone really should apply the notion of logical levels in a more practical everyday sense." As soon as the words left my mouth, it was as if I had given myself the command. This led to my development of the notion of NeuroLogical Levels, which, though controversial to some, has become an integral part of many modern NLP trainings.

Another key influence in those early years of NLP has to do directly with the "programming" aspect of NLP. Historically, neuro-linguistic programming was brought into existence in California at the same time as another important technological and social revolution was being born – the personal computer. As has been true in other periods in history, developments in our understanding of the mind mirror developments in technology (and vice versa). In many ways, NLP and Apple grew up side by side. Apple's philosophy and products emerged in the same time frame as NLP. NLP was bringing psychology and personal change out of the laboratory and institutionalized settings at the same time that Apple was doing the same thing with computing. Steve Jobs was, in fact, a contemporary of mine, born less than a month after me.

Apple sold its first personal computers from a garage in 1976. Bandler and Grinder were both interested in the details of programming. Richard's fascination with mathematics and John's background in formal linguistics made them both quite attracted to the emerging new technologies and the power of the formal structure of programming. They were some of the first purchasers of Apple's products. In those days, if you bought five or more Apple computers from the company, you were automatically a "dealer" and got a dealer discount. Bandler and Grinder bought more than five and sold the extra ones to us to "play" with. I got my first Apple computer from them and was pleased to discover that I could upgrade from 8 kilobytes of memory to 16 kilobytes. (When the 48kB computers came out, we couldn't imagine what we would need all of that memory for.) We could see that this was not just a fad and, like NLP, could "change the world." We had many ideas for how NLP and the new technology could work together, envisioning, for instance, a "phobia booth" at airports and software that could calibrate and anchor resource states.

I designed a number of educational programs applying NLP concepts and strategies and, in 1982, Apple sold my programs Spelling Strategy, *Math Strategy*, and Typing Strategy for the Apple II computer. These later became the core products for a software company that I started with John Grinder and NLP Trainer David Gaster named Behavioral Technology.

As another thread in the burgeoning technology world, I had delved into biofeedback as part of my studies at UCSC. This started me on a journey that culminated in my developing the circuitry for a device on which I have a patent. This device read "autonomic" body responses, such as the electrical activity in the skin, heart rate, skin temperature, and blood pulse volume. These measurements were fed into a personal computer and could be used to calibrate internal states and even play games through apparent "thought control." The first application was named Mind Master, which was followed by the NeuroLink and a commercial computer game called MindDrive. Today, these applications are available through Somatic Vision.

By 1977, it had become obvious to me that NLP would be the essential component of my career. Jim Eicher and I began teaching NLP programs together in early 1977. In those days we always taught with a partner, following the lead of John and Richard. As Todd Epstein (a guitarist and co-founder with me of NLP University) liked to say, "the teaching of NLP was originally written as a duet, not a solo." Jim and I did workshops and individual coaching/therapy sessions in Santa Cruz and even made the local newspapers.

The following year, I began working together with Terrence McClendon. In 1978 we were hired by John O. Stevens (now known as Steve Andreas) to come to Boulder, Colorado to teach our first out-of-state NLP program, and my career as an NLP trainer was launched.

I had not yet completed a degree at UCSC, but believed in NLP and was sure it would make a difference in the world. At UCSC you could make your own degree. It was much more difficult than getting a traditional degree, but it was possible. I had to get at least five professors to support me and write a substantial thesis. It took an immense amount of effort, but I was determined to take advantage of that opportunity and created a degree in Behavioral Technology, integrating cybernetics and systems theory, psychology, biofeedback, neurophysiology and, of course, NLP. As it turns out, my senior thesis was an early draft of *NLP, Volume I.*[23] I was finally awarded my degree in 1979.

This was the same year we started creating the first formal NLP certification programs. Richard and John got together to form the Society of Neuro-Linguistic Programming and bought a former church that they transformed into the first NLP institute. I designed the now familiar NLP logo (the letters NLP arranged over a moiré interference pattern) and my father, who was an intellectual property attorney, did the original work to try to establish it as a certification mark. Leslie Cameron (or Cameron Bandler as she was at that time), David Gordon, Judy DeLozier, and I put together the contents for Practitioner and Master Practitioner certification.

The next stages of this journey, however, are a story for another volume.

Conclusion

At the University of California at Santa Cruz, at the same time NLP was being developed by Bandler and Grinder, there was a psychology professor named Frank Baron. Baron spent his career studying creative genius. Ultimately, he synthesized what he had learned into three fundamental characteristics. Creative geniuses are:

1. Comfortable with uncertainty
2. Able to hold seeming opposites or paradoxes
3. Persistent

One of the lessons I learned from those early days of NLP is that deeply creative people, like Erickson, Bateson, Satir, Bandler, and Grinder, do not need to know the answer ahead of time. Not only are they able to tolerate uncertainty, they even enjoy not knowing.

Creative people can also hold differing viewpoints and multiple realities. The great Danish physicist Niels Bohr pointed out that there are two types of truth: superficial truth and deep truth. According to Bohr, "In a superficial truth, the opposite is false. In a deep truth, the opposite is also true." Bohr was referring to the fact that the most fundamental units of physical reality, such as photons and electrons, present a paradox. At times they behave like waves of energy and other times they behave like tiny particles of matter.

Such deep truths are also at the foundation of our subjective experience. The fact that we can experience someone as beautiful does not mean that they cannot also be simultaneously ugly. Joy does not come without sadness. The worst thing that has ever happened to you can also be the best thing that has ever happened to you. Where there is light, there are also shadows.

The capacity to be aware of these seemingly opposite realities without one of them having to be "right" and the other "wrong" is an essential aspect of generativity. Gregory Bateson maintained, "Wisdom comes from sitting together and truthfully confronting our differences, without the intention to change anything." When we can hold different perspectives with curiosity, new and surprising solutions often emerge.

This is where the quality of *persistence* is also important. Creative geniuses don't give up, even in the face of uncertainty and dilemma. They remain curious to discover what is possible and continue searching.

This combination of beginner's mind (not knowing), curiosity, and persistence was at the core of NLP at its beginnings and remains there to this day.

Note

The reader will note that while I (John Grinder) offered comments on the articles by Gilligan and Eicher, there is no corresponding commentary here associated with the Dilts article. This lack of comment reflects, from my point of view, profound differences between the style and substance of the article by Dilts as compared with those of Gilligan and Eicher.

There are serious and substantive differences between my perceptions and what is offered in all three of the articles in this section with respect to what occurred in the period under discussion. I accept that this is not the appropriate place for a discussion of these differences.

What occurs in the article by Dilts is, however, that, in addition to the significant differences referred to above, the comments about which I will forgo in the case of all three articles, is that Dilts uniquely presents two classes of statements that are wholly unacceptable to me in an article purporting to present historical descriptions, such as this book. In particular, Dilts' article contains, for example, the attribution to me of intentions and actions that simply did not occur. There are two such classes of statement:

1. Statements that ascribe to me personally intentions and actions that simply never occurred.

2. Statements that attempt to redefine the field of NLP in a manner that differs significantly from the original intentions of the co-creators of NLP.

I trust that the alert reader will be capable of identifying these statements for themselves and, by comparing them with the remainder of the descriptions offered by the entire group of people who have taken the time and effort to offer their stories, decide for him or herself.

Note

When I wrote my article for this book, I understood that it was intended as a type of personal "memoir" of my unique experience of the time. Thus, I was a bit surprised at the inclusion of the statement on the preceding page regarding the account of my experiences during that period as if it was presented as a historical description and attempted to somehow define the field of NLP or represent the intentions of the co-creators. I had no such intention and do not expect my contribution to be read as such. While NLP, and especially my experience from those early days, has continued to be an ongoing inspiration in my life, I have gone on to develop my own work. Although these developments are deeply inspired by the experiences described in this book, I do not intend for these descriptions or later developments to be a redefinition or reflection on the original formulations of the co-creators of NLP.

Robert Dilts

CHAPTER 11

"The Answer, My Friend, is Blowin' in the Wind"[1]

Bob Dylan

John Grinder

During times of universal deceit, telling the truth becomes a revolutionary act.

George Orwell

Bandler, Pucelik, and I met in the early 70s. At the time, I was in my first year as a professor at Kresge College, University of California, Santa Cruz (UCSC) and each of them were students at the same college and university. The Santa Cruz campus was relatively new and, in particular, Kresge College was forming itself when I arrived.

Robert Edger, a biologist of note, was the provost of Kresge, which itself was in its first year. He was influenced profoundly by a NTL (National Training Laboratory) associate, Michael Kahn, and had decided to develop and run an innovative experiment in academic organization, using Kresge College as a test case. The experiment was a living/learning model for Kresge – a model of how to develop community within the boundary conditions of a college at a university. This model proposed forming a community that included with equal status, the professors, the staff and the students of Kresge College in this Living/Learning Community. All voices were to be welcomed and respected and conventional hierarchies were officially to be avoided.

The particular form used to develop this Living/Learning Community was a model of communication lifted from the NTL called the T-Group or sensitivity training. Originally a form of group psychotherapy, the T-Group was adapted for non-therapeutic purposes: the development of community and studies in small (8–15 members) group dynamics. Thus, at a minimum of once a week for several hours (often more frequently and with longer hours), T-Groups assembled consisting of a faculty member, a trained T-Group facilitator, and a mix of staff and students.

Officially, the T-Group had no rules. However, in practice, there were rules and they were quite simple and transparent to those not trained to not notice them. Basically, all obvious judgments were eschewed and high value was placed on the production of statements reporting the kinesthetic state of the speaker and what s/he understood to be the source of that state to be – phrases such as:

> You not responding to my questions makes me feel bad.

> My stomach gets churned up when you look at me that way.

> The group is angry with you because you were not on time for the meeting.

It turned out, entirely by accident, that the T-Group in which I was assigned as the faculty member also contained as a member an undergraduate student at UCSC by the name of Richard Bandler.

This format, this highly confessional form of declaring kinesthetic responses that were being experienced by various members of the T-Group as a consequence of the various forms of attention and inattention from other T-Group members, was apparently as peculiar to Bandler as it was to me.

Feelings, yes, of course, were an essential part of the flavor, the texture, the joy of life. However, the injunction to express (nearly exclusively), verbally, descriptions of these feelings and, most disturbingly, to assign the responsibility for such feelings to the actions or failures to act in certain ways by the other members of the T-Group present, was at least unsettling. It ran deeply against the principle of taking personal responsibility for the consequences of one's own behavior (or failure to act, including what one experienced at the level of feelings). The underlying ideology of these sessions contained the presupposition that these kinesthetic states in one person could be attributed to and were the responsibility of some other member or members of the T-Group struck both Bandler and myself as highly questionable, even bordering on the pathological.

One of the consequences of this response to the rules of the T-Group encounter was a growing tension between the group facilitators (especially Kahn) and number of other participants, including both Bandler and myself. Quite frequently, when one of these exchanges – what would come to be called *Cause-Effect* or *Mind Reading* or both in the Meta Model that the two of us, along with Frank, would later create – would occur, it was easy for me to calibrate Bandler's mixed response of puzzlement, irritation and, finally, amusement at what had just occurred. No doubt this calibration was in large part so obvious to me because it matched my own responses to what we were observing and listening to.

Thus, our initial communication was an extended non-verbal running commentary on the form of these expressions, so highly valued in the T-Group. For example, when a group member made a statement such as:

The way that you look at me when I speak makes me feel stupid

one or the other of us would explore the specifics of this, to us, astonishing claim with deep curiosity and amusement, such as:

Could you show me exactly how I look at you that makes you feel stupid?

Needless to say, such questions were not well received in the T-Group setting and, typically, were challenged by the facilitator with statements from the same approved class of expressions, such as:

Your asking Jim to show how exactly you look at him that makes him feel stupid makes me uneasy about your commitment to the group process.

Such statements were most often met with an apparent question along the lines of:

Makes you feel uneasy, how specifically?

I leave it to the reader to imagine how bizarre such sequences of exchanges could and, in fact, did become.

One unintended consequence of both Bandler and myself being subjected to the patterning of the T-Group was a growing friendship (based initially primarily on how amusing the activity seemed to us in the group).

All this was occurring inside of an extremely dynamic context – this was the era of drugs, sex, and rock 'n' roll (jazz, too); this was the era of the counterculture challenge to the Vietnam War, to racism, sexism, and damn near every other -ism we could identify (except, of course, unfortunately, Marxism as expressed in the Soviet Union and China). This was an era in which we actually had debates (primarily between PL (Progressive Labor – a movement *inspired* by the Chinese communist revolution) and the leftists following the Russian *revolutionary* model). The dispute was whether activists would best support and accelerate movement towards an American revolution by resisting the right-wing reactionary elements and with direct action in the streets (the Russian model as represented, for example, by SDS (Students for a Democratic Society), or to (apparently) join forces with and assist the more reactionary elements in modern US politics, thereby exacerbating the deteriorating political situation and accelerating the arrival of the coming revolution (the PL position).

About the same time (1971/72), my first year as a professor at Kresge, I met Frank Pucelik. The connection to Frank was immediate. I had been in an elite military group (10th Special Forces Group, Bad Toelz, Germany) and I'd had the pleasure of working under conditions of extreme pressure and danger with guys like Frank. I immediately recognized him as a brother, someone in whose hands I was willing to place my life – a man who could be trusted. This personal connection was easy and immediate – it has remained that way ever since.

This period was transformational for me. It is amusing, in retrospect, to muse about the way that I employed the same tactics and strategies that I had acquired in Special Forces and related organizations that I ran missions for, to the issue of challenging the Vietnam War and working to stop what I perceived to be an unjust and inappropriate military action. It represented the opposite to the commitment I had made and acted on in running Special Forces and related operations: the principle being that the people have the right to determine their own forms of local governance and the right to freely choose their leaders and insist on accountability by those leaders. This was the personal and political commitment that I had made, and operated congruently with, during my years in the 10th Special Forces Group in Europe and other parts of the world. From my perspective, Vietnam was itself a violation of this principle of local determination. I refused to accept this military action as legitimate and appropriate and focused my competencies on challenging it and winding it down as quickly as possible.

Frank, of course, had seen serious action in Vietnam – it is interesting that the connection between Frank and me was so strong that even though we had quite different views on the war in Vietnam, it never constituted a barrier between us. Perhaps this is one of the simplest and clearest examples of the primacy of process over content which would later become one of defining characteristics that distinguishes NLP patterning from the other forms of patterning purporting to work in the context of change.

Frank, Richard, and I came together easily and the collaboration was natural: Frank had a quite similar response to the patterning of the T-Group (he was a member of a parallel T-Group in Kresge College) and we would regale one another with the strange and bizarre tales of T-Groupings.

As an example of the style with which the three of us would operate and often collaborate, consider this description from *Whispering in the Wind*:

> Frank Pucelik (the third man in the initial modeling and testing of patterning in NLP) was offering a demonstration before

some hundred or so people at a seminar in San Jose in the mid 70s during which he was demonstrating some anchoring format: probably, phobia cures. He was approached by several people at the end of the demonstration and asked,

How can you take such risks?

In genuine bewilderment, Frank asked what risk they were talking about. They went on to explain that to do such a demonstration in front of all these people was to take a nearly (for them) unacceptable risk.

At the end of their explanation, Frank was speechless and simply walked away. For Frank (given his Vietnam experiences) and equally for Bandler and me with our own back stories of risk taking, such challenges were simply a welcome and required opportunity to test ourselves and learn what we could accomplish in various contexts. Frank was still incredulous about the question the participants had asked him when he returned from his work and recounted his experience to me.[2]

We also engaged in such socially progressive actions such as spray painting the windows of the parking meters on campus to defeat the attempt to charge money for and control the parking: one of the milder forms of irresponsibility we carried out.

The playing field was large and full of strange and fascinating curiosities and possibilities and there was little that we were unwilling to approach through straight trial and error. The three of us confronted the world about us in a manner and with a style perfectly consistent with the philosophy of Hans Vaihinger.

Bandler introduced Vaihinger's work into the mix and while it played little part in shifting our actions at the time, it was a fine explication of what each of the three of us had practiced unconsciously and intuitively for years. It became an explicit platform for continuing in our pursuit of patterning that would ultimately become NLP. It was an open ticket to ride and we continued to do so, delighted to explore as living embodiments of Vaihinger's bold philosophy.

Prior to my connecting with either Frank or Richard, they had formed a Gestalt therapy group and ran groups of people (mostly students from UCSC but some members of the Santa Cruz community as well) through the Gestalt process as presented by Fritz Perls, the creator of this particular change method. The specifics of my becoming involved with Frank and Richard have already been described in *Whispering in the Wind*:

> It was a spring evening in the early 70s when an unexpected knock at the door pulled me (JG) reluctantly from my deep focus, reading a text (*Monopoly Capitalism*) which I was devouring in an attempt to deepen my understanding of economics – preparation for a course I was scheduled to teach in economics beginning in a few months for Kresge College at the University of California, Santa Cruz. Opening the door, I was surprised to find a fourth year undergraduate student, Richard Bandler, standing there. I invited him in, wondering mildly what the occasion for his visit could possibly be. It was not unusual for a student to drop by, as the newly founded college (Kresge) had instituted an integrated living/learning environment shared (in principle, at any rate) by students, faculty and staff.

> I had met Richard some months before on the occasion of his having been assigned to be a member of a T-Group (the so-called encounter group, a contribution in semantic ill-formedness by the people from National Training Lab (one of the original American sources for group therapy) for which I had the responsibility of serving as the faculty sponsor. The rapport between the two of us was immediate – each of us sensed quickly that there were a number of shared patterns between us – not least of which was a profound commitment to do nearly anything rather than be bored.

> Up to this point, our experiences together had been relatively limited and while thoroughly enjoyable, had given no indication of the highly productive, even revolutionary collaboration that would ensue. These experiences consisted primarily of activities such as painting the windows on parking meters to make it impossible for the University of California campus police to issue parking tickets; playing strange mind games in the required T-Group sessions; getting our fair share of abuse

at anti-Vietnam war rallies and sampling local Santa Cruz herbs.

On this particular evening, Richard's conversation moved rapidly from one topic to another in his usual amusing and entertaining way without revealing what, if any, specific purpose the visit entailed. After we had passed a pleasurable 20 minutes bantering together, he abruptly rose to his feet and made to leave. I accompanied him to door where we both paused, and with an uncharacteristic show of self-consciousness, he hesitated and then asked me if I would like to go with him. He went on to explain that he and a friend, Frank Pucelik, were doing a Gestalt therapy group nearby and that he was inviting me to come along. He said that it might be interesting to me to observe the group. I was genuinely amused by the invitation. I thanked him and explained that I had no intention in participating in any therapy of any kind. Further, although I had absolutely no experience in these matters, it was clear to me that one of the primary consequences of therapy was to adjust people to the social, economic and political context in which they found themselves exploited; and further as a committed revolutionary it was obvious to me that such activity (therapy) was highly counter-revolutionary. I explained to him patiently that the adjustment of people to an inequitable system had the negative effect of reducing revolutionary potential.

This ritual – a visit ending in an invitation to accompany him to the Gestalt therapy group – was repeated several times over the next few weeks until finally, I asked what it was that he thought my visiting the Gestalt group would accomplish. Haltingly, he explained that he had listened to me describe in detail, at great length and with precision, the processes of natural language (my doctorate is in transformational linguistics) and its relationship to the structure of the human mind. He described his frustration in the Gestalt group work saying that he and Frank were excellent Gestalt therapists; but their actual goal was to teach others to do what they did, and in this portion of their endeavor, they had thus far failed miserably. Richard stated that he had hoped that I might be able to figure out how to describe what they were doing so that they might accomplish their goal of training others in the art form of Gestalt.

With the challenge thus revealed, I found myself curious enough to accompany him to the Gestalt group he and Frank were doing. A single evening was more than adequate to capture my attention. It was clear to me that each of them, Frank and Richard, while engaging in strange and (to me) hilarious behaviors were superb at assisting others in making rapid and, as far as I could determine, profound personal changes, in which their clients succeeded in liberating themselves from the limitations they had imposed upon themselves. Their work was excellent. Indeed when I later compared their work with Perls' work presented on film and audio tape, I found Pucelik and Bandler's work to be significantly more effective than the model (Perls) they were imitating.[3]

We resolved to collaborate – both Frank and Richard expressed their strong desire to work out how to pass their skill sets (Gestalt) on to their students and this was to be the explicit goal of my collaboration with them. I was fascinated by the work that they were doing and recognized that portions of their work covered parts of what was missing in the processes used by radical left groups (the anti-Vietnam War movement, for example) in the expression of their political and personal actions. Most tellingly, this occurred within a lack of ability to develop and exercise choice in how they approached making the differences that they espoused.

It was always the system that required, necessitated, left no choice about how to behave; little responsibility was assigned to what people actually did and did not do in addressing the issues of the day. They were not CHOOSING to challenge the Vietnam War (or the more recent wars of choice that the US government has waged) or challenge the rampant sexism or racism that crowded in to close down choices and movement towards something closer to exercising choice. They HAD TO do these things – choice in the matter was bourgeoisie, a betrayal of the coming revolution.

My perception was (and continues to be) that anyone promoting a mission/cause, and who displays an utter lack of choice about their pursuit, immediately disqualifies themselves as a representative of anything I would subscribe to.

Rarely in my life had I witnessed people so driven by what they perceived to be their mission and simultaneously so unable or unwilling to exercise personal choice in their own lives. In particular, they found it nearly impossible to promote in others, as well as in themselves, the acceptance of the responsibility for the consequences of their actions. In these left-wing groups (SDS, Tuesday the Ninth, etc.), the flurry of modal operators (applied both to their personal and their political actions) made seeing clearly and moving effectively to where we wished to go, and what possible paths might serve to guide us there, very difficult.

I recognized that the skill sets that I witnessed Pucelik and Bandler employing had significant consequences for creating choice where choice had previously been unavailable or not exercised. This struck me as an excellent strategy to pursue and a welcome clean-up of some of the left-wing group practices that made them so grim and humorless. I was determined to explore these new skill sets and determine how they might well serve the same intentions that had I carried through my Special Forces experiences as well as the radical left-wing politics and political actions that had characterized my public actions during graduate school (University of California at San Diego) and first years as a professor at UCSC.

In this quite precise sense, I viewed the Meta Model as a bullshit detector. Anyone who has employed the Meta Model to determine whether someone knows what they are talking about can verify that within the first half a dozen specifier challenges iteratively to some topic will reveal the limits (or not) of the knowledge base of the person speaking about that topic. This tool, and especially the challenges to modal operators, operate as a breath of fresh air in highly inflated and emotional displays of belief systems, whether based in fundamentalist Christian/Muslim/Jewish or far-left or right-wing politicos – and therefore function as a healthy antidote to these world-encompassing belief systems.

These explorations (the Meta Model, representational systems, anchoring – the basic patterning of the Classic Code) represented for me an extended exercise in bringing my own behavior into alignment with what I was promoting in the world – a movement towards congruity.

The initial avowed goal was the extraction of patterning from the geniuses of late 20th century agents of change in order to create choice for individuals and small groups seeking liberation from their self-imposed limitations. But the track I was running behind this activity was a challenge to the processes by which ideologies were promoted in the world and the congruity (or lack thereof) of the people promoting these ideologies – a calibration exercise that continues to be a reflex in my wanderings about the world even today.

The collaboration with Frank and Richard was superb. Some years ago I wrote the following piece (included in *Whispering in the Wind*) partially in response to some nonsense being promoted along the lines that Richard Bandler was the sole and unique creator of NLP. I reproduce it here for the reader's review – the only amendment to what I wrote then and what I offer here is that the piece was originally written in response to the claim that Bandler was the creator of NLP and therefore failed to accord either myself or Frank Pucelik the appropriate position in the history of the creation and testing of what has come to be known as NLP. I correct the omission below in this amended statement:

Personal Statement by John Grinder

The creation of Neuro-Linguistic Programming (NLP) represents a superb example of collaboration. I could not have created NLP by myself, nor do I believe could have Frank Pucelik or Richard Bandler. Each of us brought specific talents and capabilities to the endeavor, not the least of which was the ability to work as a team. For some six years, we worked side by side as researchers, provoking, supporting, challenging and amusing one another in our efforts to mode and codify patterns of excellence in terms that made it available to the rest of the world.

Both as individuals and as a team, we followed the strategy of "Acting As If" impeccably and offered one another continuing challenges, stimulation and feedback as we developed the representations of the patterns that presently define the Classic Code in NLP. While it may be possible to distinguish partially the initial strengths of each of us, there was a deep cross-training that occurred in our collaboration through which we learned from one another how to carry out the extraordinary feats that have set the historical standard for NLP practice – both in the activity of modeling as well as in its applications. I therefore recognize with pleasure the essential historical contributions by Frank Pucelik and Richard Bandler as the co-creators alongside myself of the technology of NLP, and I specifically offer them even now my congratulations and best wishes in their continuing work, even as it deviates significantly from my own present work.

Those readers in search of a model of excellent collaboration will do well to step past the present state of affairs among the three of us and focus on the work accomplished by the three of us in the period 1972–1975; followed by the work of Bandler and I through 1979.

The descriptions that follow are designed to offer the attentive reader access to portions of the events involved in the creation of the field of that Bandler and I named NLP with special emphasis on the variables that defined the contexts and processes of discovery. Naturally the following description is uniquely from my point of view as one of the three co-creators of NLP.[4]

This is, to me, an important statement and one I freely make. Let me hasten to add to this statement a comment about the actual processes that informed the endeavor. There is a strong tendency (hindsight is easy) in presenting important events or sequences of events from the past in a way that creates the impression of a rational and well-thought out program of research and investigation – smoothing over the rough spots in the journey and focusing on the ultimate effectiveness of the product.

Let me reassure you that nothing like this actually occurred in the creation of NLP. Perhaps the easiest way to offer you a taste of how that enterprise actually played itself out is for me to simply quote a statement (again from *Whispering in the Wind*) that captures for me the flavor of our experiences together as a three-person team:

You will not find in such accounts [textbook reconstructions of the discoveries in various sciences] recognition of the role of chance, the random actions, the unconscious cunning, the outrageous irreverence necessary to shatter old habits of perception, the awkward first steps, the unjustified and congruent acting As If, the bemused recognition of a wholly flawed hypothesis, the long, deep, quiet, desperate nights, the fortuitous personal friendships and connections, the quickening that accompanies powerful and wholly unexpected consequences, the camaraderie that holds the enterprise together, the dead ends, the leaps of logic, the irrational and unjustified assumptions, the accidents of personal history and not least, the gifts and accidents of unconscious metaphor – all of which in the end allow you to stumble over the distinctions that then become the fundamental variables of the new discipline as in the end against all odds, it does succeed.[5]

Yeah, that's pretty much the way it unfolded. From speaking to other people who have been present at and/or participated in the creation of other new disciplines, it seems quite a common description of such adventures. This is in sharp contrast to what you will read in the approved academic representations of such important advances. Such publications promote a set of images and descriptions that were certainly no part of my personal experience, nor did I note either Frank or Richard carefully laying out such research programs and pursuing them.

And so the dance began. It took many forms. At times, we insisted on not repeating anything that we had ever done before; at other points (sometimes for months on end), we would limit ourselves to a couple of patterns (e.g., rapport plus Meta Model) to determine in a more refined manner what actual consequences the application of those patterns alone were.

We threw wild Christmas parties where the nominalization *gift* was returned to its full verb form *to give* and the potential recipient of this *giving* process had to decide whether to accept the experience on offer or not (without knowledge of what it was) – what we were prepared to give them as their Christmas present.

We would set people up to act with issues that matched the issues actually carried by the agent of change, and watch and listen with fascination to the interactions. We formed a group called the "whiz kids" – a side group that contained the crème de la crème of the people who had assembled themselves around us. Here, we simply did strange and weird things – the restoration of visual acuity or the sensing colors through the skin without visual access, and so on.

The world turned around us and the group that we had assembled (there were too many research and investigative groups to even keep track of) and several times each week, the three of us would gather together with our various groups to figure out answers to that constantly re-occurring question:

I wonder what would happen if I did X?

Where X could range from anything, such as the application of a new finding reported in one of the journals of neurological research, or a possibility suggested by an image that had occurred in a strange dream, or a metaphor that had spontaneously surfaced whilst working with a client, all the way to an intuition that erupted during a piece of change work – even a purely syntactic exercise in which we took the odd numbered elements in some putative pattern we had coded and tested successfully and moved these odd numbered elements in the format (1, 3, 5, etc.) over the even numbered elements and applied the resultant "pattern" to discover what the hell did happen.

But the terrible trio was coming apart. Frank was less and less frequently present at the weekly gatherings and had opened other application areas – for example, he alertly seized upon the opportunity afforded by access to the student counseling center as a worthy opportunity to test and refine the patterning that we were generating. He developed and cultivated a separate group – the Meta Group (initially in Santa Cruz and subsequently in Oklahoma and San Diego) – with both overlapping and non-overlapping members relative to what Bandler and I were doing in Santa Cruz.

Until I read it in Frank's account (see Chapter 1), I was unaware of the meeting between Pucelik and Bandler that apparently initiated the break-up of the team of the three of us who had been instrumental in the creation of NLP.

It was about this time that the encounter (described in *Whispering in the Wind*) between Bateson, myself, and Bandler occurred – the incident that sent Bandler and me off on the momentous modeling experience of assimilating, mastering, coding, and testing the enormously effective hypnotic patterning of Dr. Erickson:

> In 1975, Bandler, Grinder and Bateson all had their individual residences at 1000 Alba Road, Ben Lomond, California.
>
> The manuscript version of what would be published that year as *The Structure of Magic, Volume I* had been circulating among an excited group of people who had collected around the three men, Bandler, Grinder and Pucelik and who were assisting them with their research. Bateson had been provided with a copy of this manuscript some weeks earlier – Grinder and Bandler hoped that he would recognize what they had attempted to accomplish. Their hopes were more than met when they were invited by phone to come over to Bateson's place where they were treated to an intellectual feast: a remarkable and stimulating discussion with Bateson that lasted hours.
>
> Gregory had a long wooden table in his dining room – one worthy of a mythical Norseman, rough-hewn of dark wood and sturdy. Gregory pointedly positioned himself at one end of this monstrosity as if conducting court and indicated to the two younger men to seat themselves immediately at his right (Grinder) and left (Bandler). The conversation that ensued was enchanting.
>
> It is noteworthy (and it seemed so even at the time to Grinder and Bandler) that Bateson's command of the patterning worked up in the manuscript was so complete that little time was spent on actually discussing it.
>
> Gregory offered a soliloquy, in large part reminiscences of the research he and his colleagues at MRI had conducted and then

a strangely semi-apologetic rendering of (as he later clearly stated in his Introduction to *The Structure of Magic*) how he and his associates could have missed what we had, in fact, discovered and coded in the book:

"How well the argument flowed from the linguistics, how confusing it had been to attempt what he had done starting with pathology and cultural patterns."

He graciously offered to write a Preface to the book and then, as if rousing himself from an old and repetitive dream no longer of relevance, he fixed each of us in turn with his deep intellectually unforgiving eyes glinting with curiosity and intelligence and said,

> "OK, boys, what you have done is very good, but I am certain that what's in *The Structure of Magic* happened some time ago – my question is what have you found since coding the Meta Model?"

We were enchanted – here was a man, easily recognizable as an intellectual giant, who understood well enough what we were about, to leap to the new sets of patterning that were obsessing us at the time.

Richard and I listened to his question in awe, looked at one another with perfect agreement, paused like cliff divers to mark the importance of that point of punctuation in experience before committing and then released a great wave of descriptions that flowed from us without effort.

Buoyant now, Gregory orchestrated us beautifully – he would sit listening intently to the two of us as we rushed forward into the patterning as if pursued. Sometimes one of us spoke, sometimes the other, sometimes both of us simultaneously as if attempting to fill his vast intelligence with our observations. He sat there between us, his eyes fixed at that special point above the horizon, processing thoroughly the reports of months of our work.

From time to time, he would freeze the cascade, breaking the spell, leaning back in his chair, dropping his gaze to point on the great table forward and to his left, shaping the question that would guide these two madmen into shallower water – the question that would complete the pattern that connects in his rich internal kingdom, assembled over 7 decades of participation with intelligence in the world about him, the answer he wanted to continue his incomprehensible process.

We were like two dogs, attempting to guide their master to where they believed he wanted to go, sometimes dashing on ahead, sometimes nipping at his heels, always attentive to his cues, always loyal to his intention.

The three of us arrived together then finally at the end of our long climb, exhausted and exhilarated. We sat back now, more thoughtful, no longer driven into the new, and presently curious about the now.

There was a new tone in his rich voice – one suggesting deeper emotions than thus far expressed. The sharp edge of his intelligence that had flashed brilliantly throughout the long climb was sheathed. No doubt, among the dozens of case studies, the life stories, each with its own compelling set of metaphors, something had stirred deep within him for the first time in a long time. He quietly recounted certain events from his youth, the loss of his dear brother John and of choices in Switzerland not pursued: all as if musing to himself, comfortable in our attentive, but passive presence. He worked it out finally then to his own requirements; and turned his attention once again to us.[6]

This incident – the one that sent Bandler and I off on a journey to master the patterning of Erickson through the technology of NLP modeling – curiously marks the closure of the original collaborative work done by Pucelik, Bandler, and myself – and, simultaneously, was a classic example of the graciousness of the original models for NLP patterning. This personal relationship between myself and Pucelik continues to this day – that of the one between Pucelik and Bandler much less so, nearly absent.

From my point of view, it is impossible to tease out the various individual contributions to the creation of NLP that occurred and were necessary parts of the enterprise coming together successfully. Yes, of course, we each had our special interests, intentions, back stories, and talents which contributed to what NLP is today. But of more importance, in my opinion, is the overlapping of events and the consistent and congruent commitment of each of the three of us to pushing the rapidly moving game now called NLP to its limits on every opportunity. I regard this collaboration as the essential component of the actual creation of the field of NLP – and to this effort, there were equally important contributions by each of the three of us to the creation of the original patterning which forms the basis of this field.

The game moved on. Bandler and I were anxious to test the modeled and coded patterning that we had extracted through the NLP modeling process to as many domains as we could gain access to. Two of my favorite examples are offered below as representative of this search for the edge of the effectiveness of the patterning: (1) the impossibles practice and (1) my work with Bandler at Napa State Mental Institution, in California.

The impossibles practice was a superb series of experiences for us in which we offered to any psychiatrist, therapist, counsellor, minister, social worker – whatever title these agents of change had selected for their work – the following arrangement. If you, in your role as an agent of change, have a client with whom you have done your best to assist in developing and exercising choices and have thus far failed to succeed in making this happen, we invite you bring your client to us. You will be invited to sit in on the session or sessions to observe the patterning that we use and for taking responsibility for the follow-up with this, your client, after we have succeeded with that client.

We offered follow-up support if necessary. The intention was for us to gain access to the more challenging cases that were being presented to the various professionals in the San Francisco Bay area in order for us to discover the limits of the effectiveness of the patterning we had modeled, coded, and were testing. On the professionals' side, it was an opportunity to learn additional patterning that they could then use with other clients, as well as a clear demonstration of how to succeed in creating a context in which their present clients could achieve their aims.

This stream of clients was a wonderful gift to us! We had guessed that this class of client would be most challenging (we hoped this would be true). Contrary to these expectations, we were treated to a series of wonderfully bizarre and wild presenting problems – many that we had not yet been exposed to. Surprisingly, we were faster and more effective (as measured by the time and effort on our part) with them than with the "average" off-the-street client! The difference – something that we worked out inductively through our encounters with this stream of clients – was that these were TRAINED clients. They had typically been to see a series of professionals and while they had not yet developed the choices that they were pursuing, they had been sorted and re-sorted by these professionals into whatever classificatory schemas these professionals were trained to stuff their clients into. So, these were already well-sorted clients. However, many of the initial sorting techniques of that era (see especially section II of *The Structure of Magic, Volume II*)[7] were available to us but unnecessary as these clients were already decomposed into *parts* induced by the preferred classificatory pigeon-holes that were the favorites of the professionals that they had met and defeated. I use the term *defeated* only in the sense that these clients had more ways to remain the same when challenged by the professionals that they had encountered, than the professionals that they had seen had in inducing change.

Our experience with the impossibles is a clear example of the Law of Requisite Variety (see W. Ross Ashby's *An Introduction to Cybernetics* for an explication[8]). We were untrained agents of change in any formal sense; we obviously had our chops and riffs – namely the patterns modeled and coded, plus the wild card – requisite variety. However, we were outlaws and not constrained by the conventional boundary conditions accepted by trained professionals. We did what worked without overly concerning ourselves with any theory or investigations into the history of the individual (the no-archeology condition) in front of us. It was an existential encounter and we were going to succeed – the only question was how long it would take us to find the key to unlocking the particular cage into which this client had locked him or herself. The double teaming of these clients – typically, either an overload approach (like the double induction) with both of us operating simultaneously and overwhelming the client with far more inputs that they could manage to process, or one of us in the active role of change agent (what would later be developed as first position) and the other scanning (from what later would become a clean third position) for what was missing or alternative paths to the set of choices that the client was seeking.

I raise a warning flag at this point. I stated above that we were surprised to find the impossibles simpler to work with than the off-the-street clients more common in therapeutic practice. I then went on to propose what I regard as the difference that, in this case, made the difference between the impossibles and the more common group of clients – namely, the simple consequence of the fact that the impossibles had seen a number of professionals who had *sorted* these clients into *parts* induced by their preferred taxonomy, pigeonholes, and categories that were the favorite of the professionals that they had met. This is the standard practice in medicine and is mirrored to a significant degree in psychiatry and psychotherapy – it is the practice of diagnosis.

Now, in an ideal world where diagnostic categories are well-defined and replicable, the practice of diagnosis would take advantage of the accumulated observations of experienced and (hopefully) successful clinicians. In a world such as the one we confront at present as agents of change, where the diagnostic categories are not well-defined but rather depend on the individual interpretations of individual practitioners with all their inherent biases and differences – and further, are not based on the observations of successful clinicians but rather historical population samples – diagnosis becomes a dangerous endeavor. I pose a simple question.

> What possible positive intention is served by the application of ill-defined diagnostic categories requiring interpretation by individual clinicians and based on practices that are only partially effective?

A key piece of the resolution to this puzzle is the analytic methodology applied in the construction of these content categories: the diagnostic categories in play at the moment (including so-called evidence-based medical procedures) are statements about populations of patients/clients. But the physician, the psychiatrist, and the psychotherapist NEVER treat populations of patients/clients – they are faced with a real human being, a person who turns to them for help in a time of crisis. Herein lies the problem with the diagnostic practice of that time (and little has changed since).

The diagnostic categories create an illusion of certainty. The agent of change – the physician/psychiatrist/psychotherapist – is faced with a series of decisions that will ultimately strongly impact the life course of the human being in front of them. There are two possibilities: use the diagnostic category that the symptoms presented by the patient/client (note, a highly interpretive process) most fits and then apply the treatment that has been found to be most successful for the largest number of people in the historical sample; or use the tacit knowledge of the clinician. Unfortunately, the tacit knowledge of different clinicians varies significantly. If the clinician follows the standard practice, s/he is treating the individual as a population. If the clinician follows her or his tacit knowledge, the effectiveness of what occurs is dependent on the tacit clinical skill of the particular clinician.

Look, the diagnostic category is obviously the best guess for how to diagnose and treat the population of people sampled with the symptoms presented. The individual patient/client is a member of the population sampled. This, however, does NOT imply that the best diagnosis and treatment for the population is the best treatment for this particular member of that population!

Unfortunately, under pressure to perform, and with litigation promoting actions by the professional that are inherently conservative, the result is that once the diagnosis has been arrived at, it takes a whole lot of counter-indications (and some ingenuity and courage) for the professional to apply his or her tacit knowledge, especially as this knowledge cannot, by definition, be explicated. The result is that the professionals easily slip into treating the diagnostic category rather than the individual right in front of them. A further analysis of this dilemma is outside the scope of this work.

Consider the above as a frame for the issue of parts as used in the explanation of how it was that the impossibles were simpler to work with. One of the essential defining characteristics of the NLP that I am describing in this book has been from its inception (and still is) has been the rejection of the imposition of content and an unwavering focus on process patterning. Many examples are offered throughout this book.

The critique I offer above (and the stories I have recounted) clearly address content impositions – in particular a finger I am pointing, at the diagnostic categories that are ill-defined, that require interpretation by the professional clinician, and that are based on samples of populations. What then is the difference between this class of content impositions and the parts that are used in NLP?

The preferred method for the development and use of parts in NLP is through intensive definitions. There are two possibilities for defining a set or class: extensive definitions and intensive definitions. An extensive definition for any arbitrary set is a listing of the members of that set. For example, using an extensive definition, I can define the set of Arabian horses that I own simply by listing them: *Zebula*, *Magic*, *Dakota*, *Ben*, and *Chase*. Or I may choose to use the alternative method for defining that same set: namely, all the horses that reside at my ranch in Bonny Doon.

Both of these methods yield the same set. A moment of reflection reveals that intensive definitions (also known as set membership rules) are the only choice available if the set involved is an infinite set. Similar considerations will lead to the recognition that if the set is finite but very large and/or the members have not been explicated, then the intensive definition is the choice to be exercised.

The Betty Erickson technique for self-hypnosis is a well-known format for people who have studied NLP – one that offers a concrete practical example of the use of intensive definitions.

When using this (or any) technique for self-induction of an altered state, it is prudent prior to beginning the exercise to both set a time for reorientation from the altered state and to make arrangements for protection when using altered states. The first is as simple as explicating in your communications with the unconscious processes when (the number of minutes) you wish to reorient from the altered state. The second task is more complex and provides a good example of the practical use of intensive definitions.

Note, that in attending to this second task, the person using a self-induction could attempt to use an extensive definition; that is, listing the conditions under which s/he wants to reorient from the altered state. Such a list might look something like:

The smell of smoke

Screams

The sound of sirens outside the building where you are located

The sound of breaking glass

However, the task would be both tedious and you would never be quite certain that you had listed all the appropriate conditions. More effective for this task is the deployment of an intensive definition – something like:

... anything that calls into question my safety and well-being

Now, with this linguistic tool in hand, consider its application to the notion of *parts* – here are several examples:

The part responsible for your health

The part that knows how to cure the condition you are seeking relief from

The part who can best support you in your presentation on Friday

It is clear that these *parts* do not in any serious sense have any permanent (ontological) status – they are temporary stories we tell ourselves.

When effectively arranged, they are temporary impositions of language on experience for the purposes of achieving leverage – leverage that can then be used for the purposes of creating change; a purely Archimedean leverage point, as ethereal as the infinite lever and the imaginary fulcrum.

The notion of *parts* is an imposition by the left brain onto the flow of experience. This is equally true of the terms *conscious* and *unconscious* and any number of other distinctions of the same logical type made in NLP. And, like all these impositions, they are ultimately fictions; simple punctuations on direct experience, segmentations of an essentially analogue process, pieces of an integral whole, snipped out, isolated and used as a leverage point to accomplish some task. These are the work of the left hemisphere.

As with all such impositions, the notion of *parts* is useful *until you start to believe in them*. And then, the game is over, and you will fall into acting continuously as if they are actual distinctions in experience, rather than temporary distinctions for leverage in the change process. The world of human experience, relationships, and activities is far richer and fundamentally more unpredictable than we will ever capture with language impositions.

Yes, of course, use these punctuations on experience as leverage points, and when you have achieved what you set out to accomplish, throw them back into the vortex of ongoing experience. I recall for the reader's consideration, Gilligan's remarks about fixed beliefs and the deadly consequences of believing in them as opposed to a cyclic movement into what he calls the *creative unconscious*.

Returning now to the subject of the impossibles practice, I describe two examples to give the readers some insight into this class of pattern testing: one simple and short; the other simple and more extended.

> A psychiatrist in the Bay area called and made an appointment for himself and a female client in her forties. The psychiatrist had, with great effort and dedication, succeeded in inducing changes in the behavior of the institutionalized patient such

that the patient was judged functional and ready to return to her normal life – married, no children, a teacher. She seemed stable (unverified report by the people around her, including her psychiatrist).

However, in the previous months, when she returned to her home and usual activities – for something like a month or so, all went well (or at least well enough that no one complained) but then there was the return of certain bizarre patterns of behavior, perhaps the most distinctive of which was the kinesthetic hallucination she experienced of insects crawling all over her body – the report of which was most alarming and upsetting to those around her. She would be readmitted. This cycle had already occurred three times when we got involved.

When we asked the psychiatrist what it was that he was pursuing – what he needed to finish the job by getting the patient to make and hold a viable transition back to "normal" life, he explained that he was baffled by what it was that reactivated the same bizarre behaviors, after about a month, that got her locked up.

After this short interview with the psychiatrist to ensure that we appreciated what he wanted, we sat down with the woman and established, with humor and irreverence, a fine relationship of rapport – she accepted us. To our amazement, within a few minutes of achieving this significant relationship of rapport with her, in a conversation about how she managed to create this experience of insects crawling all over her, she leaned forward and in a conspiratorial semi-whisper, simply said: "You know, my husband really bugs me!"

Game over!

The second case I want to mention was somewhat more demanding in terms of time. A team including a psychiatrist, the patient, the patient's husband, and the pastor of the church that she and her husband attended arrived for an appointment with Bandler and me.

The woman was in her mid-forties. She was Dutch and had been living in the United States for some 20-plus years, no children. She was a large, very strong woman, with a sunny disposition and full of humor. She had a strong commitment to her religious practices and was devout in her beliefs; a thoroughly enjoyable person.

In a private pre-meeting, the psychiatrist and the pastor had insisted on explaining the backstory. It seemed that some months before our meeting together, the woman acting as the patient had developed a bizarre set of behaviors when she was out in public. When shopping, traveling on the bus to meet friends, or conducting business for herself and her husband, various men (the bus driver, the clerk at the grocery store, some passing male on the street, etc.) would proposition her, proposing various sexual activities. She explained with congruency that she had done nothing to warrant such approaches; her dress style was appropriately modest for a woman in public; her behavior was in no way flirtatious or inappropriate; she offered no signals of interest and she was deeply upset and disturbed by all this unwanted attention.

She stated with genuine conviction, as a "clean" woman, that some of what was said to her on these occasions she didn't even understand. They were not words that even existed in her vocabulary. As any proper decent woman would do, when so accosted, she defended her person and reputation, in most cases by slapping the offending male involved. Given this woman's strength, this was a non-trivial event for the men involved.

The difficulty was, of course, that none of these males were actually saying or doing anything inappropriate – she was projecting a voice from within onto these hapless men and reacting as if they had actually said such things to her. The males, quite understandably, found this objectionable. In several cases, the police had been called and she had missed appearing in court only by the graciousness of the men involved. Once the situation was explained to these men, and an apology (begrudgingly) was offered by her they did drop the charges that were pending. Obviously, this pattern had to change.

We verified all this with the woman directly while securing a profound rapport relationship with her. Bandler and I chose to close this first encounter at this point – rapport was deep, we had the full attention of the client's unconscious, and the case was interesting enough that we wished to consider how we would proceed. Of even more interest to us at the time was our independent calibrations with respect to the husband – he twitched every single time the descriptions of what had occurred reached the point where she described striking one of the men involved in these incidents. We were certain that there was a connection.

We sent the party out, with the exception of the husband, asking him to remain behind for a moment. Once we were alone, we stood in front of him, regarding him with what might be described as an incredulous fixed stare and with little sympathy.

A long, couple of minutes passed in this frozen tableau of the three of us, until, with a partially inhibited sob, high muscular tension, a ragged breathing pattern, and the clenching and unclenching of his fists, the husband confessed that he'd had an affair with a woman some 10 years previously, of which he claimed his wife knew nothing about. He hastened to further confess his guilt and took full responsibility for his ill-advised transgression (he himself was quite religious). He reassured us that the affair was well in the past and nor had there been any other such episodes. He stated that he had learned his lesson and was committed to remaining faithful to his wife. He congruently said that he was quite fearful of the reaction of his wife if she were to discover this. The party was invited to return later in the week for a session. With our usual arrogance, we announced it as the final session.

The second session was attended by the psychiatrist (who we had in the meantime briefed about the information that we had uncovered), the husband, who attended very closely to what we were doing with a look of fear of a possible disclosure spread across his face, and the patient herself. The pastor did not attend: probably a good idea given what occurred next.

The session itself was quite short in duration. About 10–12 minutes into the session, and without any obvious external cue or stimulus, I suddenly rose to my feet, standing now very close to the woman, staring fixedly past her at a point roughly where the wall and ceiling met with my hands extended, palms upward, and in a deep bass tone (my channeling voice, so to speak, quite unlike my usual speaking voice), made something like the following declaration:

> *You have been wronged and your anger is righteous. The feelings you have are a healthy and natural response to your being wronged – accept them and make them work for you to restore peace.*
>
> *I SAY UNTO YOU, each and every night until this is completed, you will wreak vengeance on the appropriate offending part ... in dreams ... in which you extract every ounce of rage within you and express it by taking full and deep revenge on the guilty party until it is satisfied and all traces of the past have faded into a soft mist moving slowly and inexorably into the dark, never to be felt, seen, or heard again.*

This set of instructions were repeated a number of times in various ways with a sonorous otherworldly delivery until I was satisfied that she had gotten them. As I was *channeling*, I was, of course, acutely aware in my peripheral vision of the physiological responses that the woman was making to this extraordinary behavior and the declaration I was offering. All the signals were *go* and I went on until I was satisfied that the message had been assimilated and a state of calmness seemed to descend on the woman. The results were positive and immediate, and a phone call a month later indicated that the vengeful dreams themselves were fading.

As the reader may well imagine, Bandler and I anticipated with deep curiosity what strange and unusual challenge the next "impossible" would bring us.

It was around this same period that Bandler and I took a contract with the professional staff at Napa State Mental Institution. Our contract called for us to train the professional medical staff – physicians, psychiatrists, nurses, ward personnel – in the NLP patterning of the era (largely the Classic Code with pieces of Ericksonian patterning layered in). Our contact was one of the resident psychiatrists, a gentleman named Peter, who was fascinated by the patterning – especially the Erickson's hypnotic patterning.

Sensing an unprecedented opportunity, we negotiated the contract with Peter for a favorable fee, adding to it a clause that gave us unlimited (within operating hours) access to the chronics on the back wards. Although we had had clients who were officially diagnosed with various titles from the official handbook of psychiatric maladies (the DSM-IV-TR or *Diagnostic and Statistical Manual of Mental Disorders*), we had as yet not gained access to the chronics, stacked in the back wards and largely on a maintenance schedule of medications that guaranteed their docility and ease of ward management (think of *One Flew Over the Cuckoo's Nest*).

We would spend some four hours of each visit training the staff, and then we would roam about the back wards, throwing parties for the inmates, creating games to play with them, consulting them about aspects of curious cases, and, most of all, testing the effectiveness of the patterning we had in this context and with this class of clients.

I remember fighting my way out of one of the back wards after I had encountered a man who *confessed* (compulsively to anyone who showed the least amount of interest) to murdering his family (it turned out that the family was still alive) and who spent the majority of his *waking* experience looking at the bodies of his family floating in the air above whoever was attempting to speak to him. The fighting-my-way-out-of-the-ward comment was the consequence of an *intervention* I made with this guy.

I had noted where he had placed the internally generated visual images of each of the members of his *murdered* family in space, using the usual above-the-horizon dilated pupils gaze associated with visual accessing. Since I was wearing a top hat (I can't go to a party, even a back ward party, without dressing properly), I would reach up and grab the image from its position above me, naming the family member floating there as I did so, and stuff it into my top hat – quickly replacing my hat on my head to prevent any of the captured images from escaping. These actions, in addition to being highly unconventional, greatly agitated the patient in question and he attempted to prevent me from leaving with *his images*.

A coordination with a professional staff member led to a favorable outcome, as the patient, now devoid of the historical images, had to develop entirely new images. Under the direction of the professional, he managed to develop a set of images that allowed him to reorganize and move strongly towards classes of behavior more acceptable to the outside world. News of our ward parties spread rapidly through the informal network of communication among the patients and our ward events were well attended.

Perhaps the most unexpected consequences of these activities was a series of visits from escapees: people who we had either had contact with over the several months of our visits to Napa or who had gotten word of our activities and results at Napa from other patients interned there. These individuals succeeded in making their way out of Napa and showed up at 1000 Alba Road, where Bandler, Bateson, and I had our homes at the time.

These *visitors* were most satisfying to work with and typically made rapid changes through a series of tasks that Bandler and I gave them. They then disappeared into the general population, functioning well enough to be acceptable to (or at least, indistinguishable from) those around them.

This activity – the testing of patterning – in multiple contexts, with multiple classes of clients, consumed a huge amount of our attention and time. We were most curious about whether the patterns we had modeled and coded through the NLP modeling processes were limited to the initial context in which they had occurred. We were well aware of the difficulties of working out which pattern had which consequences during the testing.

We suspected (correctly, in hindsight) that a non-trivial part of our success with clients could well be attributed not solely to the patterning that we ran, but also to the simultaneous use of patterning of which we were personally entirely unaware. We attempted to address this flaw in our testing protocols by using our students and participants as filters between us and the clients we *worked with*, in various training events.

As mentioned in some of the articles in this volume, we would send two students into a room that contained a client with explicit constraints on what they were allowed to do; that is, which specific patterns (in addition to rapport) they were to run. One of them was charged with the task of running the pattern in question and collecting observations about the responses of the client; the other was to observe and ensure that our instructions were followed and as back-up if the student charged with running the pattern faltered.

Sometimes we gave additional tasks to the observer to create certain classes of interruptions without their partner being privy to these additional tasks until they were directly confronted with them. By absenting ourselves from any direct contact with the client and insisting that the students representing us restrict their activities to the named pattern(s), we hoped to reduce the influence that we suspected (correctly) we were exercising without an explicit conscious understanding of what we were doing. This proved useful in ferreting out what the consequences of the application of specific patterns were.

Somewhere in this mix, we had a most amusing adventure involving some of the original researchers at the Mental Research Institute (MRI) of Palo Alto, the group that Bateson had run for some years. It was the apparent birthplace of the double bind theory of schizophrenia. We received a call from Paul Watzlawick, then head of MRI. He had gotten wind of something out of the ordinary with which we were associated – either through comments by Bateson himself (or possibly by Jay Haley).[9]

Watzlawick then invited us to come to MRI the following week with the intention of demonstrating some of the patterning that we were about to publish. All this was quite cordial although both Bandler and I marked a throw-away question at the end of the phone call. Watzlawick asked whether we were licensed psychotherapists – to which, we both immediately responded, "No, thank you very much!"

We arrived at MRI, interested in how these learned people (some of the originals from the MRI group) would respond to the patterning that we had to offer. Our curiosity was intense as we had had two radically divergent opinions, one from the original team leader, Bateson, and one from a member of the MRI research group, Haley. And these opinions could NOT have been further apart in their response to the manuscript.

Watzlawick met us at the door and kindly ushered us into a special observational room (complete with one-way mirrors and unobtrusively located video and audio capture devices). After a short delay, there was a knock on the door. It opened to reveal a somewhat plump, pleasant looking man in his mid forties/early fifties who introduced himself as a professional photographer. I remember marking a sly smile that stole momentarily across Bandler's face during the introductions.

We set off on the adventure of running this *professional photographer* through his paces to determine what it was that he actually wanted in the way of change. He seemed to me to lack any serious passion about what he related to us as the unsatisfactory aspects of his life.

Like the vast majority of clients we had seen, he knew quite well what he did NOT want, but had little idea about what it was that he did want. Sitting there with the co-authors of the Meta Model, this lack of an articulated goal presented little in the way of difficulty for us. We pursued the definition of a goal with our client using the appropriate Meta Model challenges. We also threw in a number of conversational versions of Erickson's hypnotic patterning for flavoring and got some marked physiological shifts of state.

Towards the end of the session, we conversationally induced a medium level altered state of consciousness and made a series of post-hypnotic suggestions. Included in this set was the suggestion that immediately upon leaving the session, this photographer would be seized by an irresistible desire to take a leisurely and thoughtful 15 minute walk through the tree-lined streets around the institute. Our ongoing calibrations confirmed the acceptance of this set of suggestions and we closed the session, well enough pleased with the demonstration. The session then terminated.

We were then led to a long table in a conference room presided over by Watzlawick. The intention of this post-demonstration gathering was to discuss the patterning that we had demonstrated. Also present was another member of executive board (whose name I have lost along the way since) and several interns – young and highly impressionable psychiatrists who were studying brief therapy (at least, as it was presented there at the time).

There was a chair to Watzlawick's left, apparently left empty for another member of the executive team who was to join us for the discussion. Watzlawick politely requested that we await the arrival of the soon-to-be-occupant of the empty chair, Dick Fisch, then the manager of the institute. The time dragged along, with Watzlawick periodically checking his wristwatch, asking other members of the staff if they knew where Fisch was, shaking his head at the unexpected delay and apologizing to us for having to wait. After about 10–12 minutes, Bandler leaned forward and said in a confident voice that Fisch would be along in the next 3–5 minutes. This comment was greeted with some alarm by members of the group and sure enough, about 4 minutes later, the door opened and Fisch walked in and occupied the empty chair that was awaiting him.

I then realized both what the sly smile that had crept across Bandler's face upon meeting the client was about, as well as his uncannily accurate prediction about the timing of Fisch's arrival in the conference room – and what both of these incidents implied. MRI, upon learning that neither Bandler nor I had a license to practice change work, had held a meeting to decide how to handle our visit. They were unwilling to accept the risk of allowing us to work with a *real* client because of liability issues. They had therefore decided that Fisch was to play the role of a client to allow us to demonstrate our patterning without legal exposure to the institute. Bandler had seen photos of Fisch somewhere and had recognized him when he entered the room in the role of the client. I was clueless about this entire dimension of what was occurring.

Amusing as both Bandler and I found this entire incident, there was a fascinating aspect to it that I wish to call to the attention of the reader. Fisch was playing a client, assuming an identity (professional photographer) and acting as if he had some issue he wanted help to resolve. Under the impact of both the rapport patterning and especially the specification challenges coming out of the Meta Model, he was placed in a position where he had to invent (or more colloquially, lie) content under the impact of the specification questions that flowed from us out of the Meta Model.

As anyone who has had experience with the Meta Model – well and congruently applied, and under the condition of continuing rapport – can testify, the specification of any particular offering from a client moves quite quickly to ground (full specification) from the original fluffy, undefined, high level nouns and verbs. For Fisch, it had been an extended session in lying – and the only source he had to draw upon to convincingly respond to the specification questions was his own internal maps.

For Fisch, then, it was an exercise in isomorphic mapping, from his own personal history onto a legend that supported the role he was assigned to play in this charade. For me, it was simply another client struggling to develop answers to a series of precise questions, and for Bandler, a double level and most amusing demonstration that lying over an extended conversation causes a collapse of the fabricated identity onto the lying person's own actual life narrative.

How DID Bandler know when Fisch would walk through the door of the conference room so that the discussion could begin? The answer is quite simple. Both Bandler and I had calibrated the congruent acceptance by the professional photographer, now Fisch swimming strongly in his own identity, of the post-hypnotic suggestions, which included a compulsive, irresistible desire to take a 15 minute walk in the tree-shaded streets around the institute as soon as we terminated the session and this was precisely what he had done.

As Bandler already knew that the professional photographer was actually Fisch, it was simple enough to predict when he would show up in the conference room. Far more surprising to me was the fact that Watzlawick and the other members of the institute who had witnessed the work we had done with Fisch/photographer failed to appreciate where he was during that 15 minute delay while they were waiting in the conference room.

I so enjoyed this event that, for weeks afterwards, upon meeting new clients, I would instruct them as follows:

> *As part of our collaboration here to secure the choices that you have come here to get, I will be asking you a series of questions. I require only one piece of cooperation from you – namely, that you will convincingly and compelling lie to me in answering each and every one of these questions. Under no circumstances are you to tell me the truth!*
>
> *Do you understand what I am demanding of you? Do you accept this instruction?*

I was fascinated by the fact that under the impact of a model (the Meta Model), which contained a syntactically based pure process set of systematic specifications, it appeared that the recovery of deletions, the challenging of certain other syntactic patterning, the client telling the truth (easy here – the truth as they understood it to be, not some TRUTH), and the client deliberately lying in responding to the questions converged. The consequences are indistinguishable in the sense that they each get what they had come for. The only place that the client instructed to lie can go for to the answers to this pure process, unrelenting demand for specification is their own internal maps. I take this to be one of the most elegant demonstrations of the superiority of process over content-based approaches.

I invite the reader to take a full step backwards and simply note what I have described above. Is this encounter really that much different from a *regular* session with a well-intentioned client who does his or her best to answer this class of questions by telling the truth? I would wager that a significant proportion of the answers to Meta Model class questions by clients are false. False, in the sense that they are reconstructing the past from memory (itself, a reconstruction of actual previous experiences) and will unintentionally conflate distinct experiences. By remembering them as parts of a single experience, they will omit inconvenient or embarrassing aspects of what they are describing. How different then are the results of inadvertently lying and deliberately lying in such an exchange?

The point, of course, is the lies (even these inadvertent deviations from what actually happened), these reconstructions from memory, may miss the mark by a small insignificant measure or by a mile; but like dreams, while the things/nouns may vary wildly and without any seeming logic, the relationships/verbs will be stable. The presentation may speak of different people, objects, and events, unrelated in any obvious way with the people, objectives, and events they stand in for as surrogates, but the relationships will remain constant. Thus, the content is seen – in this way of appreciating both dreams and lying as a free variable in the context of a systematic extended activity – as irrelevant to the ongoing development of the encounter. Meanwhile, the process, the form, and the relationships continue to inform this encounter as a constant.

As I look back at the events described by the various authors in this volume, including myself, several things occur to me. First among these is the impression that our work, in these early days of NLP, always seemed to succeed.

This is largely, in part, an illusion that emerges from the style we utilized in this era (and in my case, continue to explore). I offer a metaphor to make the point. Suppose that we are members of a band – take your pick: a rock 'n' roll band, a jazz quartet, an African inspired polyrhythmic group. And let's say, I am the percussionist. In that capacity, I am responsible for the beat, the pulse, the timing of what we are playing. Suppose further that the rhythmic platform I am responsible for providing is in 6/8 time (think of a waltz) and the specific rhythm that the piece we are playing has the following structure:

Pulse	Beat	Beat	Pulse	Beat	Beat	Pulse	Beat	Beat	Pulse	Beat	Beat
X			X			X	X		X		X

The pulse-beat-beat corresponds to the 1–2–3 of the waltz. The X's mark the rhythmic spots that the percussionist will mark with some percussive sound. This rhythm is known as the short bell (African origin). Now, suppose that the heart part – the part that sets the rhythmic structure – is exactly the short bell as displayed above. So, here I am cruising along playing the short bell and everyone is in the groove. Then suddenly instead of playing:

Pulse	Beat	Beat	Pulse	Beat	Beat	Pulse	Beat	Beat	Pulse	Beat	Beat
X			X			X	X		X		X

I play instead:

Pulse	Beat	Beat	Pulse	Beat	Beat	Pulse	Beat	Beat	Pulse	Beat	Beat
X			X		X		X	X		X		X

This rhythm in 6/8 is called the long bell (again, African origin) – it has a distinct accent and feel to it. So did I make a mistake? What am I to do now?

Of course, I notice that the other players have heard and felt the shift, but this new rhythm, the long bell, is contained in precisely the same rhythmic space as what I originally played (the short bell). Compare the two visually as presented above.

As it fits perfectly into the same rhythmic space, the other players, while alert to the new feel in the rhythm, play right through.

Now, here comes the next cycle of the rhythm. Which will I play – the short bell or the long bell? The answer is, of course, that this is entirely up to me. As they both fit in the same rhythmic space, I can play either or some other rhythmic sequence as long as it fits inside the same rhythmic space. The only thing I must do is KEEP PLAYING. This is, of course, an example of simply rhythmic improvisation. I repeat – the only thing I must do as the percussionist (or any other member of the group) is KEEP PLAYING. As long as the group keeps playing, we will work out any number of improvisations.

This serves as a simple metaphor for much of what we did in the early days. We had little conscious appreciation about the deeper processes that we were modeling, coding, and testing but, like the rhythmic space that contains all the permutations of the rhythmic sequences, we had calibration and a sense of where the client wished to go (driven in part by verbal exchanges but definitively more frequently by the non-verbals issuing from physiological shifts in the client's body and voice quality). Everything not forbidden was permitted!

Yes, of course, countless times we would run a pattern: if the client (as appreciated through our calibration skills) moved towards the goal s/he had, we continued. If there was little or no evidence (again, deploying that mother of all skill sets in NLP, calibration), then we tossed that pattern away and threw another one at the client. The clients were far too busy dealing with their own ongoing and intense experience in the change process to have a clue that we had just shifted to another pattern, and another, and ... And, as we were operating without any explicit theory, we often had little conscious idea of what it was that we were about. The key then was simply to KEEP PLAYING.

I offer several additional comments about this issue around failing and its importance. Once a pattern has been adequately coded (and that coding has been tested rigorously), there is little value for the practitioner (except, of course, in meeting the client's requirements) in another success. I have definitely learned far more by failing than by succeeding in the application of the patterning of the Classic Code.

In *Whispering in the Wind*, Carmen Bostic-St. Clair and I proposed that there are three criteria for the presentation of a pattern:

1. The presentation in sensory grounded terms of the elements in a pattern and their sequencing. This is most frequently offered in the form of a format – a sequences of steps to follow in the application of the patterns.

2. What (range of) consequences will likely occur, given an congruent application of the pattern.

3. Under what specific conditions is pattern X to be selected and applied instead of pattern Y, for all X's and Y's?[10]

The first two of these criteria are surprisingly available, assuming that the unconscious assimilation condition during modeling is respected. The third criterion is only infrequently made explicit. There are two possible explanations for this difference. Explicitly finding the conditions that dictate which pattern to select for an application is simply a hell of lot more difficult than either of the first two criteria. Alternatively (and more intriguing), as the patterns of NLP, Classic or New Code, are pure process patterns, they adapt themselves, in the hands of an alert agent of change with calibration skills during the process of application, with astonishing flexibility to the specific requirements of the encounter with any specific client.

Certainly, there is an obvious and reasonably coherent argument to be made, for example, for the universality of the mirroring strategies for achieving rapid and deep rapport – which was supported by the discovery of mirror neurons a quarter of a century subsequent to the coding of these mirroring strategies by Bandler and myself.[11] Similarly, the Meta Model and its offspring (the Precision Model, the Verbal Package) exploit syntactic patterning that is apparently inherent in the structure of natural languages. Again, the eye movements associated with the cortical activation of the various major representational systems, relying directly on neurological structures, appear to be universal (the sole partial exception known to date are the Basques).

As I have proposed numerous times in the past, process patterning, based on deep neurological, physiological, and biochemical processes would be the most likely candidates for such universality in patterning. Indeed, the close association between pure process patterning and their apparent universality is itself a fascinating topic – one which Bostic-St. Clair and I have been investigating for some time, although not one appropriate in a book about the origins of NLP.

I turn my attention now to some examples of larger attempts from these early days in NLP that simply did not work out. Some of these are yet still unresolved.

Had I the ability to excise from the historical record of NLP all reference to any pattern, I would unhesitatingly delete the remarks made by Bandler and myself *about most highly valued representational system* or sometimes, *preferred representational system*. These terms first appear in section I of the *The Structure of Magic, Volume II* in the presentation of representational systems. What could we have been thinking! The term is itself patently ridiculous (matched only by the phrase *subjective experience* – what the hell other kind of experience is there!).

Unfortunately, references to representational systems appear all the way into the mid-80s (in *Turtles All the Way Down*[12]). The difficulty is that the idea proposes implicitly that there could be such a thing as a preference for a single representational system, INDEPENDENT of CONTEXT and RELATIONSHIP.

Never, among all the people I have met professionally and otherwise over the last 40-plus years since we coded representational systems, have I ever encountered someone who used the same representational system cross-context and in highly differentiated relationships. Worse, one apparent consequence of this coding error has been the corruption of a pure process pattern (representational systems) into a set of content categories.

This typically takes the form of using these processes as fixed categories or pigeonholes into which people stuff themselves and those around them. Statements such as: *I'm a kino* or *I'm a visual* or *I'm an auditory person* are more than adequate evidence to disqualify the speaker as someone who has any appreciation of actual NLP patterning.

As Eicher points out in his article, he clearly appreciated that the point of noting such an imbalance among one's own representational systems is not to pigeonhole or classify yourself into such categories but as an implicit invitation to use the patterning (then available in the Classic Code of the era – e.g., overlap of representational systems) to increase his competencies in the lesser developed representational systems as a way of achieving balance across these systems. The fact that he was initially more developed in his auditory skills served for him as a stimulus to attend to and develop competencies in his visual and kinesthetic systems (both input and representational systems).

In any case, the value of such calibration points is less than a couple of seconds. This strong nominalizing tendency (the mapping of a set of process patterns onto a static, permanent classificatory schema) is, again, a clear marker of a left brain run-away system. Indeed, work pretending to be NLP (and unfortunately, using its name) that makes this logical typing error removes the single most important defining characteristic of NLP – pure process patterning – converting it into a static, content-laden system indistinguishable from the host of other approaches to change work. I refer here to systems of classification that employ content impositions and nominalized categories. When this happens, NLP loses its pure process dynamic advantage as a model for change. It may as well accept such content taxonomies as *parent/ child/adult* or *id/ego/superego*.

I offer another example of an apparent cul-de-sac – this time a rather large one. Shortly after Bandler and I discovered and coded eye movements, and Pucelik, myself, and Bandler had rigorously tested their reliability and universality, I fell into a deep reverie concerning how to take advantage of precisely this discovery. What I settled on (I am speaking here of sometime in the mid to later 70s) was a program to create a syntax of thinking.

The verb *to think* is easily recognized as an unspecified predicate with respect to how specifically the thinking is occurring. It is well known that engineers and mathematicians among others are highly developed visually – perhaps Tesla is best known for this ability in an advanced form. It was said that he never bothered to build prototypes as his internal imagery was precise enough to work out the tolerances and he proceeded directly to construction of the invention. An engineer or a mathematician can and will spend extended periods of time forming and manipulating visual images – either realist or abstract. They will do this typically without the use of language – the images are the vocabulary of the visual thinker.

In an analogous fashion, dancers and athletes among others will think with their bodies – a dancer creating a choreography will use movements (macro or, more typically for the initial stages, micro muscle) to work out the sequences of movements, postures, gestures, and rhythms that will eventually become finally the artistic presentation of a dance – and again without the medium of language being engaged. Anyone observing the superb performances of Olympic athletes will have noted indications of the body "thinking" in preparation for their events.

Musicians and composers among others will spend extended periods of time manipulating rhythms and melodies, again without linguistic activity. These components (among other elements) are the vocabulary of a musician or composer developing their art.

Most of the rest of us, in many cases, spend excessive time talking to ourselves – the usual internal dialogue. It is certainly a useful choice, if, indeed, it is a choice for any particular individual, on a context-by-context basis. We also move unconsciously from one representational system to another, or from a mapping from some input channel (quite distinct from the notion of representational systems) to various representational systems through the synesthesia circuitry.

Given all this, it occurred to me that one possible approach to this syntax of thinking was to chart the indicators: the visible, audible, and other detectable traces of the underlying neurological activity (the tracks left in the snow) and, just possibly, this would lead to ordered sequences in specified contexts. It was already quite clear that people shifted the form of their processing context by context and relationship by relationship.

This was the birth of what is now referred to in NLP as Strategies. A strategy, then, is an ordered sequence of representational systems, accesses, and synesthesia mapping (input channel X to representational system Y). This was exciting stuff – all the professional work I had done in transformational linguistics, with its high demands for formal representations of patterning, had positioned me ideally to explore this possibility.

After some months of pursuing this approach, the endeavor collapsed like a house of cards. Certainly, there were some interesting generalizations – nearly all the top decision-makers in the context of business activity or organizational work demonstrated the same ordered sequences and, importantly, it was quite distinct from poor or even average decision-makers as measured by the consequences of the decisions they made. Dilts developed what is now known as the Spelling Strategy, but what occurred that led to the collapse of this exciting project?

Here is the problem: syntax is the study of the contribution of sequence to meaning in experience and the consequences we take from such sequenced experience. Perhaps the simplest examples are language, mathematics, and music. It matters very much to the overall experience in what specific order and grouping the elements in the sentence/equation/composition occur. This is the defining element in any syntactic system. The classic linguistic example runs along the lines of:

The rat chased the cat.

and

The cat chased the rat.

These two well-formed sentences are composed of precisely the same set of elements – the same words. Yet, any fluent speaker of English will insist (correctly) that they mean entirely different things. They describe two quite distinct events; they cannot both be true of the same objects at the same point in time; they mean different things. If asked (absurdly) to point to where in the pair of sentences the element that generates this difference is, the naive fluent speaker cannot do so. The difference, of course, emerges from the different *order* of the elements in the sequence. I leave it to the reader, if useful, to construct the equivalent counterparts in math and music (Bach's études is an easy example).

Let's use Dilts' Spelling Strategy as a simple example. The Spelling Strategy proposes that the best spellers (all, most?) use a repetitive ordered sequence in their experience to accomplish this simple task: namely, when asked to spell a word, they will create an internal visual image of the work requested. Once the image of the word required is stable, the speller makes a kinesthetic check: essentially, asking the question:

Does this image feel right?

or slightly more precisely:

Is the kinesthetic experience when looking at the visual image formed one of familiarity – have I seen this image before?

Note the spellers competing in a spelling bee are taught to repeat the word as the actual first step in the competition version of this spelling strategy. If they mishear the word, they will successfully generate an image of the wrong word, display the visual image of the wrong word, check the kinesthetics for familiarity, and correctly spell the wrong word and be eliminated from the contest.

There are a number of observations to be made here. Note that this strategy is limited to words seen before, so when a speller is asked to spell a word that they have never seen before, the strategy collapses and must be augmented with some alternative non-visual approach – such as phonetics (with all its attendant gaps – for example, you cannot spell *phonetics* correctly using a phonetic approach). So clearly, an excellent speller will require more than a single strategy to succeed. Let's simply step by this limitation to secure the point I wish to make: this is a quibble about the Spelling Strategy's incompleteness.

Syntax is the study of the contribution of sequence to the experience in question. How do we know that there is any sequence here and, if there is, what that sequence is? How do we know that the image occurs first and, subsequently, we get the kinesthetic sensation of familiarity? What evidence can we use to verify the sequence in which these elements occur? That is the problem. There are, at the moment, raging arguments about whether it is possible to multi-track tasks. The debate is typically cast in terms of whether the introspective experience, as well as the calibration externally by a trained observer, is adequate evidence to accept multi-tasking, or that what appears to be multi-tasking is actually nano-second switching between the two tasks being conducted.

Apparently, at present the instrumentation is not adequate to reliably determine the answer to this question. Independently, there is the question of where to sample. Both of these concerns impact the same issue. If we cannot determine with reliability whether there is a sequencing of the relevant events (activations of specific cortical areas and input channel/representational system mappings) and, further, what that sequence is, even with relatively simple processing tasks such as spelling, then the application of the ordering of such events (syntax) is not, at present in any case, a viable approach to something as complex as thinking more generally. Thus, for the present the dream I carried of the creation of a syntax of thinking is dormant.

Two additional comments: I taught my children and grandchildren the Spelling Strategy and, of course, it worked brilliantly. Thus, for the purposes of assisting children or adults acquiring a new language in mastering the task of spelling, the Spelling Strategy has much to recommend it. This suggests that while it is not at present possible to determine sequences in the case of thinking processes, it is useful in some contexts to act as if the sequence is as it appears to be – whether or not the actual sequence of events is as it appears to be at deeper levels of the neurology or is simply an artefact of the bottleneck between unconscious and conscious processes. By the way, I note in passing that spelling does not even exist as a subject in schools in which the language in question has an isomorphic mapping between the orthography (the written system) and the phonetics (the sounds actually pronounced during the speech art) of the language in question. Spanish is such as example.

This raises the question of what possible intention is being satisfied by refusing to reform the orthography to map isomorphically between the written and sound system in English – other than creating an avoidable task for people learning the language, or not awakening the general population from their slumber by introducing a written system that is simpler but unfamiliar to their eye.

There is one context of application in which this strategy work has found a home – it is proposed in some circles (Dilts, for example, from time to time) that it is possible to model a genius simply through the elicitation and installation of the observed ordered sequences of representational system accesses (usually as determined by the calibration of eye movements).

Strangely enough, there are no examples on offer, unless you consider the list of dead people that Dilts has studied and who appear in his *Strategies of Genius* series). To date, to the best of my knowledge, no one has demonstrated that the elicitation and installation of ordered sequences of representational system accesses (that is, strategies) has the consequence that the person who has installed these sequences can replicate in any interesting way the performance of the genius involved.

This is hardly surprising to me personally. It strikes me very much like a water skier attempting to use the towline to propel the ski boat forward. What I propose is the case is that if the person wishing to match the performance of the genius were to capture and replicate the series of states displayed by the genius as s/he moves through the performance, these *strategies* would likely be dragged along as part of that capture – this is testable and would require someone capable of developing and sustaining a know-nothing state for the unconscious assimilation during capture.

My personal best guess is that the experience of sequence in the Spelling Strategy is an artefact of the bottleneck (7 + or – 2 chinks of bandwidth) in the transfer as the complex unconscious processes are mapped into consciousness. It may well be that there is a sequence deeper in the neurology (pre-conscious or using the terms developed in the most recent epistemology offered in *Whispering in the Wind,* pre-FA (first access)) but what we are presently sensing and calibrating is simply an artefact of the limitations of consciousness. Perhaps with refinements in instrumentation, such a project can be resurrected. We shall see.

I ask myself where the hell this stuff comes from. Some of the sources are clear enough: the focus on form; the priority assigned to the syntactic elements in the communications; the reflex to formalize certain portions of what I had assimilated as a way of both knowing if I actually knew what I was doing as well as a way to push the patterning to its edges; and the insistence on becoming a native/fluent speaker/actor in a language or a discipline (the unconscious assimilation apparently unique to NLP modeling to achieve stable intuitions based on well-developed circuits) as a prerequisite to the coding of patterning. All these have a direct line connection, in my case personally, with both my training with the Jesuits at university, the challenges of working as a field agent, and with the rigorous demands of operating as a professional linguist.[13]

The greeting of risk, the willingness to discover through (certain classes of non-lethal) trial and error, the subordination of success to exploration and discovery, and the insistence of finding the edge of patterns; where they fail, all of these seem to contain echoes of field work in Special Forces and related intelligence organizations, the passion for languages, the recognition that much of what passes for effective communication can be achieved with very little actual understanding, the primacy of non-verbal communication in influencing face-to-face communications, a tolerance for ambiguity and vagueness, and a fascination with the unknown.

From my point of view, NLP has succeeded brilliantly in some instances and has, as yet, to deliver on its potential. Sure, it has spread throughout the world with astonishing rapidity. However, there are severe issues with its quality – something that Gilligan accurately described as the turn that NLP took in the late 70s. It has influenced in a positive manner the lives of hundreds of thousands of people – good, happy to hear it.

I propose here that NLP's most radical contribution has, as yet, not achieved its promise. The simple observation is that, what Gilligan calls the "creative unconscious," has been displaced in the majority of people purporting to be NLP trained agents of change by extended left-brain formats of increasing complexity and rigidly specified patterns, with little or no attention to the intention behind these so-called patterns. This has been mixed in an alarming manner with the imposition of content, as opposed to the pure process work characteristic of the original patterning and its sharp distinction between content imposition and pure process patterning.

Instead of seeking out new patterning from geniuses, there is a continuous movement to re-edit or reorder or make trivial variations on patterns coded from this era – the creation of NLP. This, of course, misses the point entirely – the dynamic, creative quality of these early days came primarily from the modeling of geniuses and the rigorous testing of the coded patterns derived from this fundamental activity. However, I have no doubt that a person can arrive at the requisite competencies through paths quite distinct from those that I have identified here, and continue to travel.

As I look over the articles, comments, and narratives that form this book, I am struck by a lack of description and reference to the one activity that made all this possible – NLP modeling. It is long overdue to put down in writing what I have stated for years in private and public contexts: namely, that the sources of many of the Meta Model patterns, as well as other patterning from these first stumbles towards the creation of what has come to be known as NLP, were the original geniuses that we modeled: the patterns of Virginia Satir and Fritz Perls, and, subsequently, the patterning of Milton Erickson. They are to be recognized as the sources for most of these initial patterns and an inspiration in their effectiveness in showing the way towards excellence in change work.

I gladly correct this absence of explicit recognition on our part and salute these three people – thank you! It is particularly impressive to consider that these three pioneers worked out much of their patterning without, as Bateson says in his introduction to *The Structure of*

Magic, Volume I)[14]: the tools which we (Bateson and his MRI group) did not have – or did not see how to use. This is a remarkable achievement and one I wish to recognize and congratulate them for.

Finally, it is my hope that this effort on my part, on the part of Frank Pucelik, Carmen Bostic-St. Clair, and the other contributors to this book to make available descriptions of some of the singular events that occurred during the period when NLP was created – this *Origins of NLP* endeavor – will encourage others to strike out into unknown territory and bring back something worth putting on the table and sampling with pleasure in the near future – especially the NLP modeling of new patterning of genius. If this work has that consequence, I will have been more than adequately rewarded for the efforts involved.

Epilogue

Carmen Bostic-St. Clair

An epilogue is usually the place in a book/play where the author/actor speaks directly to the reader/audience. In this book, however, you have read the writings of nine people before me who were actors playing parts in the making of this history. I did not author any of them. In fact I wasn't even there as an actor.

I, like most of you, have an interest in the field of NLP and its beginnings. During my first reading of these articles I stepped into the shoes of the writer and really used the processes I suggested in the prologue – seeing, hearing, making pictures, getting feelings, and sometimes the smells. This gave me a taste of the context.

In preparation for writing this epilogue, I stepped into the shoes of you, the reader, and re-read the articles. While I read, I jotted notes about time sequences, events and created a list of questions to ask John Grinder, Frank Pucelik, or Robert Spitzer, or to research in the historical archives and public records when I noticed gaps in the continuity or where questions naturally came up for me.[1] I then took those questions and made them into headings for each section to create a continuity to fill in the gaps in my perception.[2] The six principal headings take the form of a theater metaphor.

The period of time that is my focus in this part of the book are the events that occurred between the years of 1971 and 1979 – with emphasis on the early years of modeling, exploration, experimentation, coding, and testing (1971–1975).

I have chosen various forms in which to present the material. In some places, I have chosen a narrative form, writing an unfolding story. I have heard many stories over the years and those stories have often been great opportunities for me to gain new perspectives on the patterns and processes; I am hoping that this narrative form will be beneficial to you as well. In some places, I have written from a third position in respect to the people and the events, most of whom I have had associations with over the years. You will notice a shift in form when I write from the perspective of historical archives or public records. In other places, I have taken a second position with you, the reader, and have spoken directly to you, as I am now.

As I have mentioned above, I wrote this epilogue after two readings of all of the articles by the individual authors. I did not have access to John Grinder's articles and his comments on the articles. John's articles were written simultaneously at a different location during the time that I was writing this portion. It was my desire, since we had already co-authored *Whispering in the Wind*, to write my portion from my own reading of the articles of the eight other authors – fresh without John's influence and to avoid the possibility that his perceptions would modify my own. The only thing that I have added to the epilogue after reading John Grinder's articles and comments is the following.

After reading his "Reflections on *The Origins of Neuro-Linguistic Programming*," I looked at what I had written from the perspective of possible filters. I must confess that a primary filter when writing this epilogue was the disambiguation of the following standard line which appears in websites, recent books, and within bios or CVs of individuals in the field now called NLP: "NLP was started in the late 70s by Richard Bandler and John Grinder"; this statement is usually followed by some strange definition of NLP and then how that particular individual or group has gone on to "develop" NLP. Individuals have been purporting to be developers of NLP since 1974. It is my hope that you, the reader, after reading the time frames and processes which I have included here in answer to my own questions after stepping into your shoes, will have a back story of discovery, exploration, pure tenacity, and an opportunity to draw your own conclusions as to: "What is NLP and how did the field emerge?"

I posed many questions to John Grinder in respect to the group processes as they were referred to by various authors. I was curious as to how these groups were used by Richard, John, and Frank, which prompted me to focus on that topic and that time frame. As you read about the group processes that I have described, it would be interesting to remember from your reading of John Grinder's writing here, that even years later (and for those of you who have attended his seminars over the years), his style of writing and teaching invites us to discover for ourselves certain patterns in the processing of the information he presents and the type of questions he may have posed within these groups and which lead to some of the tasking.

Therefore, if there are redundancies in what I have written in respect to a question that I had for myself, which may have been answered in John Grinder's articles, I invite you to read them as a second account among the multiple descriptions that appear in this book.

Before beginning the narrative, I present the following frame. I know the difference between description, interpretation, and evaluation. I have studied the precise patterns from the Meta Model – mind reading and cause/effect – so anywhere that I have ventured into those territories I have warned you that that was what I was doing.

I. The Stage and the Players

To set the context, each of these three men (Richard Bandler, Frank Pucelik, and John Grinder) as they came together at the University of California at Santa Cruz (UCSC) in 1971–72, was pursuing his own path. As the story unfolds in the accounts throughout this book and in this epilogue, there were initially two students interested in Gestalt therapy applications and earning money doing interventions and trainings while finishing their education. These students were joined by a curious professor of linguistics "invited to come see what they were doing" during a turbulent period in US history. This was an exciting time that was characterized by young people returning from the traumas resulting from the country's involvement in a questionable war; some becoming students under the GI Bill who joined other students who were seeking change in the system; experimenting with substances and managing the consequences. All of these factors created the context and the interest on a campus which, in response to the times, was launching a new type of educational model at Kresge College, the sixth college of the UCSC campus.[3]

In 1971, Richard Bandler was in his junior undergraduate year and 21 years old. Frank Pucelik was just out of the military and was continuing his bachelor's degree at age 27; he had a son and was separated. John Grinder, the oldest of the three, at the age of 31, was an Assistant Professor and had written two books and many articles within the field of Linguistics; he had a son and a daughter and was separated.[4]

Each of these men was pursuing his own individual life path; they did not purposely come together to create a new field. This new discipline *emerged* over a period of time between 1971 and 1974 and was finally announced to the general public with the publication of four books between 1975 and 1976. The field which emerged was named Neuro-Linguistic Programming (NLP) in the latter part of those same years.

II. The Main Script: NLP Modeling

As I was a working my way for a second time through the articles that you have just read, I realized that none of them directly address the modeling process utilized by John, Richard ,and Frank during the modeling of Fritz Perls and Virginia Satir; and later the modeling of Milton Erickson, by Richard and John. I stepped back and asked myself a simple question: What had to be true for this omission to have occurred? What follows is a narrative on the modeling process that answers that question for me. I have included dates, where possible, as a guide.

The modeling process employed by Richard, John, and Frank in the modeling of Perls and Satir (which includes the initial stages of Erickson) occurred during 1971–1974. This process commenced prior to, and primarily without the knowledge of, many of the participants of the later "groups" which were attended by the writers of each of the articles. Early groups were formed and conducted by John, Richard, and Frank during the modeling stage for the purpose of the experimentation, exploration, and testing *of patterns which had been modeled and were being modelled – and in some cases, already coded.*

To explain this frame, I invite the reader to make the distinction between what was conscious and explicit during 1971–1974 and what was systematic in the behaviors of Pucelik, Bandler, and Grinder. These three men were immersed in a process of systematic behavior to produce an outcome – an example of a process in and of itself. Since they were not explicit as to what they were doing, a casual observer could only generalize that their behavior was systematic.

From its inception in 1971, what has become known as the field of NLP, as embodied by the systematic behaviors of these three young men, has been the *study* of the differences which make the difference between the high performance of a genius and the average performer within the same field. The domain to which this modeling was originally applied was therapy and the high performers in that field at that time were Perls, Satir, and Erickson. The application, however, quickly became generalized to other human activity well beyond therapy. I will address below the question: How did these three men select these particular individual models?

The systematic patterns of behavior on the part of Pucelik, Bandler, and Grinder was coded piecemeal, and was committed to writing during late 1973–1974. These patterns were made public in 1975 with the publication of the first two books co-authored by Grinder and Bandler. The process of coding systematic behavior was a continuous loop. These three men would model a pattern (either directly from one of the models, each other, or something they noticed in the world), then find or create opportunities to personally test that pattern for themselves in as many contexts as possible. Once they were satisfied with their direct experience of the pattern; they would put the pattern into testing groups. If the pattern held up under testing, typically Bandler and Grinder would code it, and begin to integrate it into one of the manuscripts they were writing. The typewriters were always ready to receive the latest entry. This process was continuous from the beginning of 1973 to 1976.

The coding of the *NLP Modeling process* that was utilized implicitly during this period of time, however, was not made explicit until 2001 when the first precise description of the process was offered in *Whispering in the Wind.*[5] A summary of that model is included below to assist the reader in appreciating its structure as it was used in the modeling of Perls, Satir, and Erickson.

Five-step process description of NLP Modeling

1. Identification of and obtaining access to a model in the context where he or she is performing as a genius.

2. Unconscious uptake of model's patterns without any attempt to understand them consciously.

3. Practice in a parallel context to replicate the pattern. The intention is to achieve a performance of the model's patterns which is equal to the model him/herself.

4. Once the modeler can consistently reproduce the pattern in an applied fashion with equal results, the modeler begins the coding process.

5. Testing to determine if the pattern as coded can be transferred successfully to others who will in turn be able to get equally effective results from the coded results ... and then, ultimately to teach those processes to others.

The process of modelling Perls was informal and could best be described as a derived model, as the models that John had available (i.e., Richard and Frank) had already assimilated the behavior of the model. Fritz Perls had died in 1970. When invited "to come see what we are doing" as referenced in the articles, John did not have direct access to Perls. What he did have were three representations of Perls and his patterning: (1) films of Perls that Dr. Robert Spitzer of Science and Behavior Books had available; (2) the two men who had for a period of time been running Gestalt sessions and teaching groups of people how to perform the process; and (3) during the process of transcribing Perls' films into verbal transcripts, Richard had assimilated the voice and physiology patterns of Perls from the films. To quote Dr. Robert Spitzer, M.D.: "He came out of it talking and acting like Fritz Perls. I found myself accidentally calling him Fritz on several occasions."[6] In order to satisfy the second step of the modeling process, John modeled the models of Perls which he had available and requested that Richard provide him with films of Perls – the oldest, the most recent, and what was considered the finest performance of his work. John watched these films, then compared them with what he had modeled Frank and Richard doing. John, himself, arrived at the perception that they (Richard and Frank) were "better than Perls at being Perls" (John Grinder, personal communication). Thus, the modeling of Perls continued week by week. Richard and Frank's Gestalt group met on Mondays with John initially modeling (unconscious assimilation) and later participating.

To summarize, the above describes John's modeling phase of Perls. John's criteria was, for him, that he had to be able to produce the same results as the models, in this case Frank, Richard, and films of Perls. His criteria from his modeling of natural language required that he become fluent in the language he had targeted to learn. This fluency gave him access to the intuitions typical of native speakers. The same criteria for the linguistic modeling of native speakers applied to the modeling of Perls. John approached the modeling of Perls with the intention to become a fluent speaker – to become an actor on the (stage) platform called Gestalt. In other words, his self-assigned task was to speak, to act, and to have the same intuitions as if an actor was playing Perls on stage in a Gestalt context. Without explicitly coding what he was doing, on Thursday evenings, using classrooms at UCSC, John would, in parallel, run a similar group with different people to whatever groups Richard and Frank were running. John called this group the repeat "miracle group." This was, obviously, disciplined practice in a parallel context.

Frank observes:

> It would be helpful to the reader to remember in respect to this original modeling and the steps of modeling summarized above, that the experimentation, exploration, coding and testing inside of the original "groups" of Perls patterns was occurring with only a slight gap before the modeling of Virginia Satir and the initial modeling of Milton Erickson. This was the beginning of what Frank Pucelik describes in his article as the 1st generation (1971–1973) of the Meta/NLP groups.[7]

III. The Casting Calls

John Grinder

John's undergraduate degree was in psychology; immediately upon graduation, in 1962, he married, and the next day he entered the Army as an officer. Later he became a member of the Special Forces. After more than five years, with service primarily in Europe and now speaking German and Italian, he returned the US to begin his postgraduate degree at UC-San Diego – in the field of linguistics.

When Richard invited John to "come see what we are doing," John brought with him his experience in the modeling and coding of natural languages (German, Italian, KiSwahili); a deep analytic competency from transformational grammar (the books and articles that he had written in the field); and his most recent adventure, the modeling project of 1972 which took place along the central and northern coast of Tanzania of the Wagogo tribe, whereby he became accepted as a member of the tribe. This was coupled with his previous military experience (as a field agent) which implied that he could speak foreign languages and pass as a fluent speaker. This modeling and coding experience from his acquisition of other languages combined with his background in transformational grammar (Grinder was teaching a course, Language and Mind at the time) became the *scaffolding* upon which the modeling and coding of the original NLP patterns (Classic Code) were positioned.

The link between the modeling and coding process described above and John's experience in the previous paragraph is critical to answering the question posed by Frank (in his article): What are we doing and how can we do it better?

Perls, Satir, and Erickson's work had been written about and examples of their processes were even available, including transcripts taken from their filmed work with clients. People were giving workshops. What was it about the combination of these three men who began playing with material which was *already* available to the public and therapeutic professionals? How was it that they were able to put it to use, get results, and create patterns of this material so that other people could learn to use it? What was the difference that made that difference? The answer, in my opinion, was the borrowing of certain key processes from linguistics. One of the main processes mapped across from linguistics to what these three men were doing at that time was the recognition that behavior, like language, is rule governed. The ability to map the verbal behaviors of the models they had selected from therapy onto the structure of transformational grammar (the scaffolding) provided the key to the creation of the first model of NLP, the Meta Model, and in particular its coding. This process was subsequently extended to the coding of their systematic non-verbal behavior. As an aside, *the beauty of scaffolding is that once it has served its purpose to erect a structure, the scaffolding can safely be removed.*

The *Structure of Magic, Volume I* has as its subtitle: *A Book about Language and Therapy*. It was written in late 1973 and 1974. Providing the therapist with a systematic process for utilizing the form of a client's verbal communication through the use of the Meta Model was the primary theme; thereby connecting the linguistics process to therapy. John and Richard write:

> Human language is a way of representing the world. Transformational Grammar is an explicit model of the process of representing and communicating that representation of the world. The mechanisms within Transformational Grammar are universal to all human beings and the way in which we represent our experience.[8]

Later, they state:

> This Meta Model is based on the intuitions which you already have available to you as native speakers of your language. The terminology, however, that we have adapted from linguistics may be new to you.[9]

John and Richard then proceed to direct the therapist to a process designed to detect what is well formed in therapy; and then how to map across from the rules of the well-formed sentence in English to a well-formed verbal communication with a client during the process of therapy.

A Stage of Opportunity

The 17-acre parcel of land on Alba Road, Ben Lomond, California on which John, Richard, and Gregory Bateson all eventually lived together at one point was, and still is, owned by Dr. Robert Spitzer and housed the shipping and warehousing function of Science and Behavior books. It was at this location that Richard worked and assisted Spitzer in editing and finishing Perls' book, *The Gestalt Approach and Eye Witness to Therapy*, published in 1973.[10] This book contains transcripts of selected films of Fritz Perls working with clients. In his uncompleted draft of this book, Perls chose the films which were transcribed as best representing teaching points of Gestalt therapy. Richard had access to these films.

Science and Behavior Books (formed in 1963) was a small publishing house with the intention to provide innovative newcomers to the field of therapy with an opportunity to publish their work. The company was initially owned by Don Jackson, who founded Mental Research Institute (MRI) of Palo Alto in 1958.[11] MRI was the training arm of the Palo Alto Medical Research Foundation. Jackson was joined by Jules Riskin, M.D. and Virginia Satir as the Director of Family Therapy Training. Between 1953 and 1962, Gregory Bateson and his research team, John Weakland, Jay Haley, Don Jackson, and William Fry, conducted research projects in behavioral sciences. For a period of time the Bateson Projects and the MRI shared office space as both were operating under the auspices of the Palo Alto Medical Research Foundation. When Jackson died in 1968, Dr. Robert Spitzer who also worked at MRI with Virginia Satir, bought Science and Behavior Books and published *Peoplemaking* by Virginia in 1972.[12] To create texts of Satir's work, Richard was hired to do the audio taping of Satir working with clients and families.

In summary, after my second reading of the articles in this book, I asked myself: How were these particular models selected? The answer emerged for me after doing the research, speaking with Dr. Robert

Spitzer, and writing the above, that the selection was purely fortuitous – the selection was simply made on the basis of opportunity, on what was available. An opportunity was put in front of some young men who were alert enough to seize it. The first opportunity was in respect to Perls – the films and the first draft of the manuscript. The second opportunity was that Satir had worked with Spitzer at MRI, Science and Behavior Books published *Peoplemaking*, and Satir would on occasions run family sessions at Alba Road. The third opportunity was the connection to Erickson which was provided by Gregory Bateson. The fourth opportunity occurred on a parcel of land with multiple dwellings: Richard had lived in various buildings on the land; John, who had met Bateson in 1974 at Kresge College, moved into the Japanese Tea House, followed by Bateson who occupied the main house with his wife, Lois, and their young daughter, Nora.

Richard Bandler

Richard Bandler, the youngest of the three men, was more of an entrepreneur than the others and the most vocal in his criticisms of the then current therapeutic practices (as you will have read in Steve Gilligan's article). He had lived in the environment of Science and Behavior Books since he was 17, when he caught the attention of Becky Spitzer because of his interest in philosophy and the intellectual approach he used in teaching music to her and Robert's son. He saw, heard, and read a lot as people came and went on Alba Road; Alba Road, from the inception, was a gathering place for innovative people utilizing alternative methodologies.

Richard could hear; he was a musician. He played drums and guitar, not from sheet music but from imitating songs he liked. This ability to hear and to imitate was one of the skill sets that he brought to the modeling process.

Sometime during 1972, Richard recorded sessions of Satir in Reno. John recalls Richard coming back from these recording sessions and running everything through Satir filters. He did Virginia so well that John modeled Richard being Satir. When John moved to Alba Road, where Richard had been living for some time, they spent a lot of time together. As they modeled Satir and Erickson, the world became a lab – clients at Alba Road, "groups", the supermarket, restaurants, the airport ...

In the supermarket, for example, John noticed a woman squeezing a tomato. He asked her, using a Satir pattern and using an Erickson voice tone and rhythm, "How do you think a tomato feels about you squeezing it that way?" He walked away as the woman went into a satisfactory trance while fixated on the tomato. Richard and John, using the world as a lab, no matter where they were, would do parodies – they would exaggerate Satir's process, particularly the sculpting, as described in Jim Eicher's article. Whatever she did in a therapy session, they went out into the world and repeated it whenever or wherever they found the opportunity. When John was introduced to Virginia and modeled her in person, "he found her to be totally systematic in her processes with clients with respect to representational systems predicates." She observed: "WOW! What can anyone say about having their work looked at by four fine eyes in the heads of two very capable human researchers? ... I do something, I feel it, I see it, my gut responds to it ..."[13] As in the case of Perls, John's initial modeling of Satir was a derived model. Richard's keen ability to listen and imitate voice quality was used by John, initially through the auditory channel to become Virginia.

Double Casting the Merging of Roles: JohnRichard Team

Richard and John began to play music together, Richard on guitar and John on base guitar. Richard taught the basic riffs. The process of playing music together spontaneously brought the two men together at a different level, as discussed above, where the world became their lab. If any readers have played music in an improvisational manner, such as jazz, you will immediately "feel" the connection to which I am alluding. Two musicians improvising create a rhythm with each other, without words; they can shift leads and come back together. This type of improvisational relationship could well have been the basis for the "JohnandRichard" comments in Jim Eicher's article, and the point at which Frank felt that his role within the team had changed.

The Second Casting Call: Frank Pucelik's New Role with the Groups

Just as John and Richard improvised with music, they improvised on the stage with the play that was unfolding in the theater of NLP. What part in this play was left for Frank, who had been there from the beginning? I would like to propose that his new role was critical at that time to the field that has become known as NLP. Frank became responsible for the "groups". What exactly did that entail? Not only did it involve leading, teaching, and delegating organization, but also the responsibility for the passing, supervising and collecting of data in respect to tasking instructions to group members. During the exploration and experimenting stage, Frank led groups and did debriefs with Richard and John in the same fashion as Richard and John did with Frank after they each led groups. These debrief sessions typically contained two important processes. First, was the choice point lying exercises: each of the men in turn would describe various choice points during the encounters in that session, or invented descriptions of what might have happened at those various choice points. Often times, even as one of them was describing an actual or fabricated experience, one or both of the others would interrupt with statements like, "No, that is not what you did. What you did was ..." This was an amusing experience multiplier and, simultaneously, preparation for what they would do in the next groups. The three men had built, through years of trial and error, sharp intuitions about what would or would not work. The one presenting the fabricated experience would watch carefully in his peripheral vision for the non-verbal reactions of the other two, based on their intuitions as to whether the fabrication would actually work or not. If it was judged by these intuitions to be plausible, it became a template for the three of them to test at the next earliest opportunity. The second process used in these debriefing sessions was the isolation and description of apparent counter-examples to the patterns being experimented with and simultaneously an agenda item for the next opportunity to test it.

Frank's military experience leading the "troops," as he has stated; his work at the counseling center where he did whatever it took to get results with a client; his natural ability at leading to accomplish tasks to achieve a goal; coupled with his Semper Fi demeanor,[14] were the skill sets necessary to accomplish the task of taking the coded patterns and running them through the testing stage. He accomplished this through three generations of Meta/NLP groups, as he describes them. Even though these group members are mentioned in many articles, I have included Frank's list.[15] During the inception of Youth Services in Santa Cruz, the First NLP Community Testing Ground from David Wick's article, Frank served as the lead teacher of the group of students from NLP/Meta who trained the first counselors of the Youth Services Center in Santa Cruz until he left Santa Cruz to establish the San Diego Branch of M.E.T.A. as Director. At the time that Bryon Lewis joined M.E.T.A. in San Diego, California, around 1978, Marilyn Moskowitz, Steve Lorei, and Jeff Paris, along with Paul Carter and Steve Gilligan, all had been working with Frank at M.E.T.A.

When I stated above that Frank's role was critical to the founding and development of the field, I am referring to the fact that these groups, initially using the Gestalt platform, were the beta test sites for patterns as they were being coded by John and Richard. Testing, an essential step for the modeler in the five-step NLP modeling process, is the step designed to answer the question: Can this pattern, as coded, be successfully transferred to others such that it achieves results as effectively as the original model? Frank had participated in the modeling of Perls and in some of the modeling of Satir. He himself served as a beta test site on some patterns. Frank's natural response to a puzzle or to a role play, as an insider with Richard and John, could become the basis for a puzzle, exercise, or role play for a group session. Using the above as a frame, this is the perfect place in this narrative to offer a discussion of the Gestalt platform and how the initial groups operated within that platform.

IV. Group Improvisations: The First and Second Stages Utilized for Rehearsals of the Play

The First Stage used for Rehearsal

The brief introduction to Gestalt and Perls which you are about to read has as its purpose to provide a backstory for the reader. The platform upon which each of the early patterns, as they became coded, explored, experimented with, and tested on a daily basis inside the groups was Gestalt therapy. Gestalt itself was relatively novel with respect to the then current practices in the field of psychotherapy.

As you read the following description it may be fun to note the differentiators and type of process utilized by Gestalt, and then recall from your reading of the articles some of the processes and terms used by the various writers to describe their experience within the groups. The actual process of the Meta/NLP groups will be explicated after this initial discussion of Gestalt.

Fritz Perls, and his wife and collaborator, Laura Perls, created the New York Institute for Gestalt Therapy in the early 1950s, rejecting Freudian methods and exploring methodology which he called Gestalt.[16] His work in the United States began from their New York apartment from which he conducted groups, seminars, and workshops.

After the solo arrival of Perls in California in 1960, he began presenting Gestalt therapy training workshops at the Esalen Institute during the summer of 1964 – these trainings continued through 1968. The principal differentiator between the types of therapeutic interventions which were being utilized by traditional psychotherapists and Perls' Gestalt at the time was the relationship between therapist and client.

The methodology used by Perls was designed to have the client become actively involved by interacting with the therapist; not through the use of free association, which utilized no interaction with the client, but rather through exploration with the therapist. This began by inviting the client in each session to state what they were experiencing in that moment, rather than make an interpretation about events which occurred 10 minutes or three years ago. The therapist would then experiment with and explore the client's responses.

Few books had been written about the methodology which contained a limited set of patterns.[17] This methodology was employed in individual sessions or group sessions with approximately 10 participants. During the group sessions, a therapist worked with one client on the "hot seat" while other group members observed; at the end of usually a 20 minute session with the "hot seat" individual, the other group members gave feedback about how the work with that individual had impacted their personal issues.

The philosophy of Perls' Gestalt placed emphasis on what the client was experiencing in the present moment and upon the relationship between the therapist and client – the *therapists' role was to utilize spontaneous ways to explore* the client's experience.[18] The therapist did not attempt to modify behavior. It was upon this platform within the groups that the language patterns from the models were first explored, experimented with and, after initial coding, tested by the first generation Meta/NLP groups.

I will provide a brief summary to remind the reader of the chronology and to supply some additional details which more fully provide a context for this discussion of the group process.

Richard had met John at the UCSC T-Groups in approximately September 1971, and they maintained the connection on a casual social basis. It would not be unusual for Richard to drop into some of John's classes during the period of time that he and Frank were co-leading the Gestalt groups. Frank and John had yet to meet. In the fall of 1971, John was teaching Introduction to General Linguistics, followed in the winter quarter by Language and Mind[19] and in the spring quarter (of 1972) Structure of English.

It is now the fall quarter of 1972, and Richard invites John to "come see what we are doing." John had just returned from some months in Africa. Richard and Frank had embodied Perls' work. Richard had either taken or sat in on some of John's classes, particularly Language and Mind. When John questioned Richard's invitation in regard to Richard's intention for him "to come see what they were doing," John recalls Richard responding: "I have heard you talk with precision about how language and the human mind work."

Frank states the following in his article: "Richard invited a new 'hot-shot' linguistics professor to come visit our groups to see if there were linguistic or other patterns he could observe from our behaviors, and/

or ideas that could help us be better than we already were." (This phrase, by the way, could have been the original intent of Frank for inviting John: to have the ability to improve their Gestalt practice. It may not have been Richard's intention.) I include this quote from Frank's article to tie in the Gestalt platform of the initial groups. I have emphasized Frank's comment in order to remind the reader of an important feature of Gestalt therapy regarding the relationship between the therapist and the client as described in Gestalt discussion above. The key point here is that the therapist's role was to *utilize spontaneous ways to explore* the client's present experience. From the experiences presented by the writers – to utilize spontaneous ways to explore – it was a process that all three men were utilizing within these groups to explore and experiment with and, ultimately, test the original set of coded language patterns.

The term groups seems to have been a popular theme on Kresge College campus in those lively formative years. The college had instituted the process of T-Groups, frequently described as a form of sensitivity training. "The participants are encouraged to share emotional reactions (such as, for example, anger, fear, warmth, or envy) that arise in response to their fellow participants' actions and statements."

It is plausible that as a result of these T-Groups, that the on-campus market for Frank's Gestalt sessions was ripe for the plucking; it is equally plausible that Richard, with his exposure to Perls, who, having heard of Frank, joined forces to take advantage of this market. By running two or three Gestalt groups per week, Frank and Richard gained valuable experience. John, even though his undergraduate degree was in psychology, had never been exposed to clinical psychology. The T-Groups fascinated, intrigued, and irritated him all at the same time. He not infrequently had dramatic encounters with Michael Kahn about the processes of the T-Group.

During the T-Group sessions, John and Richard would exchange looks, which, if said aloud, would sound something like, "You've got to be kidding." Frank, a member of the student governance board, was connected to the student counseling center at UCSC, where he met Richard and from which he did peer counseling for students in need of assistance. I ask the reader to please note that the above are my own interpretations from reading historical documentation and may, or may not, have anything to do with the intentions of the parties.

It was from the T-Group experiences that these men were *primed* to recognize, assimilate, and finally code the Meta Model patterns of mind reading and cause/effect – patterns that were so systematic and transparent in the context of T-Groups.

The Second Rehearsal Stage : Rehearsals Moved to New Stage

I have mentioned the time gap between the modeling of Perls and Satir. The importance of this marker in respect to the process of the groups is that during this gap the emphasis began to shift away from running Gestalt therapy type groups, where students were working on their own "stuff," to an emphasis on experimenting with, exploring and testing each new pattern, from whatever source, as it was either modeled or coded – or patterns that occurred spontaneously while working within the groups. These patterns were the patterns of John, Richard, and Frank, and were not systematic in the models or even available from the models. The form of rehearsal had changed.

The students of first and second generation, as identified by Frank, were the students who were shifted to this new format, thereby leaving Gestalt behind. The discovery of the modal operators of necessity is a perfect example as to how these student groups were utilized by Frank, John, and Richard. The transition began as they began to notice patterns (both linguistic and non-verbal patterns) of what they themselves were spontaneously doing during the Gestalt sessions which were not exhibited by the models. This process occurred by the constant running of groups for each of the models, first Perls, then Satir, and ultimately Erickson. For example, the identification of the modal operators of necessity and possibility was evident in the behavior of each model. However, their behavior was not systematic either in detecting or challenging them (none of them challenged the modal operators in ALL instances) and nor did any of them have well developed challenges to them. There were examples of effective challenging by non-verbal gestures to full-out verbal exchanges to explore the implications or consequence of the pattern on the part of the models. However, it was primarily through the rigorous testing and experimentation within the groups, driven by exercises, that the identification and coding of the modal operators became systematic, and specific verbal challenges were developed. The creation of specific challenges was largely an original contribution by John, Richard, and Frank. This was the process that was utilized within the groups on many of the patterns. Only after rigorous testing in the groups through role playing, puzzles, and direct context setting, along with explicit coding, could the behavior of the agent of change leading the groups become systematic enough for the challenges to ultimately become standardized.

As more and more of the patterns became coded, especially during the process of writing (*Magic I*, *Magic II*, and *Patterns I*) in late 1973 and 1974 the character of the *processes* utilized within these groups changed again, depending upon how long the group had been together. (Note in note 15 the addition of new members during a specific time frame.)

The majority of the initial testing phase of the coded patterns which appear in *The Structure of Magic, Volume I* occurred within first and second generation groups. Primarily, the recovery of deletion (e.g., comparative deletion), specification of nouns and verbs, modal operators of necessity and possibility, cause/effect, mind reading, lost performative, complex equivalence, which were the focus of *The Structure of Magic, Volume I*, as they related to therapy, were the patterns that, having been coded, were tested.

Representational systems, including both eye movements and predicates, had already been coded and then tested by these same groups. *The Structure of Magic, Volume II* had been mostly written between 1974 and 1975 but not published until 1976 as Richard and John chose to publish *The Patterns of the Hypnotic Techniques of Milton Erickson, Volume I* under their own publishing company, called Meta Publications, Inc., in 1975. Most of the patterns of the Meta Model and the wave of nonverbal patterns (i.e., rapport, calibration points, and the beginnings of anchoring) had been coded and tested by 1975.

Representational systems had also been completed as is evident from a passage in *The Structure of Magic, Volume I*:

> The power of the technique of shifting the client's experiences from one representational system to another can hardly be overestimated. In Volume II of *The Structure of Magic*, we present an explicit model for the identification and utilization of the client's most frequently employed representational system.[20]

When one of the contributors makes reference to group membership, by the time the third generation arrived on the scene, some in late 1974 and others in early 1975, we see many of the names reoccurring from the first and second generations. This group of individuals is joined by David Gordon and Leslie Cameron in 1974, both of whom declined to write articles for this book. We know of their presence as they are mentioned by the various writers. The contributors have placed themselves within the following time frames: Steve Gilligan 74, James Eicher 74, Terry McClendon, David Wick 74, Bryon Lewis 75, Judith DeLozier 75, and Robert Dilts 76. Please note that some of the dates in the Terry McClendon article are in variance with the other reports.[21] Some of these individuals arrived during and after the second modeling of Milton Erickson and all of them after the writing of *Magic I*, *Patterns I* and the initial writing of *Magic II*.

Frank, John, and Richard began to utilize additional processes with the third generation groups. I mention three of them here. In some groups, participants were given exercises designed to sharpen the skill sets that they would need to actually model. In some groups, especially during classes conducted at UCSC, group students were given a pattern and directed to run the pattern over and over in different contexts to discover the consequences of running the pattern. In some groups, the students were given tasking exercises; for example, to name something that had no name and note the consequences of such a naming on their behaviors and especially their attention.

Since many of these processes are described in one way or another within the articles by each individual writer, my intention for discussing this process has been to provide the reader with a frame of reference.

The modeling, with the exception of the second phase of Erickson for *Patterns II*, was done; much of the exploring and experimentation was done; much of the coding was done; and the original testing was done by first and second generation groups. What remained was the rigorous re-testing, the extension of the patterning into new contexts, and patterns for the transfer of the patterning to participants new to the game.

This is when Frank's third generation – Meta/NLP (in late 74–77) arrived on the scene. Some of these group members, who had been around since the first and second generation, became the "whiz kids," as John called a few; and others became members of the "inner circle", as referred to by Bryon Lewis in his chapter. These were the people who led groups, taught the patterns to new groups and/or became teacher assistants.

You may have noted while reading these articles various instances where the writer refers to the "discovery" of some of the patterns by themselves (i.e., Eicher, DeLozier, and Dilts). Such discoveries often refer to the successful completion of a task or exercise designed and assigned to the students in a group or with clients (as described by Byron Lewis). These tasks or exercises were designed by Richard, John, and Frank with two purposes: (1) the continuing rigorous testing of the patterns themselves, and (2) the transfer of the skill sets actually required for modeling. As an aside to the reader, only one of these students has mentioned in their article, that they went on to do, by their description, NLP modeling and that was Steven Gilligan in his modeling of Milton Erickson.

These discovery exercises were derived from the model utilized in the teaching of advanced linguistics students, in advanced linguistics patterning. These discovery exercises were used to assist graduate linguistic students in the development of pattern detection competencies – a necessary element in language modeling and coding. This process, utilized by John, in his Linguistics 194A Senior Seminar, Advanced Topics in Linguistics, was a process whereby he would generate a small, finite, highly structured data set which contained a pattern for the students to discover – a method that is frequently used as a didactic method in phonology and syntax.

When I mention above that the character of the processes utilized within these Meta/NLP groups changed, I am referring specifically to the introduction of the discovery process exercises which were built upon these highly structured data sets. These data sets were designed and created and sometimes written down and passed out in ditto form. The third generation Meta/NLP groups were given closed, carefully constructed data sets, especially true in the case of the linguistic patterns and the representational predicate testing, to determine whether the students in the "groups" could discover the same patterns that Richard, John, and Frank had already discovered and coded. This is the difference between an exercise that has been designed to train a practitioner to discover patterning (already patterned and coded) and an *actual original discovery*. This rigorous testing process of the patterns derived from all the models and from Richard, John, and Frank's own contributions, continued through most of 1976 with each of the groups.

V: Unscripted Parts

The Naming of the Play

It is unclear as to the precise date that the field was named Neuro-Linguistic Programming (NLP). The name does not appear in *Magic I, Patterns I,* or *Magic II* which were all written in 1974 and published in 1975–1976. I started to go through *Patterns II*, which was written in 1976, and by some use of terminology and by direct reference it appears that John and Richard had begun to write a large portion of *Neuro-Linguistic Programming, Volume I*[22] (much in the same way that they wrote *Magic II* almost two years in advance of its publication) and were planning to publish it immediately after the publication of *Patterns II*.

In *Patterns II* we have:

> Finally, we mention the choice of re-framing, either meta-phorical or literal. This is an extensive area containing many interesting patterns some of which will be contained in a forthcoming publication (*Neuro-Linguistic Programming I.*).[23]

Again, in *Patterns II* there is a listing in the bibliography for:

> Grinder, J, Bandler, R. and Cameron, L. *Neuro Linguistic Programming I* (in preparation).[24]

These references seem to coincide with Jim Eicher's recollection in his article that the name, neuro-linguistic programming, was coined some-time after the publication of *Structure of Magic II* as a way to respond to the question: "How can I become more like JohnandRichard? How can I successfully model the modelers and their 'magic'?"

After reading Eicher's article, doing the research, and writing this Epilogue, I have concluded that sometime during late 1975, while writing the draft of *Patterns II* and the initial drafting of *Neuro-Linguistic Programming, Volume I*, that the rapidly growing sets of patterns that Richard, John, and Frank had modeled, experimented with, and coded reached the point where it seemed to call for a name – a title of its own. This new set of patterns no longer fit within the container of Perls' Gestalt therapy, and certainly not within Satir's work. I posited this hypothesis to John in an e-mail and asked him to comment on the naming of the field. What follows is an excerpt from that e-mail:

> One fateful evening, at the Tea House at Alba Road, Bandler and I were continuing to work on the written descriptions of the patterns. My memories of the evening are the following:

> Bandler was convinced that it was time to brand (in retrospect I am sure that he was correct – that is, it WAS time to brand – what we were doing – I had resisted similar proposals from him for some months). This evening, his presentation was forceful enough (congruity) that I accepted the challenge of having a run at working this naming thing out.

As was often the case in the collaboration between Bandler and myself, it fell to me to generate a set of choices from which Bandler would then make a selection of what he considered preferable. Once this selection had occurred, we would typically discuss the advantages and disadvantages of what he had selected from the list enumerated by me and decide together how to proceed. In this case, I remember running off a set of possible labels for what we had created, the three of us. Something like:

"OK, here are some possibilities: Radical Patterning, Meta-Moves, Incantations, Paths into the Future, Integrative Therapy, E Pluribus Unum, The New Generation, Neurolinguistics, Natural Language Patterning, Theatre of the Absurd." Bandler halted this stream of terms and said, *"Neurolinguistics, I like the way that sounds!"*

I explained to him that there already was a discipline called *neurolinguistics* – a field established in the 19th century, having its base in aphasiology (the study of the syndrome called aphasia – typically after some traumatic insult to the temporal lobes) – and other natural experiments – studies of the consequences of cerebral insults through accidents to the cortex and the tracking down of the behavioral consequences of such "natural" experiments. With his usual arrogance, he dismissed this objection as trivial. The conversation drifted into other areas of interest. Either I or Bandler left the following day on some trip and it was approximately a week later when we got back together that I discovered that he had simply added the word *programming* onto *neurolinguistics*, and with a punctuation change – separating the *neuro* from the *linguistics* with a hyphen, he had coined the name of the present field *Neuro-Linguistic Programming*; a term that was such a mouthful that it was almost immediately shorted to *NLP*. I demurred.

Meta to What?

As you have read in the articles, the term *meta* appears frequently in Frank's article and in any article referring to Frank or the groups. The original patterns as modeled, explored, tested by the student groups and then coded in *Magic I* and *Magic II* were primarily the Meta model distinctions, the set of representational systems (eye movements, predicates, and overlap), calibration, and nominalizations, to name but a few.

This was during the discovery, exploration, experimentation, and coding period as each new model appeared in the matrix – Perls, Satir, and Erickson. Further evidence of this reference to the word meta is the lack of mention of NLP in *Magic I*, *Magic II*, and *Patterns I*, and the fact that John and Richard formed a publishing company in late 1974 or early 1975 which published as its first book *Patterns I* and later *Patterns II* (1977). This company was called Meta Publications. *Magic II* uses terms like Meta – So What, Achieving Meta-Position, Meta-Tactics for incongruity, and Meta Tactics for phases 1–6. This book was largely written in late 1974 and completed in early 1975 and is referenced in *Patterns I* along with, reference to *Magic I*, urging the therapist to consult these two books for processes to reintegrate the client's model of his world fully before the hypnotic relationship is ended.[25] This reference provides more information that *Magic II* had been written before *Patterns I* and during 1974–1975 before the name NLP was created. It appears that Frank called the groups for which he became responsible, Meta groups, therefore, when Frank left to go to San Diego, it was natural that he would set up an organization called M.E.T.A. San Diego to offer trainings in the work that he had been doing with Richard and John.

The Consequences of Naming *Play*

The naming function has always been an interesting phenomenon within the field now known as NLP. Perhaps this phenomenon stems from the dilemma or consequence which arises for innovative individuals when linguistically coding an experience. The act of doing and experiencing is dynamic. Whenever there is an imposition of language onto the flow of experience, the flow is interrupted and something dynamic is transformed into something static. The naming function therefore operates analogously to the linguistic process of nominalization, in which a verb (representing something dynamic) is transformed into something static (a noun or, technically, a pseudo noun called a nominalization). The observation of this phenomenon comes to us from linguistics. All natural languages thus far analyzed contain this nominalization function (and is, indeed, the recursive element).

The process of nominalization has multiple consequences. Let's consider, then, the word *programming* as part of the name *Neuro-Linguistic Programming*. If you don't have an immediate association to Big Brother, you obviously have not read Orwell's *1984*. I did, and as I began my training in 1986 from a down-line that relied heavily on the utilization of Erickson's patterns from the stage prior to the teaching of the processes of NLP within sessions led by assistants, I felt that I was being programmed to "decide now." My next course was with John Grinder and Judith DeLozier. I was delighted to note the ecological utilization of the Erickson patterns – with emphasis on personal choice.

As another example of the consequences of the naming function, consider a phenomenon within the field now known as NLP: the pattern that bridges Classic Code to the New Code, which is historically known as six-step reframing. Anyone who has ever used this pattern or simply intellectually analyzed this pattern will recognize that there is no change in the original frame (positive intention); but rather, that the frame is held constant, and the behavior is shifted to alternative behaviors which satisfy the frame of positive intention which is held constant. This process is named – defined from – the inside-out, backwards. Reframing would more accurately be called its inverse – re-behaving. Think about the term *meta programs*, I have asked myself; what are these programs meta to?

What was the consequence of naming the first book, *The Structure of Magic, Volume I* and the subsequent one *Volume II*? Apparently, the booksellers only looked at the covers, rather than the subtitles or contents of each book: *The Structure of Magic I: A Book about Language and Therapy* and *The Structure of Magic II: A Book about Communication and Change*. These books were placed on the bookshelves under the category of New Age and Occult in almost every bookstore I have ever visited.

To close this section on the consequences of naming, I would like to ask the reader to think about the consequences of any naming function.

The naming function, the act of labeling, is an act that places a left brain imposition upon the active flow of one's experience. Labeling could, in a deep sense, prematurely make a nominalization of a person's ongoing experience rendering it static – thereby limiting the *scope* of the exploration or experimentation. With this definition, perhaps it will be easy for the reader to understand the time lapse on the part of Richard and John for naming the field. If the field had been named during the modeling, exploration, coding, and testing of 1972–1974, would this labeling not have been akin to "pinning the graceful butterfly to a piece of black velvet" – as, perhaps, with all the redefining of the patterns and the definitions of the field, that it ultimately has turned out to be?

VI. The Epilogue of the Play

Each of the chapters in this volume end with what the writer went on to do as a result of the experiences they have captured within their article from this period in their lives as students – and some go on to comment about the field today. Each of these writers was young, eager, and willing to explore to develop their own life paths after graduation from UCSC.

Frank went to San Diego and set up M.E.T.A. followed by some of the students from first, second, and third generations. Richard and John, who had been modeling, exploring, experimenting, coding, and writing for years together, after the formation of Meta Publications and having named the field, began to travel together to present seminars on their processes. Even though the great work of these two men continues in their individual discoveries and explorations today, what follows is a brief description of the period from 1976 to 1979 – the transition from the initial process of discovery.

Richard and Leslie Cameron-Bandler formed a corporation called Not Ltd in September 1977. A division of that corporation, the Division of Training and Research (DOTAR) vested responsibility in Leslie Cameron-Bandler and its function was the certification, testing, and delivering of seminars on Neuro-Linguistic Programming. In October 1977, John Grinder and Judith DeLozier formed a corporation called Unlimited, Ltd.

In 1979, these two entities, Not Ltd and Unlimited, Ltd, became equal partners in the Society of Neuro-Linguistic Programming, whose purpose was to engage in the business of teaching and training others in the techniques and art of NLP, including the certification and credentialing of others in this art. At this time, there were many conversations among the officers of these corporations regarding the advantages for the formation of the Society of Neuro-Linguistic Programming in order to establish formal criteria for the training and certification of training in NLP. As you have read in this book, many of the students who had tested the patterns in groups at UCSC were teaching courses in the processes. Perhaps the training programs began to warrant formal guidelines and standardization for branding.

Since memories can be altered by present filters, it is important to clarify the sequence of events and correct some of the dates and facts that appear in some of the articles. To do this, I went to public documents on file. The formal certification programs and the parameters were begun by Leslie Cameron-Bandler in her own hand and were developed later with David Gordon and Robert Dilts under DOTAR as originally formed in 1977. The first use of a trademark differentiation Neuro-Linguistic Programming (NLP) occurs one year later in November 1978. The partnership agreement for the Society of Neuro-Linguistic Programming occurred nearly two years after the initial incorporation of Not Ltd and Unlimited, Ltd in November 1978. After the execution of the partnership agreement between Not Ltd and Unlimited, Ltd, Robert Dilts became involved officially with DOTAR, and the respective officers of those corporations, along with David Gordon, to carry forth the mission of the partnership as described above. The logo about which Robert Dilts writes was part of the intellectual property that was transferred into the Society's partnership agreement in 1979 from Not Ltd and Unlimited, Ltd.

So, at the end of this epilogue of the Play what was the importance of the word MAGIC? When I began my interest in the field, before I went to my first seminar with John Grinder, I purchased all the books that John and Richard had written. When the books arrived from Grinder and DeLozier associates, I tore open the box and immediately selected *Frogs into Princes, Richard Bandler and John Grinder Live*, published in

1979. Perhaps I selected it because of the "Live" or perhaps the covers of *Magic I* and *Magic II*, with the wizard, were less appealing than the picture of the handsome prince on the cover of *Frogs*. When I finally read *Magic I* and *Magic II*, I was enchanted. I had briefly studied some linguistics books many years back while I was a teacher. I remember musing, "If only I'd that book then – how differently I would have approached English grammar as a teacher!"

As I reread the books to write this Epilogue, I was intrigued about the metaphor of magic. I did not pay much attention to it years ago at my first reading; the language patterns were what intrigued me back in 1986.

At the time of writing *Magic I*, John and Richard had just modeled Perls, Satir, and the initial modeling of Erickson. They behaviorally *became* these models. They confirmed for themselves the magic of acting *as if* and experienced the magic that occurred in groups as they become fluent speakers and actors within the field of therapy. The Preface to *The Structure of Magic, Volume I* begins:

> Down through the ages the power and wonder of practitioners of magic have been recorded in song and story. The presence of wizards, witches, sorcerers, shamen and gurus has always been intriguing and awe inspiring to the average person ... In modern time, the mantle of the wizard is most often placed upon those dynamic practitioners of psychotherapy who exceed the skill of other therapists by leaps and bounds, and whose work is so amazing to watch that it moves us with powerful emotions, disbelief, and utter confusion.
>
> Just as with all wizards of the ages of earth whose knowledge was treasured and passed down from sage to sage – losing and adding pieces but retaining a basic structure – so, too, does *the magic of these therapeutic wizards also have structure.* (my emphasis)[26]

They became excited about the response of clients that their communication elicited (the meaning of a communication is the response that it elicits). They found and coded the structure of this magic and wanted to pass it on in a learnable way to anyone interested.

Further on in *The Structure of Magic, Volume I*, they write:

> This book is a manual to teach you a set of tools which will increase your effectiveness as a therapist. Since this book, the first of a series, is primarily concerned with the verbal techniques, most of the techniques are questions based on the *form* of the clients' communication in therapy. (my emphasis)[27]

Ultimately, the magic that they demystified became a field for innovative people willing to explore something new:

> One of the mysteries in the field of therapy is that, although the various schools of therapy have very different forms, they all succeed to some degree. The puzzle will be solved when the effective methods shared by the different psychotherapies can be described in a single set of terms, thus making the similarities explicit and thereby learnable by therapists of any school.*[28]

With the hope, as described by Jay Haley, of "providing the most effective strategy possible to induce a person to spontaneously behave in a different manner,"[29] this is a hope that perhaps lives on.

I end with this quote from Virginia Satir from the foreword to *The Structure of Magic, Volume I*:

> The knowledge of the process is now considerably advanced by Richard Bandler and John Grinder, who can talk in a way that can be concretized and measured about the ingredients of the *what* that goes into making the *how* possible.[30]

---

* We highly recommend the excellent work by Jay Haley, Gregory Bateson and his associates, Paul Watlawick [*sic*], Janet Beavin, and Don Jackson. Their studies appear to us to be, at present, the closest approximation along with the *Meta-model to achieving this goal.* (my emphasis)

Notes

Introduction: Reflections on *The Origins of Neuro-Linguistic Programming* – *John Grinder*

1. Richard Bandler and John Grinder, *Patterns of the Hypnotic Techniques of Milton H. Erickson, M.D., Vol. I* (Cupertino, CA: Meta Publications, 1975); John Grinder, Richard Bandler, and Judith DeLozier, *Patterns of the Hypnotic Techniques of Milton H. Erickson, M.D., Vol. II* (Cupertino, CA: Meta Publications, 1977).

2. Thomas Kuhn, *The Structure of Scientific Revolutions* (Chicago, IL: University of Chicago Press, 1970).

3. Kuhn, *The Structure of Scientific Revolutions*, pp. 114–117.

4. Thomas Kuhn, *The Essential Tension* (Chicago, IL: University of Chicago Press, 1979), pp. 66–71.

5. Carmen Bostic-St. Clair and John Grinder, *Whispering in the Wind* (Scotts Valley, CA: J & C Enterprises, 2001), pp. 61–138.

Part 1

Chapter 2: My Road to NLP – *Terry McClendon*

1. John Grinder and Richard Bandler, *Frogs into Princes: Neuro Linguistic Programming* (Moab, UT: Real People Press, 1979); eidem, *Reframing: Neurolinguistic Programming and the Transformation of Meaning* (Moab, UT: Real People Press, 1983); John Grinder, Richard Bandler, and Connirae Andreas, *Trance-Formations: Neuro-Linguistic Programming and the Structure of Hypnosis* (Moab, UT: Real People Press, 1981).

2. Barry Stevens, *Don't Push the River (It Flows By Itself)* (Moab, UT: Real People Press, 1970).

3. Fritz Perls, *The Gestalt Approach and Eyewitness to Therapy* (Palo Alto, CA: Science and Behavior Books, 1973).

4. John Grinder and Richard Bandler, *The Structure of Magic, Vol. I: A Book about Language and Therapy* (Palo Alto, CA: Science and Behavior Books, 1975).

5. John Grinder, Richard Bandler, Judith DeLozier, and Robert Dilts, *Neuro-Linguistic Programming: The Study of the Structure of Subjective Experience, Vol. I* (Capitola, CA: Meta Publications, 1980).

6. Terrence McClendon, *The Wild Days: NLP 1972–1981* (Terrence McClendon, 1989).

7. Terrence McClendon, *Happy Parents Happy Kids: Words and Actions for Parents and Kids* (Terrence McClendon, 2012).

Chapter 3: The Early Days of NLP – *Judith DeLozier*

1. John Grinder and Richard Bandler, *The Structure of Magic, Vol. I: A Book about Language and Therapy* (Palo Alto, CA: Science and Behavior Books, 1975).

2. Gregory Bateson and Margaret Mead, *Balinese Character: A Photographic Analysis* (New York: New York Academy of Sciences, 1942).

3. Virginia Satir, John Grinder, and Richard Bandler, *Changing with Families: A Book about Further Education for Being Human* (Palo Alto, CA: Science and Behavior Books, 1976).

4. John Grinder and Richard Bandler, *Patterns of the Hypnotic Techniques of Milton H. Erickson, M.D., Vol. I* (Cupertino, CA: Meta Publications, 1975) and John Grinder, Richard Bandler, and Judith DeLozier, *Patterns of the Hypnotic Techniques of Milton H. Erickson, M.D., Vol. II* (Cupertino, CA: Meta Publications, 1977).

5. John Grinder and Judith DeLozier, *Turtles All the Way Down: Prerequisites to Personal Genius* (Portland, OR: Metamorphous Press, 1995).

Chapter 5: My Parts Party: Early Dissociated Therapy – *Byron Lewis*

1. Little did I know at the time that Frank was one of the three original creators of what would grow to become NLP. Along with Richard Bandler and John Grinder, they were pioneering a whole new range of therapeutic interventions based on their observations and modeling of master therapists such as Virginia Satir and Milton Erickson. It is striking to me today that, other than a few citations, such as Carmen Bostic-St. Clair and John Grinder's *Whispering in the Wind* (Scotts Valley, CA: J & C Enterprises, 2001), Frank appears to have been systematically left out of most accounts of the early development of NLP.

2. I was recently delighted when I ran across a description of this process in Paul Tosey and Jane Mathison's *Neuro-Linguistic Programming: A Critical Appreciation for Managers and Developers* (London: Palgrave Macmillan, 2009). In their discussion of the need for more "appraisal" of the Meta

Model, they cite information by Bostic-St. Clair and Grinder (*Whispering in the Wind*) who wrote that Richard and John tested the patterns they were developing by setting up a "pseudo-therapist" (such as myself) who was "primed by them on exactly what questions to ask to elicit the structure of the problem, while the 'real' therapists [presumably Richard and/or John in my case] listened in. The pseudo-therapist would then leave the client, and confer with Grinder and Bandler on the best approach to the presenting problem [and receive instructions on how to intervene]."

3. I apologize to those who decry the dearth of "legitimate case histories" in the various publications that talk about successful applications of NLP. Here is yet another glamorous description that is only as valid as the reader decides it is true because I said it is. As Frank and I work on the revised edition of *Magic of NLP Demystified*, we hope to be able to guide readers to the growing body of scientific research on various techniques and applications of NLP across a broad spectrum of disciplines, from psychotherapy and coaching to teaching and medicine.

4. With a notable exception in the very recent past, our book has been in continuous publication since its release in 1980. I know that it has been reprinted in a number of different languages around the world, and I am extremely pleased to have been invited recently to complete a second edition, to be released by Crown House Publishing. While it is a simple introduction to the field of NLP, our book also addresses very early on such issues as the *ethics* of persuasive communications, the validity of models of the world, and the underpinnings of its basic precepts.

5. The program we developed focused primarily on the works of Maxie Maultsby: *Rational Behavioral Therapy* (Englewood Cliffs, NJ: Prentice Hall, 1984); Maxie Maultsby and Allie Hendricks, *You and Your Emotions* (Appleton, WI: Rational Self-Help Books, 1974); T. Gorski and M. Miller, *Counseling for Relapse Prevention* (Independence, MO: Herals House/Independence Press, 1982). I expanded on their works and integrated my experience with NLP into my second book, *Sobriety Demystified: Getting Clean and Sober with NLP and CBT* (Saratoga, CA: Kelsey & Co., 1996) – now available from Crown House Publishing.

6. See Walter Isaacson's *Steve Jobs: The Exclusive Biography* (New York: Little, Brown and Co., 2011).

Part 2

Chapter 6: The Middle of Know Where: My Early Days in NLP
– *Stephen Gilligan*

1. I have done my best to accurately recall events, including dates, people involved, and so on. Memory is undeniably a constructive process, always in revision, so my apologies for any significant distortions or deletions.

2. To my knowledge, the original groups were led by Bandler and Pucelik, with Grinder joining in after several years. The first groups I was in were, I believe, at the time when things shifted from Bandler and Pucelik to Bandler and Grinder.

3. John Grinder and Richard Bandler, *The Structure of Magic, Vol. I: A Book about Language and Therapy* (Palo Alto, CA: Science and Behavior Books, 1975).

Chapter 7: Commentary on "The Middle of Know Where"
– *John Grinder*

1. See Carmen Bostic St. Clair and John Grinder, *Whispering in the Wind* (Scotts Valley, CA: J & C Enterprises, 2001), pp. 9–49.

Chapter 8: "It's a Fresh Wind That Blows Against the Empire" –
James Eicher

1. Quote by Robert Heinlein.

2. Norman O. Brown, *Life against Death: The Psychoanalytical Meaning of History* (Middletown, CT: Wesleyan University Press, 1959); idem, *Love's Body* (New York: Random House, 1966).

3. John Grinder and Suzette Haden Elgin, *Guide to Transformational Grammar: History, Theory, Practice* (New York: Holt, Rinehart and Winston, 1973).

4. Fritz Perls, *The Gestalt Approach and Eyewitness to Therapy* (Palo Alto, CA: Science and Behavior Books, 1973).

5. John Grinder and Richard Bandler, *The Structure of Magic, Vol. I: A Book about Language and Therapy* (Palo Alto, CA: Science and Behavior Books, 1975).

6. Richard Bandler and John Grinder, *Patterns of the Hypnotic Techniques of Milton H. Erickson, M.D., Vol. I* (Cupertino, CA: Meta Publications, 1975).

7. Alfred Korzybski, *Science and Sanity: An Introduction to Non-Aristotelian Systems and General Semantics*, 5th edn (Brooklyn, NY: Institute of General Semantics, 1994; orig. pub. 1933).

8. Virginia Satir, *Peoplemaking* (London: Souvenir Press, 1990; orig. pub. 1972).

9. Gregory Bateson, *Steps to an Ecology of Mind: Collected Essays in Anthropology, Psychiatry, Evolution, and Epistemology* (Chicago, IL: University of Chicago Press, 1972).

10. Gregory Bateson and Margaret Mead, *Balinese Character: A Photographic Analysis* (New York: New York Academy of Sciences, 1942).

11. George A. Miller, "The Magical Number Seven, Plus or Minus Two: Some Limits on Our Capacity for Processing Information," *Psychological Review*, 63 (1956), 81–97.

12. George A. Miller, Eugene Galanter, and Karl H. Pribram, *Plans and the Structure of Behavior* (New York: Adams Bannister Cox, 1960).

13. John Grinder and Richard Bandler, *The Structure of Magic, Vol. II: A Book about Communication and Change* (Palo Alto, CA: Science and Behavior Books, 1975); eidem, *Patterns of the Hypnotic Techniques of Milton H. Erickson, Vol. I*; John Grinder, Richard Bandler, and Judith DeLozier, *Patterns of the Hypnotic Techniques of Milton H. Erickson, M.D., Vol. II* (Cupertino, CA: Meta Publications, 1977); Virginia Satir, John Grinder, and Richard Bandler, *Changing with Families: A Book about Further Education for Being Human* (Palo Alto, CA: Science and Behavior Books, 1976).

14. Gregory Bateson, "A Theory of Play and Fantasy," *Psychiatric Research Reports*, 2 (1955), 39–51.

15. Erving Goffman, *Frame Analysis: An Essay on the Organization of Experience* (London: Harper and Row, 1974).

16. Paul Watzlawick, Janet Beavin-Bavelas, and Don Jackson, *Pragmatics of Human Communication: A Study of Interactional Patterns, Pathologies, and Paradoxes* (New York: W.W. Norton, 1967).

17. James Eicher, "Linguistics and the Problem of Serial Order," *Papers in Linguistics*, 10 (1977), 151–183.

18. John Grinder and Richard Bandler, *Frogs into Princes: Neuro Linguistic Programming* (Moab, UT: Real People Press, 1979).

19. Daniel Goleman, "People Who Read People," *Psychology Today*, 13 (July 1979).

20. Philip Slater, *The Pursuit of Loneliness* (Boston, MA: Beacon Press, 1990; orig. pub. 1970) and *Earthwalk* (New York: Anchor Books, 1975).

21. Robert Lorber and Ken Blanchard, *Putting the One Minute Manager to Work* (New York: Berkley, 1985).

22. James Eicher, *Making the Message Clear: Communicating for Business* (Santa Cruz, CA: Grinder, DeLozier and Associates, 1987).

23. James Eicher, John Jones, and William Bearley, *The Neurolinguistic Communication Profile* (King of Prussia, PA: HRDQ, 1990); eidem, *Rapport: Matching and Mirroring Communication* (King of Prussia, PA: HRDQ, 1990).

24. James Eicher, *Rapport-Based Selling* (Dallas, TX: Get to the Point Books, 2009); idem, *No Need for Conflict!* (Dallas, TX: Get to the Point Books, 2010).

Chapter 9: Commentary on "It's a Fresh Wind that Blows against the Empire" – *John Grinder*

1. Carmen Bostic-St. Clair and John Grinder, *Whispering in the Wind* (Scotts Valley, CA: J & C Enterprises, 2001), pp. 164–172.

2. George A. Miller, "The Magical Number Seven, Plus or Minus Two: Some Limits on Our Capacity for Processing Information," *Psychological Review*, 63 (1956), 81–97.

3. Noam Chomsky, "A Review of B. F. Skinner's *Verbal Behavior*," *Language*, 35(1) (1959), 26–58.

4. George A. Miller, Eugene Galanter, and Karl H. Pribram, *Plans and the Structure of Behavior* (New York: Adams Bannister Cox, 1960).

Chapter 10: My Early History with NLP – *Robert Dilts*

1. The origin of neurolinguistics dates to the work of Broca (1861, 1865) and Wernicke (1874) who localized the neurological mechanisms underlying the storage and perception of language to certain areas in the left hemisphere of the brain. Most early neurolinguistic studies were made as the result of observations of people with aphasia – speech disorders brought about by damage to particular parts of the brain. Later research involved the technique of electrically stimulating areas of the cortex of conscious patients undergoing brain surgery in order to locate which

areas of the brain were connected with various types of general cognitive and linguistic phenomena.

Russian neuropsychologist Alexander Luria extended the field of neurolinguistics by attempting to identify basic language processes and functions (naming, syntax, word recognition, etc.), and then ascribing these language components to particular brain regions.

In 1941, Alfred Korzybski mentioned "neurolinguistics" as an area of study relating to General Semantics. Korzybski saw neurolinguistics as a key element in developing a better understanding of the role and limitations of language in how we build our maps of the world, and in distinguishing the "map" from the "territory."

Much of the contemporary work in the field of neurolinguistics has been in the area of representational models, which was stimulated by Noam Chomsky's theory of transformational grammar (1957). The notion of "computational neurolinguistics," proposed by Michael A. Arbib (1972, 1979), attempts to make a bridge from artificial intelligence programs which process speech to principles of "synapse-cell-circuit" neuroscience.

2. According to John Grinder, the name emerged one night when he and Bandler were musing about what to call what they were doing. Typical of their collaboration in those days, John would propose possible names, Bandler would select his preferences and then they would make the final decision together. When John mentioned "neurolinguistics," Richard got excited and declared that that was what he wanted to call it. John objected that there already was an established field called neurolinguistics. Bandler thought about it for a while and then said that he wanted to call it Neuro-Linguistic Programming, adding the "programming" and hyphenating the first word. John had his doubts about it, but Richard persisted and the rest is history.

3. The Santa Cruz campus of the University of California opened in 1964. The visionary founder of the university was Dean McHenry, who had a dream that an environment could be created which encouraged the interaction between departments and would promote interdisciplinary studies and projects. This had not previously been the case in many institutions of higher education. McHenry went through great efforts to get the best, brightest, and most innovative professors and students. The effect of this intense emphasis on intellectual "cross pollination" yielded many benefits in that it unleashed creative thinking in many areas; symbolizing in many ways the dramatic social and intellectual changes of the 1960s. It was this environment that spawned the creation of NLP and supported its early development.

4. Robert Dilts, *Strategies of Genius, Vol. I* (Capitola, CA: Meta Publications, 1994).

5. John Grinder and Richard Bandler, *The Structure of Magic, Vol. I: A Book about Language and Therapy* (Palo Alto, CA: Science and Behavior Books, 1975).

6. Robert Dilts, *Applications of Neuro-Linguistic Programming* (Capitola, CA: Meta Publications, 1983).

7. Gregory Bateson, *Steps to an Ecology of Mind: Collected Essays in Anthropology, Psychiatry, Evolution, and Epistemology* (Chicago, IL: University of Chicago Press, 1972).

8. Bateson's earlier work, to which he referred in his preface to *The Structure of Magic, Volume I,* was his attempt to apply principles of cybernetics and communication theory to psychotherapy and the understanding of psychological pathology. Stimulated by Norbert Wiener (the founder of cybernetics), Bateson had adapted cybernetic thinking to human communication and interaction in order to develop generalizations about the behavior and mental characteristics of individuals, groups, and families, and the influences behind functional and dysfunctional systems. Bateson's ideas fueled a whole generation of behavioral scientists and psychotherapists. People such as Virginia Satir, Mara Selvini Palazzoli, Jay Haley, John Weakland, and others, for example, applied Bateson's formulations to the treatment of individual and family problems.

9. Gregory Bateson and Margaret Mead, *Balinese Character: A Photographic Analysis* (New York: New York Academy of Sciences, 1942).

10. John Grinder and Richard Bandler, *Patterns of the Hypnotic Techniques of Milton H. Erickson, M.D., Vol. I* (Cupertino, CA: Meta Publications, 1975).

11. My early work with eye movements culminated with a research study at the Langley Porter Institute in San Francisco in 1977 correlating EEG recordings of brain waves with eye movements and representational systems. This study was written up in *Roots of NLP* (Capitola, CA: Meta Publications, 1983) and also appears in the *Encyclopedia of Systemic NLP* (Santa Cruz, CA: NLP University Press, 2000).

Judith DeLozier and I point out in the *Encyclopedia of Systemic NLP* that the notion that eye movements might be related to internal representations was first suggested by American psychologist William James in his book *Principles of Psychology* (New York: Henry Holt, 1890). Observing that some forms of micromovement always accompany thought, James wrote: "I cannot think in visual terms, or example, without feeling a fluctuating play of pressures, convergences, divergences, and accommodations in my eyeballs … When I try to remember or reflect, the movements in question … feel like a sort of withdrawal from the outer world. As far as I can detect, these feelings are due to an actual rolling outwards and upwards of the eyeballs" (pp. 193–195).

It is also the case that there was a surge of interest in the meaning of eye movements in the early 1970s when psychologists such as Kinsbourne (1972), Kocel et al. (1972), and Galin and Ornstein (1974), began to equate lateral eye movements to processes related to the different hemispheres of the brain. They observed that right-handed people tended to shift their heads and eyes to the *right* during "left hemisphere" (logical and verbally oriented) tasks, and to move their heads and eyes to the *left* during "right hemisphere" (artistic and spatially oriented) tasks. That is, people tended to look in the opposite direction of the part of the brain they were using to complete a cognitive task.

It was the brilliance of Grinder and Bandler, however, that was responsible for the initial coding of the visual, auditory, and kinesthetic accessing cues along the up, lateral, and downward axis of eye movement.

12. Another significant influence on Bandler, Grinder, and the members of the "Meta" group at that time were the writings of Carlos Castaneda. Castaneda's works provided explicit descriptions of different states of consciousness, and outlined specific steps to achieve perceptual flexibility and explore the relationship between conscious and unconscious processes. They relate his experience of the visionary reality of the Native Americans guided by the character of Don Juan, a Yaqui Indian who introduced Castaneda to different states of consciousness by means of hallucinogens. For instance, some of the interactions between Don Juan and another Yaqui "sorcerer," Don Genaro, inspired Bandler and Grinder to create the NLP "double induction" process.

Castaneda's first book, *The Teachings of Don Juan: A Yaqui Way of Knowledge* (Berkeley: University of California Press, 1968), was submitted as a master's thesis in anthropology at UCLA. In his later works – *A Separate Reality* (1971), *Journey to Ixtlan* (1972), *Tales of Power* (1974), *The Second Ring of Power* (1978) – Castaneda described an epistemology of being a "warrior." According to Castaneda's Don Juan, for instance, *fear* is the first of life's four "enemies." Fear is overcome through *clarity*, which in turn becomes our next "enemy." Clarity must be overcome through the development of *power*. Power is eventually overcome by *old age*, which is the final, undefeatable enemy. The ultimate goal of the warrior is to manage these transitions while maintaining a state of "impeccability" or congruence, always keeping death as an advisor.

13. Robert Dilts and Judith DeLozier, *Encyclopedia of Systemic Neuro-Linguistic Programming and NLP New Coding* (Santa Cruz, CA: NLP University Press, 2000); eidem, *NLP II: The Next Generation* (Capitola, CA: Meta Publications, 2010).

14. Robert Dilts and Stephen Gilligan, *The Hero's Journey* (Carmarthen, Wales: Crown House Publishing, 2009).

15. Beecher, 1955; Evans, 1984.

16. More recent studies (Angell, 2011) have shown that, as judged by scales used to measure depression, placebos were 75–82 percent as effective as antidepressants.

17. Robert Dilts, Tim Hallbom, and Suzi Smith, *Beliefs: Pathways to Health and Well-Being* (Portland, OR: Metamorphous Press, 1990).

18. John Grinder and Richard Bandler, *The Structure of Magic, Vol. II: A Book about Communication and Change* (Palo Alto, CA: Science and Behavior Books, 1975); Virginia Satir, John Grinder, and Richard Bandler, *Changing with Families: A Book about Further Education for Being Human* (Palo Alto, CA: Science and Behavior Books, 1976).

19. John Grinder and Richard Bandler, *Patterns of the Hypnotic Techniques of Milton H. Erickson, M.D., Vol. II* (Cupertino, CA: Meta Publications, 1977).

20. Grinder and Bandler, *Patterns of the Hypnotic Techniques of Milton H. Erickson, Vol. II*, pp. 210–212.

21. According to Bateson, the issue is not so much whether a person is schizophrenic or not. He believed that we are all schizophrenic to a large degree. For him, the critical distinction was whether one was 96% schizophrenic versus 98% schizophrenic and how that difference was responded to and held within the larger system surrounding us.

22. In a paper I wrote in November 1976 (published in *Roots of NLP*), for instance, I attempted to distinguish between logical types and logical levels.

23. John Grinder, Richard Bandler, Judith DeLozier, and Robert Dilts, *Neuro-Linguistic Programming: The Study of the Structure of Subjective Experience, Vol. I* (Capitola, CA: Meta Publications, 1980).

Chapter 11 "The Answer, My Friend, is Blowin' in the Wind"
– John Grinder

1. "Blowin' in the Wind" appears on Bob Dylan's album, *The Freewheelin'* (Columbia Records, 1963).

2. Carmen Bostic-St. Clair and John Grinder, *Whispering in the Wind* (Scotts Valley, CA: J & C Enterprises, 2001), pp. 126–127.

3. Bostic-St. Clair and Grinder, *Whispering in the Wind*, pp. 142–143.

4. Bostic-St. Clair and Grinder, *Whispering in the Wind*, pp. 120–121.

5. Bostic-St. Clair and Grinder, *Whispering in the Wind*, p. 140.

6. Bostic-St. Clair and Grinder, *Whispering in the Wind*, pp. 173–174.

7. John Grinder and Richard Bandler, *The Structure of Magic, Vol. II: A Book about Communication and Change* (Palo Alto, CA: Science and Behavior Books, 1975).

8. W. Ross Ashby, *An Introduction to Cybernetics* (London: Chapman & Hall, 1956).

9. Robert Spitzer, then the owner of Science and Behavior Books (SBB) in Palo Alto, and Bandler's employer (Bandler at the time was the guy who packaged, addressed, and sent out orders from a warehouse housing the titles carried by SBB on the property at 1000 Alba Road) as well as a close personal friend of Spitzer, knew that Bandler and I were experimenting with some notoriety with some unconventional patterning. And, further, that we were in the process of writing a book with the intention of presenting these patterns. He approached us and offered to *consider* publishing our book (*The Structure of Magic, Volume I*) through his publishing company. We seized upon his marked use of the verb *consider* contained in the phrase *consider publishing* and waited for an explanation.

    Spitzer, well aware that Bandler had considerable influence on him (and in ways that he sensed but couldn't make explicit for himself), went on to disclose that as he himself was too close to the work (through his association as Bandler's employer), he would seek the counsel of someone whose opinion he trusted to advise him as to whether he should publish our book or not. He had selected Jay Haley, one of the former members of the MRI group under Bateson for this task. He requested that we give him a clean copy of the draft of *The Structure of Magic*. He then sent this copy to Haley, requesting that he read it and offer his opinion about publishing it. Several weeks passed – during this interim, the well-known meeting at Bateson's long Norse table (described in *Whispering in the Wind*, pp. 173–176) at which the initial offer to connect us with Erickson occurred. It was at this same meeting that Bateson had offered to write and then had, indeed, written an introduction to *Magic I*. In this introduction he explicitly recognized that we had created a worthy solution to the challenge that he and his team (including Haley) had confronted but failed to resolve in a manner satisfactory to him at MRI).

We now had our first official recognition for the patterning that we had created and from none other than the man who was recognized as the intellectual leader in the field we were addressing. Fortified with this endorsement, we could hardly suppress bursting into laughter when Spitzer sheepishly approached us with the *bad* news that Haley had judged our manuscript unworthy of publication and quoted a line from Haley's letter to the effect that we demonstrated a woeful lack of appreciation for Bateson's work at MRI and were impossibly naive when it came to the patterning we were proposing.

The look on Spitzer's face was priceless as we handed him a copy of Bateson's laudatory remarks in his introduction to the book and watched him digest its contents directly from the recognized master. Spitzer, bolstered by the direct and unambiguous commentary by Bateson, re-considered his decision and published *The Structure of Magic* in 1975 – the first of a series of books by Bandler and me that established this new body of patterning, NLP.

10. A deeper analysis reveals that these steps in the application of any coded NLP patterns are fundamentally a sequence of attention fixing points, directing the attention of both the agent of change and, through his or her actions, of the client him or herself.

    Please note also that both the elements and their sequencing could in principle be replaced by an alternate set of elements and sequencings. The coding of patterns is a deeply arbitrary endeavor, answering only to the criterion, does this coded pattern congruently applied deliver the set of outcomes typical of the genius whose patterning has been so coded, i.e., does the damn thing work?

11. Arbib, 1996.

12. John Grinder and Judith DeLozier, *Turtles All the Way Down: Prerequisites to Personal Genius* (Portland, OR: Metamorphous Press, 1995).

13. The interested reader is invited to read a more extended comment on this in *Whispering in the Wind*, pp. 120–138.

14. John Grinder and Richard Bandler, *The Structure of Magic, Vol. II: A Book about Language and Therapy* (Palo Alto, CA: Science and Behavior Books, 1975) p.x.

Epilogue – *Carmen Bostic-St. Clair*

1. These are my questions as I jotted them:
   - How did each of these guys meet? Where were they in their life paths? What were they like? What did each of these guys contribute?

- When, where, and how did the modeling occur? Why did they do Gestalt? What is Gestalt what does it mean?
- How did the groups fit in? Who was where, when?
- When did they notice that this could be a field? Where did the name NLP come from? How come Frank calls it Meta? Why was *Magic I* called "magic," and although mostly written, why was *Magic II* published after *Patterns I*?
- What was the context of discovery? How did Perls, Satir, and Erickson get selected? How did Bateson fit in?

2. At one point, I began to create a timeline from the articles and to piece together what was missing for me, the reader. The timeline became chaotic and contradictory – I then began a process of re-reading all the books and researching at UCSC and university websites which archive original papers of the Perls, Satir, and Erickson models.

3. Kresge College was founded in 1971 – the same time John Grinder was hired. According to UCSC's website: "The college was designed with the concept of participatory democracy as a means of encouraging a strong sense of community. The vision was for the college to be a place where students enjoyed a sense of creativity, community and individuality."

4. Books and articles by John Grinder on linguistics:

John Grinder and Suzette Haden Elgin. *A Guide to Transformational Grammar: History, Theory, Practice.* (Austin, TX: Holt, Rinehart and Winston, 1973).

John Grinder. *On Deletion Phenomena in English.* (The Hauge: Mouton, 1976).

John Grinder. "Conjunct Splitting in Samoan," *Linguistic Notes from La Jolla* (University of California, San Diego, Dept. of Linguistics) 2 (1969), 46–79.

John Grinder. "Super Equi-NP Deletion," *Papers from the Sixth Regional Meeting, Chicago Linguistic Society* (University of Chicago, 1970), pp. 297–317.

John Grinder. *On Deletion Phenomena in English.* PhD Dissertation University of California, San Diego (1971).

John Grinder and Paul Postal. "A Global Constraint on Deletion," *Linguistic Inquiry* (MIT Press) 2(1) (1971), 110–112.

John Grinder. "Double Indices," *Linguistic Inquiry* (MIT Press) 2(4) (1971), 572.

John Grinder. "Chains of Co-reference," *Linguistic Inquiry* (MIT Press) 2(2) (1971), 183–202.

John Grinder and Paul Postal. "Missing Antecedents," *Linguistic Inquiry* (MIT Press) 2(3): (1971), 269–312.

John Grinder. "A Reply to Super Equi-NP Deletion as Dative Deletion," in A. Douglas. *Papers from the Seventh Regional Meeting, Chicago Linguistic Society* (Chicago, IL, 1971), pp. 101–111.

John Grinder. "On the Cycle in Syntax," in John P. Kimball, *Syntax and Semantics I* (New York: Academic Press, 1972), pp. 81–112.

John Grinder and Suzette Haden Elgin. "Bully for Us," *Syntax and Semantics* (Los Angeles, CA: Academic Press) 4 (1975), 239–247.

5. Carmen Bostic-St.Clair and John Grinder, *Whispering in the Wind* (Scotts Valley, CA: J & C Enterprises, 2001), p. 349.

6. Dr. Robert Spitzer, "Virginia Satir & Origins of NLP," *Anchor Point Magazine.* July 1992, pp. 1–4; and direct conversation. These two sources led me to go to other research locations to braid together the strands.

7. From an e-mail from Frank Pucelik: 1st Generation (1971 to 1973) *(Apartment Kresge – Kresge – Cowell – Medical center)*

    Trevelyan Houck
    Bill Polansky
    Lisa Chiara
    Joyce Michaelson
    Marilyn Moskowitz
    Jeff Paris
    Terry Rooney
    Patrick Rooney
    Ken Block
    Ilene McCloud

8. Richard Bandler and John Grinder, *The Structure of Magic, Vol. I: A Book about Language and Therapy* (Palo Alto, CA: Science and Behavior Books, 1975), p. 37.

9. Bandler and Grinder, *The Structure of Magic, Vol. I*, p. 57.

10. Fritz Perls, *The Gestalt Approach and Eye Witness to Therapy* (Palo Alto, CA: Science and Behavior Books, 1973).

11. Available at the Mental Research Institute (MRI) website: www.mri.org/about_us.html and through direct conversation with Dr. Robert Spitzer.

12. Virginia Satir, *Peoplemaking* (London: Souvenir Press, 1990; orig. pub. 1972).

13. Virginia Satir, "Foreword," in Bandler and Grinder, *The Structure of Magic, Vol. I*, pp. vii–viii, at vii.

14. "Semper Fi" (shortened from *Semper Fidelis*, the Latin for "Always Faithful" or "Always Loyal") which is the motto of the US Marine Corps.

15. The following list of each generation is Frank Pucelik's response to a request by e-mail. My comments preface Frank's list.

    The Meta Model (the first pattern of NLP) provides the user of the pattern with certain linguistic choices to obtain precision from verbal statements. In line with the intention behind the Meta Model, I offer the following: The classification of the groups as *generations* is Frank's terminology. Frank's extension of this biological metaphor is perfectly acceptable as a *metaphor*. A more definite assignment of meaning to this term would require an identification of the key characteristics (genes) which were passed from one generation to the other (generational transmission). This classificatory distinction is a metaphor and as such does not quite rise to meet the criteria necessary to qualify these groups in a *literal sense* as *generations first*, *second*, and *third*. You may have noted other examples in these articles where the same metaphor of generation has been utilized. One possible consequence of this use of the metaphor for the reader of this history could be a contradiction of time and sequence.

    First generation (1971 to 1973) *(Apartment Kresge – Kresge – Cowell – Medical center)*
    Trevelyan Houck
    Bill Polansky
    Ilene McCloud
    Lisa Chiara
    Joyce Michaelson
    Marilyn Moskowitz
    Jeff Paris
    Terry Rooney
    Patrick Rooney
    Ken Block

    Second generation (1973 to 1974) (early 1973 to mid 1974) *(Kresge – Medical Center – Edgars)*
    Michael Patton
    Peter Gaarn
    Gary Merrill
    David Wick
    Devra Canter
    Jody Bruce

Joyce Michaelson
Marilyn Moskowitz
Ken Block
Terry Rooney
Patrick Rooney
Lisa Chiara
Trevelyan Houck

Third generation (1974 to 1977) (late 1974 through mid 1977) (during late 1976 and into 1977 several people from SJ began to be involved from time to time including Robert Spitzer) *(Edgars – Kresge – Alba – SJ Highway)*
Steve Gilligan
Judy DeLozier
Robert Dilts
Leslie Cameron
David Gordon
Byron Lewis
Jim Eicher
Paul Carter
Terry McClendon
Jody Bruce
Ken Block
Marilyn Moskowitz
Gary Merrill
Devra Canter
Terry Rooney
Joyce Michaelson
Trevelyan Houck

16. The word *Gestalt* in German refers to "a configuration, pattern, or organized field having specific properties that cannot be derived from the summation of its component parts; a unified whole" (source: Collins English Dictionary).

17. Fritz Perls' first book was published in South Africa in 1942 and was titled *Ego, Hunger and Aggression: A Revision of Freud's Theory and Method*. Perls then re-published with Paul Goodman and Ralph Hefferline, essentially the same material with a new sub-title: *Ego, Hunger and Aggression: The Beginning of Gestalt Therapy* in 1951, which in turn was re-published again in 1969 by Random House. In 1969, a second book, based on film transcripts of Perls' work at the Esalen Institute during 1968, entitled *Gestalt Therapy Verbatim*, was compiled and edited by John O. Stevens (Lafayette, CA: Real People Press, 1969). (John O. Stevens, is now known as Steve

Andreas who first entered NLP in 1977). This book includes four lectures in which Perls presents a clear explanation in simple terms of the basic ideas he believed underlie the philosophy and methodology of Gestalt therapy. The lectures are followed by verbatim transcripts of work Perls had done with workshop participants.

18. "Perls often times was regarded as provocative, abrasive or aggressive; while other times, he seemed patronizing. In recent years, Gestalt therapists have attempted to soften these interactions with the client." (various gestalt websites)

19. Research performed by Laura McClanathan, an Information Services Specialist at UCSC. Laura, at my request, searched the following resources: UCSC – General Catalog 1971–1972 to 1976–1977); Kresge College Newsletters; Kresge Town Crier; City on a Hill indices and UCSC Course Review evaluations 1973–1977. My sincerest thank you! Your contribution assisted me greatly in weaving together the strands of this history.

20. Bandler and Grinder, *The Structure of Magic, Vol. I*, p. 174.

21. When Terry McClendon writes the following in his article, "In 1973, Robert Dilts and I were invited to conduct introductory NLP training courses in a number of Western/Mid-West states," the date which matches his book (*The Early Days*) is 1978. I am not sure what date he became involved with the groups, as the dates in his article are at variance with Frank Pucelik's list of generations.

22. Robert Dilts, John Grinder, Richard Bandler, and Judith DeLozier, *Neuro-Linguistic Programming: The Study of the Structure of Subjective Experience, Vol. I* (Capitola, CA: Meta Publications, 1980).

23. John Grinder, Richard Bandler, and Judith DeLozier, *Patterns of the Hypnotic Techniques of Milton H. Erickson, M.D., Vol. II* (Cupertino, CA: Meta Publications, 1977), p. 108.

24. Grinder et al., *Patterns of the Hypnotic Techniques of Milton H. Erickson, Vol. II*, p. 244.

25. Richard Bandler and John Grinder, *Patterns of the Hypnotic Techniques of Milton H. Erickson, M.D., Vol. I* (Cupertino, CA: Meta Publications, 1975), pp. 234–235.

26. Bandler and Grinder, *The Structure of Magic, Vol. I*, p. xiii.

27. Bandler and Grinder, *The Structure of Magic, Vol. I*, p. 3.

28. Bandler and Grinder, *The Structure of Magic, Vol. I*, p. 39.

29. Jay Haley, *Strategies of Psychotherapy* (Carmarthen, Wales: Crown House Publishing, 2006) p. 85. The quote as it appeared in *Structure of Magic, Volume I*. "A more rigorous science of psychotherapy will arrive when the procedures in the various methods can be synthesized down to the most effective strategy possible to induce a person to spontaneously behave in a different manner."

30. Satir, "Foreword," in Bandler and Grinder, *The Structure of Magic, Vol. I*, p. vii.

Appendices

Appendix 1

Santa Cruz City Schools

February 4, 1976

TO WHOM IT MAY CONCERN:

Youth Services Bureau of Community Counseling has been working with a
number of Branciforte Junior High students - students whose behavior
has indicated pronounced emotional and behavioral problems. There has
been improvement, sometimes dramatic improvement, in attitude, and therefore behavior, with these students. Workers from Youth Services Bureau
have spent hours with them and with their families in their homes, and
in activities outside the homes such as camping trips, field trips of
various kinds, swimming, etc. Some of these children have never had
these experiences before. We have found that the approach Youth Services
Bureau is taking toward their clients has resulted in very positive
changes. They reach families who can or will not accept the usual clinic
type of therapy (going to an office at a certain time of day - in a
clinic setting).

We strongly support Youth Services Bureau and hope that, not only will
they continue to be funded, but that their service can be expanded.

Very truly yours,

Elizabeth A. Bennett
School Psychologist

EAB:lw

133 Mission Street Santa Cruz, California 95060 (408) 426-6000

273

Appendix 2

SANTA CRUZ CITY SCHOOLS

Branciforte Junior High School

Santa Cruz, California

February 3, 1976

Santa Cruz Community Counseling Center
271 Water
Santa Cruz, California

Attention: Mr. David Wick

Dear Mr. Wick:

I wish to state my gratitude for all the services that the Community
Counseling Center -- Youth Services -- has given Branciforte Junior High
during the 1975-76 school year. Mr. Ken Block and Mr. Frank Pucelick have
been working closely with several of our students this semester. These
students have indicated a definite behavior pattern change that would allow
them to function and cope with their academic, social, and personal lives
at a greater level of self-understanding and maturity.

In 14 years of dealing with youngsters, I have never observed such definite
behavioral pattern changes in such a short period of time (6 weeks to 3
months). Therefore, I am writing this letter of commendation for the benefit
of any individual persons or agencies that will be working with Youth Services
in the near future. In my opinion there will be definite positive changes in
the youngsters referred to this agency.

Sincerely yours,

James Whiteley
Principal

JW/jc

Appendix 3

Course Curriculum for Primary Prevention Project

Unit Goal I - The Primary Prevention Program course, "Peoplemaking" will assist secondary school students (grades 7-12) in developing awareness of self and others in the cognitive, interpersonal, and affective domains.

Section Goal I - To provide students with an understanding of the developmental processes that create a sense of selfworth and human potential.

Objective I - Students will learn to identify the five (5) modes of communicating as developed and described by Virginia Satir.

Objective II - Students will list and identify the rules by which they operate in their families and society.

Objective III - Students will be able to transform their rules into "guides" for successful survival.

Objective IV - Students will be able to recite the "Five Freedoms" as discussed by Virginia Satir.

Section Goal II - To enrich students awareness of their present and possible "models of the world" through the theory and form of communication and language patterns.

Objective I - Students will be able to differentiate between and identify at least three (3) "Meta-Model" distinctions as developed by Dr. John Grinder and Richard Bandler and discussed in *The Structure of Magic, Volumes I and II.*

Objective II - Students will learn to compare, contrast, and translate between the primary "representational systems" by which human beings structure their reality (i.e., kinesthetic, visual, and auditory).

Objective III - Students will participate in a variety of experiences designed to enhance their knowledge about the pragmatics of human communication.

Section Goal III - To assist students in having more choices in the way they interact with peers of both sexes.

Objective I - Students will be able to list and identify characteristics by which they distinguish between the sexes, and thereby develop new choices for defining roles usually "tied" to gender.

Objective II - Students will learn to recognize and identify unwritten "contracts" that influence the way s/he relates to peers.

2

Objective III - *Students will be able to list and describe the characteristics of the social peer groups within which they interact or avoid.*

Objective IV - *Participants will be able to differentiate between monadic, dyadic, and triadic relating (i.e., individual, couples, and groups).*

Section Goal IV - To present students with a variety of perspectives regardin care and development of the mind and body.

Objective I - *Students will participate in at least two experiential activities in the realm of consciousness and cognition (e.g., creative writing and/or reading, meditation, comparative philosophy, guided fantasy).*

Objective II - *Students will participate in at least two (2) experienti activities designed to promote increased body awareness (e.g., Yoga, martial arts, backpacking, dance).*

Objective III - *Students will be able to list and identify two (2) ways of harmonizing the mind and body.*

Section Goal V - To aid students in the development of strategies that lead to effective and useful clarification of personal values and priorities.

Objective I - *Participants will be able to list, identify, and utilize the seven (7) steps that lead to values clarification.*

Objective II - *Students will take part in at least one clarifying exercise in each of the following domains: cognitive, social, and affective.*

nit Goal II - The Primary Prevention Program course, "Peoplemaking" will assist econdary school students (grades 7-12) in creatively gaining accurate and useful nformation regarding chemical substance use and abuse.

Section Goal I - To provide students with information pertinent to the structure, physiological effects, and psychological manifestations of substances identified by the Controlled Substances Act (CSA).

Objective I - *Students will participate in at least two (2) basic instructional sessions on the history, uses, and abuses of drugs and alcohol.*

Objective II - *Students will demonstrate cognitive and affective awareness regarding drugs as measured by the Pennsylvania State University Drug Education Evaluation Scale (Pre/Post Test).*

Section Goal II - To assist students in defining and clarifying values and priorities regarding personal poly-drug use.

Objective I - *Students will be able to list and identify seven (7) alternative activities that might provide diversion from substance abuse.*

Objective II - *Students will be able to utilize their new skills in Values Clarification to determine personal perspective on poly-drug use.*

Unit Goal III - The Primary Prevention Program course, "Peoplemaking" will assist secondary school students (grades 7-12) in understanding their role and potential for full participation as citizens in the Santa Cruz County community.

Section Goal I - To aid students in gaining awareness of the legal rights of young people, the functions and operations of the local law enforcement agencies, and the juvenile justice system in general.

Objective I - *Students will be able to construct the basic organiza-tion and workings of the juvenile justice system.*

Objective II - *Students will be able to distinguish between, compare and contrast the 600, 601, and 602 categories of the California Welfare and Institutions Code that pertain to juveniles.*

Objective III - *Participants will be able to identify the basic jurisdiction of the local law enforcement agencies.*

Section Goal II - To provide students with increased knowledge of community resources that enhance their ability to fully participate in recreational, educational, vocational, and social service programs within Santa Cruz County.

Objective I - *Students will be able to identify at least two (2) recreational programs in Santa Cruz County.*

Objective II - *Participants will be able to demonstrate knowledge of the Youth Employment Service (Y.E.S.) and identify two (2) means of "making money" for their age group.*

Objective III - *Students will be able to contruct the basic hierarchy of authority in their school, district, and County, as it pertains to job titles and function.*

Objective IV - *Students will be able to list and identify three (3) organizations within the Santa Cruz County community that provide social service assistance to/for young people.*

Text: The text for this course will be Peoplemaking by Virginia Satir, Science and Behavior Books, Inc., Palo Alto, California, 1972.

Methods of Achieving Objectives will include didactic lecture, demonstrations, seminar, audio-visual media presentation, and experiential participation.

Credit will be established by conjoint planning with the sponsoring school teacher and administration.

Bibliography

Angell, M. "The Epidemic of Mental Illness", *New York Review of Books*, June 23, 2011.

Arbib, M. A. *The metaphorical brain; an introduction to cybernetics as artificial intelligence and brain theory* (New York: Wiley-Interscience, 1972).

Arbib, M. A. *Neurolinguistics Must be Computational* (Cambridge: Cambridge University Press, 1979).

Arbib, M. A., Bonaiuto, J., and Rosta, E. *The mirror system hypothesis: From a macaque-like mirror system to imitation*. In Proceedings of the 6th International Conference on the Evolution of Language, p.3–10 (2006).

Ashby, W. R. *An Introduction to Cybernetics* (London: Chapman & Hall, 1956).

Bandler, R. and Grinder J. *Frogs into Princes: Neuro Linguistic Programming* (Moab, UT: Real People Press, 1979).

Bandler, R. and Grinder J. *Patterns of the Hypnotic Techniques of Milton H. Erickson, M.D., Vol. I* (Cupertino, CA: Meta Publications, 1975).

Bandler, R. and Grinder J. *The Structure of Magic, Vol. I: A Book about Language and Therapy* (Palo Alto, CA: Science and Behavior Books, 1975).

Bateson, G. "A Theory of Play and Fantasy," *Psychiatric Research Reports*, 2 (1955), 39–51.

Bateson, G. *Steps to an Ecology of Mind: Collected Essays in Anthropology, Psychiatry, Evolution, and Epistemology* (Chicago, IL: University of Chicago Press, 1972).

Bateson, G. and Mead, M. *Balinese Character: A Photographic Analysis* (New York: New York Academy of Sciences, 1942).

Beecher, H. K. "The Powerful Placebo" *Journal of American Medical Association* 159 (17) (1955).

Bostic-St. Clair, C. and Grinder, J. *Whispering in the Wind* (Scotts Valley, CA: J & C Enterprises, 2001).

Brocca, P. "Loss of Speech, Softening and Partial Destruction of the Anterior Left Lobe of the Brain". *Bulletin de la Société Anthropologique*. 2, (1861) 235–238.

Brocca, P. "Sur le siége de la foulté du language articulé" (15 juin) *Bulletin de la Société Anthropologique de Paris* 6, (1865) 377–393.

Brown, N. O. *Life against Death: The Psychoanalytical Meaning of History* (Middletown, CT: Wesleyan University Press, 1959).

Brown, N. O. *Love's Body* (New York: Random House, 1966).

Castaneda, C. *Tales of Power* (London: Simon & Schuster, 1974).

Castaneda, C. *The Second Ring od Power* (London: Penguin, 1978).

Castaneda, C. *A Seperate Reality* (London: Penguin Books, 1971).

Castaneda, C. *Journey to Ixtlan* (London: Simon & Schuster, 1972).

Chomsky, N. "A Review of B. F. Skinner's Verbal Behavior," *Language*, 35(1) (1959), 26–58.

Chomsky, N. *Aspects of Theory and Syntax* (Cambridge, MA: MIT Press, 1965).

DeLozier, J. *Patterns of the Hypnotic Techniques of Milton H. Erickson, M.D., Vol. II* (Cupertino, CA: Meta Publications, 1977).

Dilts, R. *Applications of Neuro-Linguistic Programming* (Capitola, CA: Meta Publications, 1983).

Dilts, R. *Roots of Neuro-Linguistic Programming* (Capitola, CA: Meta Publications, 1983).

Dilts, R. *Strategies of Genius, Vol. I* (Capitola, CA: Meta Publications, 1994).

Dilts, R. and DeLozier, J. *Encyclopedia of Systemic Neuro-Linguistic Programming and NLP New Coding* (Santa Cruz, CA: NLP University Press, 2000).

Dilts, R. and DeLozier, J. *NLP II: The Next Generation* (Capitola, CA: Meta Publications, 2010).

Dilts, R. and Gilligan, S. *The Hero's Journey* (Carmarthen, Wales: Crown House Publishing, 2009).

Dilts, R., Hallbom, T., and Smith, S. *Beliefs: Pathways to Health and Well-Being* (Portland, OR: Metamorphous Press, 1990).

Dilts, R., Grinder, J., Bandler, R. and DeLozier, J. *Neuro-Linguistic Programming: The Study of the Structure of Subjective Experience, Vol. I* (Capitola, CA: Meta Publications, 1980).

Eicher, J. "Linguistics and the Problem of Serial Order," *Papers in Linguistics*, 10 (1977), 151–183.

Eicher, J. *Making the Message Clear: Communicating for Business* (Santa Cruz, CA: Grinder, DeLozier and Associates, 1987).

Eicher, J. *Rapport-Based Selling* (Dallas, TX: Get to the Point Books, 2009).

Eicher, J. *No Need for Conflict!* (Dallas, TX: Get to the Point Books, 2010).

Eicher, J., Jones, J., and Bearley, W. *Rapport: Matching and Mirroring Communication* (King of Prussia, PA: HRDQ, 1990).

Eicher, J., Jones, J., and Bearley, W. *The Neurolinguistic Communication Profile* (King of Prussia, PA: HRDQ, 1990).

Evans, J. K. "Unraveling the Placebo Effects" *Advances*, 1 (3) (1984) 11–20.

Galin, D. Oistein, R. "Individual Differences in Cognitive Style— Reflective Eye Movements" *Neuropsychologia*, 12, (1974) 376–397.

Goffman, E. *Frame Analysis: An Essay on the Organization of Experience* (London: Harper and Row, 1974).

Goleman, D. "People Who Read People," *Psychology Today*, 13 (July 1979).

Gorski, T. and Miller, M. *Counseling for Relapse Prevention* (Independence, MO: Herals House/Independence Press, 1982).

Grinder, J. "Conjunct splitting in Samoan," *Linguistic Notes from La Jolla* (University of California, San Diego, Dept. of Linguistics) 2 (1969), 46–79.

Grinder, J. "Super Equi-NP Deletion," *Papers from the Sixth Regional Meeting, Chicago Linguistic Society* (University of Chicago, 1970), pp. 297–317.

Grinder, J. "A Reply to Super Equi-NP Deletion as Dative Deletion," in A. Douglas, *Papers from the Seventh Regional Meeting, Chicago Linguistic Society* (Chicago, IL, 1971), pp. 101–111.

Grinder, J. "Chains of Co-reference," *Linguistic Inquiry* (MIT Press) 2(2) (1971) 183–202.

Grinder, J. "Double Indices," *Linguistic Inquiry* (MIT Press) 2(4) (1971) 572.

Grinder, J. *On Deletion Phenomena in English*. PhD Dissertation, University of California, San Diego (1971).

Grinder, J. "On the Cycle in Syntax," in John P. Kimball (ed.), *Syntax and Semantics I* (New York: Academic Press, 1972), pp. 81–112.

Grinder, J. *On Deletion Phenomena in English* (The Hauge: Mouton, 1976).

Grinder, J. and Bandler, R. *Patterns of the Hypnotic Techniques of Milton H. Erickson, M.D., Vol. I* (Cupertino, CA: Meta Publications, 1975).

Grinder, J. and Bandler, R. *The Structure of Magic, Vol. II: A Book about Communication and Change* (Palo Alto, CA: Science and Behavior Books, 1975).

Grinder, J. and Bandler, R. *Reframing: Neurolinguistic Programming and the Transformation of Meaning* (Moab, UT: Real People Press, 1983).

Grinder J., Bandler, R., and Andreas, C. *Trance-Formations: Neuro-Linguistic Programming and the Structure of Hypnosis* (Moab, UT: Real People Press, 1981).

Grinder, J., Bandler, R., and DeLozier, J. *Patterns of the Hypnotic Techniques of Milton H. Erickson, M.D., Vol. II* (Cupertino, CA: Meta Publications, 1977).

Grinder, J. and DeLozier, J. *Turtles All the Way Down: Prerequisites to Personal Genius* (Portland, OR: Metamorphous Press, 1995).

Grinder, J. and Elgin, S. *A Guide to Transformational Grammar: History, Theory, Practice* (Austin, TX: Holt, Rinehart and Winston, 1973).

Grinder, J. and Elgin, S. "Bully for Us," *Syntax and Semantics* (Los Angeles, CA: Academic Press) 4 (1975), 239–247.

Grinder, J. and Postal, P. "A Global Constraint on Deletion," *Linguistic Inquiry* (MIT Press) 2(1) (1971), 110–112.

Grinder, J. and Postal, P. "Missing Antecedents," *Linguistic Inquiry* (MIT Press) 2(3) (1971), 269–312.

Haley, J. *Strategies of Psychotherapy*. (Carmarthen, Wales: Crown House Publishing, 2006).

Holt, H. *Principles of Psychology* (New York: Henry Holt, 1890).

Isaacson, W. *Steve Jobs: The Exclusive Biography* (New York: Little, Brown and Co., 2011).

Kingsbourne, M. "Eye and Head Turning Indicates Cerebral Laterialization," *Science*, 179, (1972) 539–541.

Kocel, K. et al. "Lateral Eye Movement and Cognitive Mode," *Psychonomic Science*, 17, 223–224.

Korzybski, A. *Science and Sanity: An Introduction to Non-Aristotelian Systems and General Semantics*, 5th edn (Brooklyn, NY: Institute of General Semantics, 1994; orig. pub. 1933).

Kuhn, T. *The Structure of Scientific Revolutions* (Chicago, IL: University of Chicago Press, 1970).

Kuhn, T. *The Essential Tension* (Chicago, IL: University of Chicago Press, 1979).

Lewis, B. *Sobriety Demystified: Getting Clean and Sober with NLP and CBT* (Saratoga, CA: Kelsey & Co., 1996).

Lewis, B. *Magic of NLP Demystified* (Carmarthen, Wales: Crown House Publishing, 2012).

Lorber, R. and Blanchard, K. *Putting the One Minute Manager to Work* (New York: Berkley, 1985).

Maultsby, M. *Rational Behavioral Therapy* (Englewood Cliffs, NJ: Prentice Hall, 1984).

Maultsby, M. and Hendricks, A. *You and Your Emotions* (Appleton, WI: Rational Self-Help Books, 1974).

McClendon, T. *The Wild Days: NLP 1972–1981* (Terrence McClendon, 1989).

McClendon, T. *Happy Parents Happy Kids: Words and Actions for Parents and Kids* (Terrence McClendon, 2012).

Miller, G. A. "The Magical Number Seven, Plus or Minus Two: Some Limits on Our Capacity for Processing Information," *Psychological Review*, 63 (1956), 81–97.

Miller, G. A., Galanter, E., and Pribram, K. H. *Plans and the Structure of Behavior* (New York: Adams Bannister Cox, 1960).

Perls, F. *Ego, Hunger, and Aggression: The Beginning of Gestalt Therapy* (New York: Random House, 1969; orig. pub. 1942).

Perls, F. *Gestalt Therapy Verbatim*, compiled and edited by John O. Stevens (Lafayette, CA: Real People Press, 1969).

Perls, F. *In and Out of the Garbage Pail* (Lafayette, CA: Real People Press, 1969).

Perls, F. *The Gestalt Approach and Eye Witness to Therapy* (Palo Alto, CA: Science and Behavior Books, 1973).

Perls, F. *Gestalt Theory* [audio recording]. Center for Cassette Studies (1974).

Perls, F. *The Gestalt Approach and Eye Witness to Therapy* (New York: Bantam Books, 1976).

Perls, F. *Three Approaches to Psychotherapy: A Film Series* [video recording]. Produced and directed by Everett L. Shostrom (Corona del Mar, CA: Psychological Films, 1990).

Perls, F. "Psychiatry in a New Key," *Gestalt Journal*, 1(1) (1978), 32–53.

Perls, F. and Baumgardner, P. *Legacy from Fritz: Gifts from Lake Cowichan* (Palo Alto, CA: Science and Behaviour Books, 1975).

Perls, F., Goodman, P., and Hefferline, R. *Excitement and Growth in Human Personality* (New York: Julian Press, 1951).

Satir, V. *Peoplemaking* (London: Souvenir Press, 1990; orig. pub. 1972).

Satir, V., Grinder, J., and Bandler, R. *Changing with Families: A Book about Further Education for Being Human* (Palo Alto, CA: Science and Behavior Books, 1976).

Slater, P. *The Pursuit of Loneliness* (Boston, MA: Beacon Press, 1990; orig. pub. 1970).

Slater, P. *Earthwalk* (New York: Anchor Books, 1975).

Spitzer, R. "Virginia Satir & Origins of NLP," *Anchor Point Magazine* (July 1992), pp. 1–4.

Stevens, B. *Don't Push the River (It Flows By Itself)* (Moab, UT: Real People Press, 1970).

Tosey, P. and Mathison, J. *Neuro-Linguistic Programming: A Critical Appreciation for Managers and Developers* (London: Palgrave Macmillan, 2009).

Watzlawick, P., Beavin-Bavelas, J., and Jackson, D. *Pragmatics of Human Communication: A Study of Interactional Patterns, Pathologies, and Paradoxes* (New York: W.W. Norton, 1967).

Wernike, C. *Der Aphesische Symptomcomplex* (Breslaw: Cohn and Weigert, 1874).